M000207990

THE
POLITICS
OF
HEAVEN

PAUL IN
CRITICAL
CONTEXTS

The Paul in Critical Contexts series offers cutting-edge reexaminations of Paul through the lenses of power, gender, and ideology.

Apostle to the Conquered: Reimagining Paul's Mission
Davina C. Lopez

The Arrogance of Nations: Reading Romans in the Shadow of Empire
Neil Elliott

Christ's Body in Corinth: The Politics of a Metaphor
Yung Suk Kim

Galatians Re-Imagined: Reading with the Eyes of the Vanquished
Brigitte Kahl

Onesimus Our Brother: Reading Religion, Race, and Slavery in Philemon
Matthew V. Johnson, James A. Noel, and
Demetrius K. Williams, eds.

THE
POLITICS
OF
HEAVEN

WOMEN, GENDER, AND EMPIRE IN THE STUDY OF PAUL

JOSEPH A. MARCHAL

Fortress Press
Minneapolis

THE POLITICS OF HEAVEN
Women, Gender, and Empire in the Study of Paul

Cover design: Laurie Ingram
Cover image: Stone carving of the Greek goddess Nike, © Digital Vision / Getty Images
Book design and typesetting: The HK Scriptorium, Inc.

Library of Congress Cataloging-in-Publication Data

Marchal, Joseph A.
  The politics of heaven : women, gender, and empire in the study of Paul /
Joseph A. Marchal.
    p. cm.
  Includes bibliographical references and index.
  ISBN-13: 978-0-8006-6300-1 (alk. paper)
  1. Bible. N.T. Epistles of Paul—Criticism, interpretation, etc. 2. Sex role—Biblical
teaching. 3. Feminist theology. 4. Postcolonialism. 5. Christianity and politics—
Biblical teaching. I. Title.
  BS2650.52.M27 2008
  227'.06082—dc22

                                                                    2008016228

Manufactured in the U.S.A.

12 11 10 09 08   1 2 3 4 5 6 7 8 9 10

Contents

Preface   vii

**Introduction: Interpretation at the Intersection
of Approaches**   1
  Context   1
  Starting Points and Parameters: Feminist and
    Postcolonial Analysis   4
  Paul, Philippians, and the Plan of This Book   10

**1. Histories of Interpretation and "People's History"
in Pauline Studies**   15
  Initial Inquiries and Imperial Intersections
    in Interpretation   15
  Introduction   15
  Gaps, Erasures, and Conflicts   16
  Procedure and Precedent   21
  People's Possibilities: Subaltern History
    and Problems of Perspective   24
  People's History and Pauline Studies   24
  Genealogies, Genders, Gaps, and Geopolitics
    in People's History   26
  Back to the Biblical: Antiquity and Feminist,
    Postcolonial Approaches   33

2. A Hymn Within and a Heavenly *Politeuma*   37
  Introduction   37
  A Heavenly *Politeuma* and a Hymn Within   39
  Rhetorical Interactions and Pauline Interpretation:
    A Postcolonial Paul?   45
  Initial Connections and Conclusions   54

3. **The Rhetorics of Imitation and Postcolonial**
   Theories of Mimicry   **59**
   Imitation Rhetorics in Paul and in Pauline Scholarship   60
   The Promise and Perils of Postcolonial Mimicry   67
   Post-Poning Any Undue Celebrations: Criticisms, Cautions,
        and Calibrations of Postcolonial Mimicry   74
   Resistance, Risks, and Replications: On the Limits
        of Mimicry for a Feminist, Postcolonial Analysis   79

4. **Women in the Contact Zone**   **91**
   Contact Zone and Transcultural Interactions   91
   Pauline Travels and the Philippian Contact Zone   96
   Euodia and Syntyche: Reconstructing Co-Workers
        in the Contact Zone   101

5. **Concluding Reflections and Connections**   **111**
   Reviewing the Present Project   111
   Elaborating Further Possibilities   117

List of Abbreviations   125
Notes   127
Bibliography   181
Index   205

Preface

While the words of this book were almost entirely written during one war, it might be said that the process that led to its creation began much earlier in a previous war, albeit one launched upon the same territory, with the same interests, and with the same elite pale-male-headed family occupying this country's White House. It was during this "first" invasion of the Persian Gulf region by U.S. forces that one could say my own specific awareness of empire began to emerge. As a middle- to upper-class pale male, living in a mid-country urban zone where inner city met middle-class state university space, I already had words to describe the racism endemic to American society. As the older son of social justice–oriented catholic parents, I was aware of the crippling effects of poverty and unemployment upon others, as these were routinely invoked in words and in actions in our community and in my family. In 1991, however, I encountered something different: previously rigid and inviolable dress codes expanded so that students of all stripes could adorn their jackets with make-shift yellow ribbons and wear mass-marketed dog-tags over their puffed-with-masculinely-American-pride chests. (Simple white ribbons or buttons of pointed critique, questioning, or chastisement were met with both formal administrative censure and informal peer reprisals.) In the hail of smart bombs, exultant news coverage, and exuberant mass assent, I could only sense that my vocabularies of racism and poverty would not adequately express my protest (and that of far too few others) of this exercise in economic and military might. My words and deeds were maladapted to resist or resituate the conditions of permissible consumption and patriotic display.

Religious communities were no less involved in these dynamics, as the stirring tones of "The Battle Hymn of the Republic" and "God Bless America" rallied the churchgoers who I had previously assumed would be outraged by the events of the time. I was beginning to be explicitly schooled in the heavenly politics of American civil religion. From my defiantly adolescent but dependably observant point of view, such ritual displays aroused such sickening ambivalences in me that I chose stock stillness and silence over my normal full-throated enthusiasm. On one such occasion, I recall my typically stoic father, leaning over to me in church, angrily meeting my irreverent indignation with the chiding admonition, "You know, there's nothing wrong with showing respect for your country."

As on so many other occasions, whether they knew it or not, such parental words would haunt and provoke my reflections for days, weeks, even decades to come. What, exactly, did my father mean by such an uncharacteristic mid-service reprimand? Guided by both my mother and my father, my siblings and I were witnesses and participants in innumerable critical conversations about our country, the government, the church, the economy, and the social good of all. Somehow, amid the efforts of these various institutions, we were expected to find fairness and respect for all people. Where this was to be found was often uncertain then, as my parents (especially my mother) alternated between hopeful belief, exasperated disappointment, clear determination, and sad resignation. Within all this, there was a clear (yet still undefined) authority to which (once found) we should show reverence and obedience.

Perhaps my father's reaction was to my own bubbling resentment and irreverence, then. Or was my sin the pride and privileged arrogance of one assuming he knew better than all others assembled? Or maybe the requisite respect was lacking in my approach, if not my evaluation. But, if respect was due to my country, what made it mine? Was it the idea of "freedom" that was due respect, or are the actions of its people the basis for constituting respect? What of the historical injustices we had so often discussed, which had so often been endorsed by both "the people" and the authorities (religious and otherwise) to whom respect was due? Surely, we had been taught, there was something wrong in that legacy of injustice. My parents had so regularly supplemented our formal education with consistent questioning, of the world and of ourselves, that these kinds of questions and concerns just came tumbling out.

Whatever part of this project addresses such persistent concerns and ethical reflections, then, is at least partially (if unexpectedly) due to the manner with which I was engaged with early expectation, and exhorted to keep an obligation to those beyond myself and those I might claim as "my own." Because of this, I cannot fail to acknowledge the unacknowledge-able impulse and impact of my parents, Andrea and Bill, on this and other life-efforts.

It is difficult to describe the beginning of this project, though, as it has more than one beginning. With the passing of time, I developed more nuanced vocabularies for resisting the forms of domination that plague our world. A dozen years after the first Gulf War, I was working as a femi-nist teacher, scholar, and activist in another time of war, as U.S. forces invaded Iraq for the "second" time (although the Iraqi people might ques-tion whether the United States ever really left). Now, not only did I have words for patriarchal and imperial authority, but I was also part of some of the largest mass protests in recent recorded history. Despite such efforts, the march of war was not to be slowed on this occasion, either. It was in this context that I completed my doctoral studies and began putting the words that follow to paper. This work was made possible by that formal training and by the many informal forms of education that occurred every day around me and others who were troubled by various interwoven formations of gender, sexuality, race, ethnicity, and empire. Thus, I find it difficult to fully and more formally thank the innumerable souls who struggled alongside me in so many of these less defined contexts, particu-larly given the speed with which I have moved from one state to another, "blue," "red," and "purple." Most of these souls know who they are, but to those to whom I have yet to express adequate thanks, I will endeavor to do so before we shuffle off these mortal coils.

Given the oscillating climates of fear and friendship for scholars work-ing on projects such as this one, I have been fortunate to find colleagues and companions in such efforts at a number of collegial stops, from Maine to Texas, from southern California to central Iowa. Students at these stops and in courses as varied as "Feminism, Rhetoric, and Paul," "Women from the Beginnings," "Interpreting Paul," "Imitations, Models, and Mean-ing," "Theory in Gender and Women's Studies," and dozens of introduc-tory sections were often curious and dogged participants in assignments and activities circling around the themes of this book. As always, teaching such material and garnering diverse responses served to clarify my per-spective and likely improved the contents that follow. Various faculty in and outside of the religious studies departments of Colby College, Austin College, California State University-Northridge, and Grinnell College have helped to provide an environment of support and encouragement for a scholar working at the intersections of feminist, postcolonial, and queer theories of interpretation. Such interests often led to odd and extended amounts of requests for research help at the libraries of the colleges and universities previously mentioned, as well as those of the Graduate Theological Union and the University of California, Berkeley. Again, given the length of this potential list of supporters, both quiet and strident, among faculty, students, and staff, I will again have to pass my genuine thanks without further extensive annotation.

The content and contours of the present incarnation of this project also benefited from multiple occasions for engagement at several professional conferences. Though I have been favored by a number of respondents in such contexts, two formal respondents from the annual meeting of the Society of Biblical Literature (SBL), in particular, stand out both in my memory and by the impact of their addresses. Abraham Smith soundly reminded me of the potential pitfalls of an analysis focused on gender and sexuality that is ignorant (or forgetful) of the processes of racialization and imperialism. I hope such concerns are addressed throughout these pages, even as my specific debts to Smith are sounded in the first chapter. Caroline Johnson Hodge responded to a rather methodologically and rhetorically heavy presentation by challenging me (and, by inference, I believe, an entire sub-set of this generation of biblical scholars) to think more concretely through the significance of our approaches for historical reconstructive efforts. If I have at all succeeded in addressing such a challenge, chapter 4 might constitute my own attempt to resituate historical-critical analyses in Pauline studies.

Alongside formal respondents, I must thank the many conversation partners who, often individually but at least cumulatively, have managed to strike the useful balance of challenge and encouragement in this present project, or closely related efforts, in both initial and advanced stages. Though this list is hardly comprehensive, thanks are due to Efraín Agosto, Yong-Sung Ahn, Sharon Betsworth, Jennifer Bird, Greg Bloomquist, Roland Boer, Mark G. Brett, Bernadette Brooten, Denise Kimber Buell, Sean Burke, Susan Elliott, Leticia Guardiola-Sáenz, Leslie Hayes, Holly Hearon, J. David Hester (Amador), James D. Hester, Avaren Ipsen, Melanie Johnson-Debaufre, Uriah Yong-Hwan Kim, Cynthia Briggs Kittredge, Sung Eun Lee, Tat-siong Benny Liew, Davina Lopez,

Francisco Lozada, Shelly Matthews, Julie Miller, Mark Nanos, Laura Nasrallah, Jorunn Økland, Christina Petterson, Jeremy Punt, Calvin Roetzel, Erin Runions, Fernando Segovia, Tricia Sheffield, Jeffrey Siker, Judy Yates Siker, Ken Stone, R. S. Sugirtharajah, Mary Ann Tolbert, Peggy Vernieu, and Vincent Wimbush. Outside the study of antiquity, religion, or theology, there also have been a number of sympathetic colleagues who have shared and sparked elements of the approach pursued in this project, including particularly friends in social history, or the history of historically under-represented people (who were also friends and fellow survivors of visiting professorships at Colby and Grinnell): Diana Shull, Crystal Lewis-Colman, and David Lewis-Colman. The support of such good-humored colleagues, their partners, friends, and children buoyed my often transitory days with temporary (but no less appreciated) solace and community.

Versions of the various contents represented in the pages that follow were presented in a number of venues. My thanks, then, must extend also to those groups, conferences, and colleagues who offered such venues for sharing the work that both directly and indirectly shaped the form of the present project. Thanks to David and Jim Hester for offering intentionally interdisciplinary and dialogical conferences in wintry southern California on topics like rhetoric, violence, and evil; rhetorics of identity: race, place, sex and the person; and the rhetorics of social formation. Colleagues at Austin College, including especially Todd Penner, encouraged and enthusiastically responded to a keynote speech for a conference on gender and humanities. Key portions of chapters 1 and 3 were presented at the International Meeting of the SBL in sections on Critical Theory and Biblical Interpretation and Methodology and the Future of Biblical Studies. This society's joint annual meeting with the American Academy of Religion (AAR) has proven the most consistent venue for presentation, contestation, revision, and exposition of my work in sessions organized by units on Rhetoric and the New Testament; Paul and Politics; Pauline Epistles; Reading, Theory and the Bible; Bible, Theology, and Postmodernity; LGBT/Queer Hermeneutics; and Feminist Hermeneutics of the Bible.

The group that has read and responded to the widest selection of materials that were eventually winnowed into the main body of this project is the working group on Philippians and the people's history of the assembly at Philippi. Though the membership has expanded and contracted in past years, all participants generously engaged my (and others') working papers with the collaborative spirit so necessary when scholars manage both to share certain fundamental assumptions and to diverge so significantly on such a wide variety of issues and approaches. It has been a wonderful venue for thinking more about "the people besides Paul," and I hope that continued collective and individual fruits might result from the labor of persistent participants like Valerie Abrahamsen, Noelle Damico, Peter Oakes, Angela Standhartinger, and Demetrius Williams. The present work has been improved due to such conversations, even as I am certain that its particulars and its departures are not always representative of the distinct rigor, vigor, or view of others in these conversations.

Thanks must also be extended to Richard Horsley, and not simply because he introduced me to this people's history project and then let me take the organizing reins for our Philippic friends. Dick Horsley is the rare scholar who responds to persistent criticisms of his writing and theorizing not only with aplomb, but also with an often unabashed enthusiasm. I hope such a disposition might never change, even as both of our approaches most definitely should. Caroline Vander Stichele and Todd Penner draw my regular thanks (and ire) for a host of reasons too difficult to recount. Their trenchant perspectives on the various proceedings of the aforementioned gatherings, large and small, have been matched by the frank but friendly engagement that has characterized our ongoing conversations. Fellow travelers in arguments against imperial and gendered oppressions, but by often different routes, Todd and Caroline have proven to be gracious organizers, editors, collaborators, and even mentors (by another mother), in and from foreign locales like Europe and Texas.

My debts to the work of Kwok Pui-lan and Musa Dube should be apparent in this study, almost from the start. From before it even started, though, two advisors have played key roles in this project's development and completion. Anne Wire has consistently modeled to me how a scholar remains both curious and committed to those things that matter most, even as the contours of our world and our perspective de- and re-materialize. My experiences teaching, reading, and just chatting with her motivate me as much after matriculation as they did before. Reading Elisabeth Schüssler Fiorenza's *But She Said* more than a dozen years ago helped me to find the foot of the path to pursue justice with suspicion and hope. Since then, Elisabeth has shown herself to be just the kind of inspiration and ally needed for the struggles we are still facing and those still to come. Her consistent advice, instruction, mentoring, and questioning improved this work, as did her gracious sharing of an advanced version of a work on closely related matters (now out from Fortress Press).

The shape and stimulation of the arguments herein have no doubt benefited in ways large and small from those named and unnamed above, even as the responsibilities for its shortcomings are the author's alone. Its appearance at all, at this time and in this form, is attributable to Neil Elliott's editorial energy and the initial recognition of its potential merits on his part. I hope it has become what we anticipated. I also want to thank the team of folks at Fortress who worked on the manuscript, including especially Marissa Bauck, Susan Johnson, and Leslie Rubin. Elements of the first and second chapters first appeared in the article, "Imperial Intersections and Initial Inquiries: Toward a Feminist, Postcolonial Analysis of Philippians," in *Journal of Feminist Studies in Religion* 22:2 (Fall 2006): 5–32. My thanks to the editors at *JFSR* for permission to reuse these materials in revised and expanded form and for providing an opportunity for colleagues to respond to this project in its intermediate stages.

Finally, I dedicate this project to my partner in all things, who constantly checks and challenges me and against whom I could never safely bandy unjustified proclamations or bloviating assertions. I know daily that matters must be explained not just passionately but convincingly, and not just to an audience of an intimate one, but to those who do not share obvious premises or privileged conditions (of which my life as an elitely educated pale male of the United States has many). To my tascha, I owe immeasurable gratitude and joy for showing love and candor, support and suspicion, charity and sarcasm, precision and incision, patience and critique, comfort and sharpness, justice and (our own kind of) faith, to me and to others in our world(s). Words fail me, but you do not.

Interpretation at the Intersection of Approaches

Context

This book both begins by and persists in examining a series of
intersections. As a concerted effort to develop a feminist, postcolonial analysis of Paul's letters and Pauline interpretation, in general,
it draws upon a variety of resources and interrogates how certain foci
have predominated in the wider orbits of both academic and public
circles. These intersections have proven most relevant in my life as both
an advocate/activist and a teacher/scholar. It should also be noted that
it has clear connections to, but even clearer departures from, my previously published work, a dissertation completed in a time inexorably
marked by invasions of distant territories and of intimately assumed
liberties, a period that continues in exacerbating inequalities and in
generating globally interconnected injustices.[1] This is also partially the
context of the evolution of the present work: as a response to the questions, confusions, and concerns of an era in which many more are now
willing to think in terms of imperialism and/or neocolonialism, but so
few still seriously and simultaneously attend to women, gender, and/or
sexuality within this critique.

This tenor of frustration, confusion, and concern is not the only
environment in which our work now proceeds, however, as it is also
conditioned by unprecedented alliances and unreasonable hopes for
another way to a different world. Since the twinned dawn of a new
millennium and of a more public doctrine of the paternally American
empire, we have witnessed some of the most coordinated mass protests
in modern memory. I can now count among my own experiences (as a
privileged citizen and resident of the United States) the commingled
sights, sounds, and smells of hooded punks and families with children

1

in strollers, of exhausted moderates and stalwart guilty white liberals, of colorful street theater and somber veterans, of Jews for peace and their pro-Palestinian partners against international racism, of United Nations endorsers and World Trade Organization resisters, of joyful drummers and women in black, all banding together in common cause.

This is not to say that these were uncomplicated events and alliances, either politically or personally. In the midst of comprehensive exams, teaching appointments, and dissertation proposals, I was a participant and low-level organizer for many such events. I did so, though, not from the vantage point of the main funding organizations, but as a point-person for a semi-radical local chapter of a mainstream liberal feminist organization. There were many occasions when my colleagues and I found ourselves called to account for why a feminist group should spend precious time and efforts in such coalitions. In turn, our commitment raised a whole host of queries as to why movements against imperial interventions and internationalized racism seldom trained our/their eyes against the coinciding dynamics of gender and sexuality.

My own research and writing as a feminist scholar of antiquity and biblical interpretation ran concurrent to and overlapped with these conversations, confrontations, and convictions. Such overlap led to puzzling, if compelling, insights. When discussing the topic of my research (identifying hierarchical rhetorics and situating them within ancient contexts that included friendship and the military) with friends academic, activist, and otherwise, they often assumed the project was postcolonial. Some of these assumptions stemmed from anticipated dynamics: believing any talk about empire would be implicitly against imperial or colonial formations. Yet, biblical scholars and classicists have been discussing the Roman Empire for centuries now without interrogating its structures or critiquing colonizing interconnections to Europe or the United States. More often, when empire was the subject, it was empire that was implicitly affirmed and validated. Thus, as will become clear throughout this present work, there have been some significant differences between developing postcolonial approaches and discussing Roman imperialism, differences that might still be effectively navigated.

Having initially read Said and Spivak, Sugirtharajah and Segovia, I knew some of these initial reactions were based on impressions of rather than encounters with such writing. But, to be honest, at that point, I clearly saw my work in coalition with but different from postcolonial interpretation.[2] I had colleagues who did significant work from that perspective, from and with whom I learned a great deal; but I was keenly aware that postcolonial work was a thriving sub-discipline and entailed its own specific set of theoretical and historical issues.[3] I noted, with others, that the efforts of postcolonial theorists often intersect with those of feminists, but more frequently these intersections have been downplayed, ignored, or obscured. Such erasures and minimizations troubled me, yet my continuing research strongly engaged the imperial attributes of Pauline rhetorics and openly wondered about its contemporary resonance alongside and within feminist approaches.

Perhaps more telling than these reactions and assumptions about postcolonial projects were the puzzled looks over why a *feminist* would be concerned with the structures of ancient imperialism or more recent neocolonialism(s). Such reactions speak volumes about some unfortunately common ideas about feminism(s); they imply that an examination of military rhetorics, for example, could only be a task for the anti-imperialist, which feminists ostensibly were or are not. These responses compel me to both continue and alter my focus so as to question how and why feminist and postcolonial scholars have been viewed as engaging in separate critical contestations. How did this come to be? It had been noted how inconsistently postcolonial or decolonizing analyses attended to dynamics of gender and sexuality, but were these reactions to feminist efforts misapprehensions? Or were they, rather, signs of how inconsistently feminists have worked both within and against imperial and colonial formations? What has gone wrong here, in coalitional politics and in biblical interpretation?

One of the main contentions of this project responds to such queries by insisting that neither will live up to its critical potential if it fails to adequately grapple with the intersecting dynamics of gender, sexuality, ethnicity, and empire. The various responses described above are indicative of a larger problem in our categories of analysis and approach: too much of critical value has been missing in our interpretive projects because we so often lack an intentionally and explicitly multi-axial focus. This becomes all the more crucial when one recognizes how these power dynamics work together not only in our world but in the ancient settings in which Paul wrote his letters. Another purpose of this project, then, is to demonstrate how both Paul's letters and Pauline scholarship are the results of imperially gendered activities. Thus, it is imperative to analyze and assess not solely on the basis of a feminist or a postcolonial approach but, rather, to evaluate the effective intersections of these approaches and develop an analytic attuned to the interconnections of sexism and imperialism. It becomes important, then, to delineate from the beginning what terms like feminist and postcolonial mean and to at least initially indicate how and why they might still coalesce.

Starting Points and Parameters: Feminist and Postcolonial Analysis

Because this project is primarily articulated as a feminist, postcolonial analysis of Paul's letters and Pauline interpretation, it seems appropriate to begin by describing its identification as feminist. From my point of view, feminism(s) can be many different things, but one of the more useful (and cheeky) ways to define it is through the common aphorism, "feminism is the radical notion that women are people."[4] Another feminist scholar notes that "at the very least, feminism, like other liberation movements, attempts a critique of the oppressive structures of society."[5] Both descriptions nicely sum up the import and the aspects of feminisms that are engaged in this project. The first ironically juxtaposes an apparently commonsense idea with the label "radical," an indication that, if followed to its core, feminism should lead to a substantial transformation of society. The second foregrounds, or stresses, the critical aspect of this effort and, in a key move for this particular project, links it to other struggles against systematic forms of oppression.[6] Both indicate how feminists can and should work toward significant changes in the world.

In its current usage, the term *postcolonial* involves considerably more variety, confusion, and even tension. First of all, the subject of postcolonial studies could be said to include both imperialism and colonialism. In most formulations, imperialism is the more general term, while colonialism is a specific form or strategy within imperialism. As Edward Said defines them, imperialism "means the practice, the theory, and the attitudes of a dominating metropolitan center ruling a distant territory," whereas colonialism involves "the implanting of settlements" on that distant territory.[7]

Conveniently enough for the student of the ancient Mediterranean, these terms have etymological predecessors with paralleled functions in the Roman Empire. *Imperium* generally refers to the authority, order, and power of one over another, but most especially in political contexts. (In extending its authority beyond matters concerned with its people (*res publica*) to other territories, Roman rule became imperial.) A *colonia* originally described an estate or farm, but came to be a more technical term for a settlement with specific connections back to Rome, like the city of Philippi. As both terms prove relevant, then, to the study of ancient texts like Paul's letters, we will try to remain aware of both imperial and colonial dynamics in history and in interpretation.[8]

A second major concern in defining the term postcolonial involves a rather clear set of tensions within postcolonial studies as a subdiscipline. Scholars remain divided as to whether it should be material or cultural in emphasis, Marxist or literary in method, and historical or discursive in focus.[9] These tensions are well illustrated by considering two different reflections on the *post* in postcolonial. At first, the term was meant simply as a chronological indicator, describing a historical era after official colonial rule. This became a useful (and highly marketable) label to append to what was previously labeled commonwealth literature, that is, the literature of the African, Asian, and Caribbean colonies of the British empire.[10] However, the impact of colonialism did not end when the British authorities left India or the Algerians gained political independence from the French. Thus, a strictly temporal meaning for postcolonial seems unsuitable, as Musa Dube argues:

> the term *postcolonial* does not denote that colonialism is over, since the latter did not simply consist of geographical and political domination but also included cultural and economic structures that persist to this day. Postcolonial, therefore, refers to an overall analysis of the methods and effects of imperialism as a continuing reality in global relations.[11]

Such an expansive description of the horizons of postcolonial studies requires, then, at least a dual focus on historical and discursive colonization.[12] Grappling with the ongoing effects of the knowledge produced in and by colonially dominated locales will be short-sighted if it fails to engage and assess historical processes, but an exclusive emphasis on the past would obscure the current continuities and particularities of (neo)colonial formations.

Such potential gaps in analysis would hinder the effort of postcolonial studies to live up to one final connotation of the term postcolonial: moving beyond and thus against the heritage and impact of imperial and colonial dynamics.[13] Here, then, the spirit and impulse of postcolonialism are most closely akin to those of feminism(s), as both are seeking to critique oppressive forms and construct liberating options for the future. One might think of them as similarly limited political movements, but that would ignore that both seek wider transformations throughout the world's cultures and societies. Such interconnections are crucial to the project at hand but are not often (enough) mobilized in either biblical studies or other fields of human activity.

This rather variegated landscape in postcolonial studies, then, might begin to explain some of the confusions, assumptions, and misapprehensions about the relation of a feminist project to postcolonialism. Such uncertainties could also be due, however, to the way one views the structures requiring critical assessment and resistance. With Elisabeth Schüssler Fiorenza, my work attempts to address the intersecting structures of oppression and domination in what she has come to call *kyriarchy*. Schüssler Fiorenza coined this term based on the Greek word for lord or master, *kyrios*, a title that also would have been used for an ancient emperor.[14] As a replacement for patriarchy and its more simplified, dualistic analysis of power in gendered terms, kyriarchy highlights how multiple and mutually influential structures of domination and subordination function together in pyramidal relations determined not only by sexism, but also by racism, classism, ethnocentrism, heterosexism, colonialism, nationalism, and militarism. Thus, a feminist project that focuses its efforts on recognizing, critiquing, and resisting kyriarchal structures (and their multiple effects) should find common cause with postcolonial efforts that grapple with gender, sexuality, and status alongside and within racial, ethnic, imperial, and colonial formations. It is for this reason that this project (and my work in general) continues to make use of this helpful analytic category and maintains that other feminist projects should do likewise.

Nevertheless, some scholars working in postcolonial feminist interpretation have remained cautious, even critical of Schüssler Fiorenza's articulation of kyriarchy. Both Musa Dube and Kwok Pui-lan have raised concerns about some situations where kyriarchy has been used to conflate dominating structures, with the result of "bracketing" or downplaying imperialism.[15] Such concerns tend to coincide with Laura Donaldson's critique of the homology "man = colonizer, woman = colonized."[16] Such an equivalence belies the complexly heterogeneous manner in which gender and colonialism construct and contest each other. Therefore, greater attention is due to the particular ways in which gendered subjects (including, but not limited to, imperial pale females) have benefited from imperial and colonial formations.

Indeed, these kinds of critiques and cautions cogently describe some of the practical and theoretical blind spots of a great deal of feminist scholarship. Yet, the concerns with kyriarchy strike this reader as quite odd, given the concept's attention to imperial dynamics and its clear potential for adaptation to the legitimate judgments of postcolonial feminists.[17] For example, Kwok highlights how the colonizers' pyramidal kyriarchy is laid over local kyriarchies so that "the people of the colonizing nation, including the rich and the poor, men and women, dominate and exert control over the colonized people by imposing their system of power."[18] Rather than showing the limits of kyriarchy as a conceptual tool, though, this potential critique demonstrates how simultaneously flexible and useful the concept can be. Continuing with its originally geometric conceptualization, one could see how the area in one larger pyramid (representing, for example, global relations) contains and is constituted by a number of smaller pyramids in a range of positions: the relatively higher and more exclusive in the pyramid (a colonizing kyriarchal system) intersecting and thus shaping the relatively lower and more populous areas in the pyramid (the kyriarchies of various colonized peoples).[19] Hence, Dube and Kwok are right to call for more complicated analyses of the relations between dominators and dominated, but in halting their interrogations of kyriarchy at this point they do not discover the clear advantages and continued utility of its explicitly intersecting and pyramidal conceptualization.[20] It is my contention that such a concept can remain a relevant and helpful tool for feminist, postcolonial analyses of biblical literature and interpretation.

In a recent work, Schüssler Fiorenza addressed some of these criticisms and, in turn, raised some concerns of her own with the current trajectory of postcolonial and, most especially, postcolonial feminist biblical

studies.[21] A good portion of her attention is drawn to the potential similarities of this tension between feminist and postcolonial studies and a
previous disciplinary debate between feminists and Marxists. Akin to
some of the stances taken in those debates about how to conceptualize the
relationship between sexism/patriarchy and classism/capitalism, Schüssler
Fiorenza is concerned that too many biblical scholars (including postcolonial feminist biblical scholars) operate with a "dual systems analysis," only
the two separate systems are now patriarchy and imperialism.[22] From her
point of view, conceptual aids like kyriarchy are more helpful since they
recognize and seek to counter the intersecting and mutually multiplicative
structures of domination, including sexisms and imperialisms as well as
racisms, classisms, heterosexisms, and other oppressive dynamics.

Nevertheless, for the purposes of this study, it no longer seems adequate
to simply call the following analysis feminist.[23] For reasons both practical
and theoretical, we can no longer assume or subsume anti-imperial or postcolonial efforts within feminisms. Though some of the misapprehensions
cited at the start of this introduction could be viewed as minor among
our concerns, specifying this work as a feminist, postcolonial analysis of
Pauline letters and interpretation addresses all of them, and the other
dynamics already addressed, in a number of ways. For example, the following analysis retains the term *postcolonial* to indicate the increased attention to the insights of postcolonial scholars. In doing so, I seek to make
explicit my commitments against imperial and (neo)colonial dynamics, as
well as foreground the relationship between patriarchal/sexist and impe-
rial/colonial relations in the examinations to follow.

In articulating a feminist, postcolonial analysis, though, the comma
as a marker of a certain pause or discontinuity between feminist and
postcolonial should not be overlooked. To the contrary, the order and
punctuation are both intentional. The comma acts as a sign of the not-so-
straightforward relations between feminist and postcolonial work given
their theoretical tensions, practical indeterminacies, and historical ambiguities (examined thus far and to be expanded upon in the following chapters). As will become particularly clear for the study of Paul, this kind of
feminist, postcolonial project represents a process of invention and impro-
visation. Beyond punctuation, the order of the terms should also indicate
my own attempts to be honest about the historical, political, and theoretical precedence of feminism(s) to my own learning and living activities. In

my scholarly training, personal experience, and public activity, feminism has had an extraordinarily transformative and thus indelible and unmistakable impact. I have moved only more recently to an appreciation of postcolonial studies, even as it has a clear relevance and resonance to this and other projects. I do not believe these factors should predetermine the course taken in such efforts, but likely they underscore their effects on my present efforts. I highlight this self-understanding to enable engagement of this work on its specific terms, so that the interested reader also can assess its relative merits and shortcomings in light of the situatedness of its author, the reader(s), and the various intervening communities of accountability and influence for all involved in the exchanges still to come. Given the current contours of both global and local relations, such reflections on and responses to analyses borne from certain social locations are sure to be relevant.

In the end, I continue to utilize the term *postcolonial* to describe the efforts of this present project because, as a distinctive set of approaches and interventions, postcolonial studies has proved to be a key resource in identifying and resisting imperial and colonial forces, often as they overlap and coincide in gendered, eroticized, racialized, and/or ethnic dynamics. Postcolonial theory, for example, is increasingly becoming a recognizable field with its own developing canon of theorists, often focusing on one or more of the postcolonial trinity of Edward Said, Gayatri Chakravorty Spivak, and Homi Bhabha.[24] Although we will have cause to comment or elaborate upon all three of these usual suspects, this study also aims to extend biblical studies' theoretical apparatus to effectively integrate insights from a wider range of theorists, most especially when and as gender and/or sexuality are treated more prominently by some within postcolonial studies. In fact, a secondary contention of this project is that biblical studies would benefit from a greater acquaintance with a larger set of extra-biblical postcolonial scholars than those currently engaged. While Bhabha, in particular, has proven to be quite popular in some circles of postcolonial biblical criticism, this study suggests that further attention to the insights and import of Rey Chow, Inderpal Grewal, Anne McClintock, Sara Mills, Chandra Talpade Mohanty, Mary Louise Pratt, and Meyda Yeğenoğlu, among others, is now long overdue. Indeed, when one aspires to a feminist, postcolonial analysis, the need for further reading becomes apparent as scholars like Said frequently manage to downplay, elide, or ignore the formative role gender and sexuality play in Orientalism, racialization, and imperialism.[25]

One might raise similar concerns about proceeding in postcolonial biblical studies only from the work of Fernando Segovia or R. S. Sugirtharajah. While highlighting the pioneering role of these scholars' work in postcolonial biblical criticism, Kwok also has demonstrated how "gender remains a marginal issue in their overall analysis."[26] Though feminist approaches are occasionally acknowledged, they are rarely (if ever) woven into their postcolonial or decolonizing efforts.[27] To find sustained attention to the gender dimensions inherent in the operation of imperial and colonial power, one must turn to the reflections of feminist and postcolonial feminist scholars. It might be helpful, then, to limit and reconsider the influence and application of some postcolonial male critics. This reconsideration would have the additional advantage of encouraging us to turn to extra-biblical postcolonial studies and assess the import and relevance of various forms of scholarship under that rubric for our own distinct purposes, instead of receiving condensed versions through intermediaries in the field of biblical, religious, or antiquity studies.

As a feminist, postcolonial analysis of Pauline letters and interpretation, this study departs from tendencies that plague not only Sugirtharajah and Segovia, but also postcolonial biblical criticism in general. The first departure, an explicit emphasis on feminist approaches and goals, should be fairly clear by now. Yet, a second difference in this analysis is also quite significant: whereas the overwhelming majority of postcolonial scholars have focused on the Gospels and apocalyptic literature, very few have developed postcolonial perspectives on Paul. This is indeed surprising given the burgeoning interest in contextualizing Paul's letters relative to the structures of Roman imperialism.[28] The potential connections and the recurrent gaps between these approaches and feminist analyses require in-depth consideration and greater contextualization, which this study aims to provide.

―――― **Paul, Philippians, and the Plan of This Book** ――――

To navigate these different "strands" of biblical interpretation and develop a focused feminist, postcolonial analysis of Pauline letters and interpretation, this study must make a few strategic priorities from the outset.

Unlike the predominant tendency evident in Pauline studies, a priority will not be placed in reconstructing Paul's point of view or lionizing his rhetorical dexterity. Given the historic and contemporary uses of Pauline argumentation toward dominating ends, there is plenty of reason to proceed with a hermeneutics of suspicion and a plan of cautious critical assessment. Indeed, one purpose of this work is to demonstrate how Paul's letters and most (elite imperial pale malestream) scholarship on Paul are the results of imperially gendered rhetorical activities. Thus, like some feminist scholarship before it, this study aims to decenter the normative focus on Paul, in order to elaborate the relevant historical and rhetorical elements for a feminist, postcolonial analysis. In doing so, the analysis does not proceed by selecting either the temporal/chronological or the political/discursive connotations of postcolonialism. Rather, it maintains that we can effectively activate both meanings by addressing and blending historical and rhetorical aspects for the study of Paul.[29] Indeed, this theoretical divide provides one element to the structure of the whole, as it proceeds from historical to the rhetorical and, in turn, from the rhetorical back to the historical.

To discuss such significant trends in biblical interpretation as they have and have not altered Pauline studies, this project also should find a way to be as widely relevant, yet as soundly focused, as possible. This could prove to be difficult since, despite centuries of interpretation that view him otherwise, Paul is no systematic theologian. Those letters that have survived are not simply chapters that proceed from previous installments to logical conclusions. Rather, each letter operates with a distinctive plan, utilizes different strategies, emphasizes select elements, and aims to address disparate and often distant communities. As a result, a scholarly focus on Paul's letters and the massive amounts of interpretation, commentary, and analysis that now accompany them might understandably be prone to either pious generalities or scattered obscurities.

For this project, we seek to navigate between the Scylla of comprehensiveness and the Charybdis of precision by focusing many of the more textual portions of the arguments on one of Paul's letters: the letter to the Philippians.[30] This strategy will be most evident when the study proceeds into the rhetorical analyses of chapters 2 and 3, and returns to historical reflections in chapter 4. This focus on Philippians should function as an excellent case study of the tensions between interpretive strands and the problems in our common categories and modes of procedure. Spanning only four chapters, the letter to the Philippians is ideal to use for the purposes of precision: it is a relatively compact and manageable selection of Pauline argumentation. In attempting to argue for a different way of proceeding, Philippians also presents us with the advantage of being less familiar and less iconically "Pauline" than other, well-trodden letters like Romans, Galatians, or the Corinthian correspondence. Nevertheless, an examination of Philippi and the letter to the community also proves relevant to the wider study of Paul because it shares similar features and reflects recurrent dynamics with these other Pauline works. Like most (if not all) of his letters, Philippians adapts ancient imperial-political language, reflects on ethnic status, uses traditional materials, discusses others in the developing communities, and in particular, argues about the role of women in these communities. In addition, themes that would be central to a feminist, postcolonial analysis of any Pauline letter are key to the development of specific arguments in Philippians, whether we consider the issues of imitation and authority or the conditions of travel and contact.

Before moving to an examination of the rhetorics of Philippians and Pauline scholarship, however, the study charts in chapter 1 some of the recent developments in the field(s) of biblical studies, especially with regard to the use of postcolonialism and the study of Roman imperialism. In surveying the history of scholarly approaches to these dynamics (most especially by those working in the Paul and Politics group), chapter 1 will demonstrate that those malestream scholars that already have focused on colonialism or empire have ignored, elided, or downplayed the formative role gender and sexuality plays. However, most feminist scholarship on Paul has also failed to engage concerns over imperial situations or the colonizing status of the field. The gaps and conflicts in this history of biblical interpretation suggest that another route must be taken, and this chapter looks specifically to the work of Kwok and Dube as resources for a feminist, postcolonial analysis. Having established some of the contours of a feminist, postcolonial analysis, the chapter also considers the potential of the "people's history" project, as it is only now being applied to studies of the communities to which Paul wrote. Some of the same tensions and gaps that plague those scholars focusing on feminism, postcolonialism, or Roman imperialism remain evident in the initial conceptualization of these groups, especially when one further reflects on the insights of Marxist and feminist historians, subaltern scholars, and postcolonial feminist critics of all three. Nevertheless, such historical contextualization and critique could prepare the way for tentative alliances, still useful for the purposes of feminist, postcolonial analysis.

The second chapter turns to an analysis of the rhetoric of the text of the letter to the Philippians, while considering the priorities certain scholars have placed in their interpretations. A great deal of focus has been directed on the Christ hymn (2:6-11) and some of the language on the heavenly *politeuma* (3:18-21). By reexamining these passages and the scholarship that claims they carry an anti-imperial resonance, the chapter demonstrates the need for a feminist, postcolonial analysis that attends to the many directions in which the power dynamics in the text run. It also addresses the question about the text's stance vis-à-vis the imperialism of its time by answering four guiding questions from the work of Dube, expanding the analysis of the text beyond these two passages. Expanding on this analysis, the third chapter remains focused on the rhetorics of Philippians, this time treating the predominant theme of imitation by exploring the resources available in colonial and postcolonial studies on mimicry. In doing so, it examines especially the utility and shortcomings of Bhabha's approach to mimicry, especially as it fails to negotiate the intersections between gender, class, ethnicity, and empire. In contradistinction, engagement with the work of Chow, McClintock, and Yeğenoğlu can elucidate how Paul argues in a cross-ethnic, cross-gendered imperial context, as the study develops a more complicated picture of colonial and communal dynamics in terms of agency, resistance, reinscription, and/or co-optation.

The fourth chapter addresses the possibilities for historical reconstruction of people's roles in the community at Philippi. It functions to decenter the scholarly focus on the role of Paul by conceiving of Philippi as an ancient, colonial "contact zone." This term, from Mary Louise Pratt, stresses that the typical mixture of peoples from disparate origins (ethnic, cultic, political, geographic) in colonial locales allows for the mutual agency of colonizer and colonized, even as the conditions are asymmetrical and conflicted. Given this *colonia*'s location on an important route for travel and the fact that Paul and his letters depend upon these conditions for travel, the previous chapters' rhetorical analyses bolster the opportunities for non-idealized historical reflections, especially on the role of women, like Euodia and Syntyche, in the community. Finally, the fifth chapter concludes by summarizing some of the main findings of the previous chapters, while reflecting upon their relevance for biblical interpretation, as well as the wider contexts of a globalized, neocolonial, and masculinely militarized world. It functions as a greater call for further multi-axial or trans-disciplinary analyses of Paul's letters, among other texts. Strategic alliances between feminist, postcolonial, and queer theoretical approaches are particularly stressed, and a variety of challenges that still remain are outlined and linked to the efforts of this project.

This kind of approach to the study of Pauline letters and interpretation requires asking new questions about the heavenly politics in this letter and far too often inscribed in biblical scholarship. If Paul argues that "our *politeuma* is in the heavens" (Phil 3:20), then we should immediately question whether and how this arrangement could be different from the imperially gendered organization of people, for either the first or the twenty-first century. Does Paul's mode of arguing suggest immediate parallels to Roman claims of an authority that descends from such locations and across their expansive empire? Does translating *politeuma* as "commonwealth" or "citizenship" manage to obscure rather than confront the kyriarchal dynamics of institutions that themselves mask imperial dynamics behind a veneer of equality and accessibility? How do we ensure that we do more than simply maintain such a status quo, particularly given the conditions of globalized injustice and systemic inequalities in our world today? In taking such conditions seriously in the chapters that follow, these questions can begin to be answered and the efforts to resist and reshape this world can be bolstered so that we might achieve, if not a heavenly realm, then at least one more closely approximating one of radically realized peace, justice, and hope.

CHAPTER ONE

Histories of Interpretation and "People's History" in Pauline Studies

Initial Inquiries and Imperial Intersections in Interpretation

Introduction

Recent developments in the fields of biblical interpretation necessitate a reevaluation of the process for and import of interpreting Pauline letters. Indeed, the persistent and pernicious conditions of globalized injustice demonstrate the urgency with which this reevaluation should occur. This urgency presses biblical interpreters in particular because the contents of our work have been utilized not only historically, but also in all too recent imperialistic situations. In response, a growing body of work on postcolonial, anti-imperial, or decolonizing approaches is emphasizing the relevance of biblical rhetorics in colonizing and colonized discourse.[1] Running parallel to and occasionally overlapping with these approaches, a number of Pauline scholars are more carefully attending to the political context of the letters written to communities within the Roman Empire.[2]

Feminist interpretation has made significant contributions in both of these strands, even as it has often been decentered in the process. In addition, postcolonial feminists (from both within and outside of our field) note how frequently white and/or Western feminists have ignored or elided imperialism in our analysis.[3] These gaps, conflicts, and erasures in and between approaches will be further explored below, as a precursor to and preparation for a specifically feminist, postcolonial analysis of Paul's letters and their interpretation. Since this chapter offers an initial pursuit of this task, it begins with an awareness of the dynamics that prompt such an analysis, while seeking how to proceed from the contributions of postcolonial feminist work by biblical interpreters, including especially Musa W. Dube and Kwok Pui-lan.[4] Hopefully, it will become clear that feminist and postcolonial analysis can and should work toward mutual goals, even as we recognize both the difference between and the intersections of sexism(s) and imperialism(s). Finally, the procedures and goals of feminist, postcolonial analysis should prove to be particularly relevant for an examination of Paul's letters.[5]

Gaps, Erasures, and Conflicts

As highlighted above, biblical scholarship that addresses postcolonialism or Roman imperialism should be relevant to the task of this project. In fact, it seems that these pursuits would have rather clear connections to the goals of feminist biblical interpretation. Yet, feminist contributions have been elided and/or decentered in both postcolonial and Roman imperial studies. Additionally, it should be recognized that a great deal of white and/or Western feminist scholarship fails to acknowledge or (worse still) implicitly colludes with the imperialist tendencies of our field and the dominant culture.

Postcolonial feminist work, both from within biblical studies and in the wider circles of postcolonial theory, has highlighted how the colonial subject has often assumed a specifically male character. Women's roles in historical movements for decolonization have been minimized or erased, and an analysis of colonial dynamics that are themselves particularly and even centrally gendered was rarely taken up. Gayatri Chakravorty Spivak has pointed out how colonized women have been used as rationales for the "saving action" of colonists, because "white men are saving brown women from brown men."[6] The circumstances of women under colonization highlight not only their doubled or tripled colonization, but also the difference(s) between the forms of patriarchal oppression.[7] Chandra Talpade Mohanty has been particularly influential in this regard, demonstrating how the categories "woman" and "Third World woman" have been homogenized "under Western eyes." Producing such monolithic pictures erases the complex roles of women and gendered argumentation in colonialism and anti-colonialist struggle. Despite efforts by most parties to cast women as passive victims or territories to claim, women have been active participants in economic, political, and military struggles in colonized locales.[8]

These gaps and erasures are unfortunate, not only for the tasks of a feminist scholar, but also for a coherent and comprehensive decolonizing project, because "gender inequalities are *essential* to the structure of colonial racism and imperial authority."[9] Even for our contemporary situation, the gendered differences of neocolonialism are apparent in both "the global militarization of masculinity and the feminization of poverty."[10] In a context where women are seen as boundary markers for empire, and distant lands are "virgin territory" (under what Anne McClintock has dubbed the "porno-tropics" of empire), it becomes clear that sexuality as a domain must also be considered in an interconnected but independent fashion with gender.[11] Treating women, gender, and/or sexuality in a peripheral fashion or appending the subject of women's colonization as a supplement to the "primary" task only increases the disconnect.[12] By not engaging with an analysis of gender in colonial and anti-colonial contexts, postcolonial theory runs the risk of replicating elements of the colonial system.

In some ways, the critiques made by Spivak, Mohanty, and McClintock (among others) to postcolonial theory and anti-imperial work have been incorporated into the fields. It is notable that feminist and/or gender critique are now acknowledged in the field, so that most introductions must include such work. It also should be pointed out, though, that such contributions are more often listed in their own subsections or chapters, rather than integrated into the whole of the arguments.[13] Nevertheless, to an increasing degree, postcolonial scholars are aware of the role of feminist predecessors to and/or feminist advocates from within their ranks. The beginnings of postcolonial biblical interpretation are not divorced from these previous tendencies. For whatever reason (the initially androcentric nature of postcolonial theory at large, the still androcentric character of biblical studies, and/or its still burgeoning condition), postcolonial biblical interpretation has not foregrounded feminist contributions or focused on gender en route to "decolonizing biblical studies."[14]

For example, scholars like Ali Mazrui noted how "God, gold, and glory" were implemented as three rationales to justify the imperial regimes of the West.[15] As Musa Dube highlights for biblical interpretation, a great deal is lacking in such an analysis, though, because women in colonized locales are doubly or triply oppressed (under multiple patriarchal systems),[16] whereas gendered representations are "central to the narrative strategies of imperialism."[17] As a result, Dube argues compellingly that "gender" should be added to the three g's of colonial analysis of biblical texts.[18] Kwok Pui-lan also has noted how, even when analyzing the connections between religion and colonialism, interpreters "have left out the gender dimension."[19] This is particularly problematic in biblical studies, given the prominent role of biblical argumentation in ancient and more contemporary forms of colonization.[20] Kwok maintains that postcolonial feminist methods would aid in analyzing and negotiating any kind of a "postcolonial bible," as this collection "must also be seen as a political text written, collected, and redacted by the male colonial elite."[21]

In a similar fashion to their colleagues in postcolonial hermeneutics, scholars focused upon the Roman imperial context for the study of the Second Testament have also failed to adequately incorporate feminist insights and methods. The Paul and Politics section of the Society of Biblical Literature has been the home base for the production of several remarkable volumes of collected papers of immediate import for the topic at hand.[22] However, in spite of a range of critiques, cautions, and concerns raised by feminist scholars in such sessions and in these volumes, it is equally remarkable that the majority of the work rarely touches upon the topics of gender or sexuality or implements feminist practices. Far from recognizing the key role of gendered rhetorics in Paul's letters and in the empire, these volumes include feminist and/or female voices only to ignore or implicitly dismiss them.[23] One striking example involves the series of concerns raised by Elisabeth Schüssler Fiorenza, Cynthia Briggs Kittredge, Sheila Briggs, and Antoinette Clark Wire in the second volume of papers, titled *Paul and Politics*.[24] Schüssler Fiorenza noted how Paul's violent rhetorics are not so different from imperial discourse, and Briggs demonstrated how ignoring sexuality when discussing slavery in Paul also evades the coercion of Roman imperial institutions.[25] Wire's responses questioned how including women would alter the liberating picture presented by some of the articles.[26] Echoing the parallel insights of postcolonial feminist work, Kittredge pointed out how feminist interpreters treating gender as a central category have already provided important qualifications to such views, qualifications that had not been accounted for to that point.[27]

An awareness of gender relations or feminist analyses, then, would seem crucial to any construction of the imperial system of Paul's time.[28] Despite what should be considered central observations to the project of comprehending the Roman imperial context of the letters, most entries in the two volumes that follow pass over or seem simply unaware of these qualifications and reservations, or for that matter, even the development of feminist biblical interpretation in the past thirty years.[29] Outside of the final article[30] of the next volume (*Paul and the Roman Imperial Order*), however, gender constructs and feminist approaches are never considered, whereas the roles of particular women are treated briefly in only two places (in the article by Agosto and in the introduction to the volume).[31] Even when feminist insights are permitted within the bounds of these examinations, their work, as well as previous feminist scholarship, is rarely footnoted and even more rarely taken into account.[32] Turning to the *Hidden Transcripts and the Arts of Resistance* volume, Richard Horsley insists that resistance aspects were "previously unnoticed" until scholars turned to James C. Scott's work.[33] However, these comments prove to be a sadly ironic commentary on malestream biblical scholarship, because scholars could only claim this lack of notice if they themselves failed to notice how years of feminist scholarship on Pauline literature had already offered a number of strategies for "reading against the grain," with a hermeneutics of suspicion, or reading for the submerged voices of the oppressed.[34] Alongside the continuing occlusion of gender, such introductory comments are even more surprising given Kittredge's contribution towards the end of the volume. Here again, Kittredge highlights the previous feminist contributions for the task at hand, while cautioning about the politics of choosing Scott's theoretical model.[35]

Still, as feminist and postcolonial feminist scholars have been making such arguments to these sets of malestream colleagues, the bulk of feminist scholarship on biblical literature has yet to address these exact same dynamics. Even rather recent feminist work on Pauline letters foregrounds neither the phenomenon of colonialism or the conditions of empire for the creation and reception of these letters. Two brief examples should suffice to make this point.[36] In Sandra Hack Polaski's recent book, *A Feminist Introduction to Paul* (2005), Roman emperors and bits of Roman law are discussed.[37] Even as Polaski often optimistically presents Paul's letters as standing in contradistinction to the structures of his day, there is no

indication that Roman imperialism might be an important or even fundamental agent of such structuring. Of the ten contributions to the *Feminist
Companion to Paul* collection (2004), only Luzia Sutter Rehmann's article
considers the particularly *imperial* context of Paul's letters.[38] Furthermore,
the only entry to critique imperialism is Luise Schottroff's analysis of
the anti-Judaism of modern Christian views of "law-free Christianity."[39]
Indeed, this might be an important connection for postcolonial feminist
approaches, as Shawn Kelley's work traces how both anti-Judaism and
Orientalism were combined in the racialized discourse of the Western
colonialist project, with very problematic results for the field of biblical studies.[40]

To be clear, this incredibly brief overview of some of the gaps, conflicts,
and erasures involved in articulating a feminist, postcolonial analysis of
a Pauline letter is not meant to repudiate certain scholars or attain some
"pure" method or vantage point from which to proceed.[41] As Kelley has
already pointed out, embracing any concept of a pristine method or pure
origins would only further implicate my own work in the racialist hierarchy that was used to align Paul with civilization, universalism, and exis-
tential authenticity.[42] To be even more candid, this colonial and racialized
heritage went unacknowledged in my own attempt (in a previous meeting
and the subsequent article) to work out a feminist analysis of Paul's mutuality rhetorics.[43] This sketch, then, is not meant to be a game of academic
"gotcha." Rather, it should be an indication of some of the gaps in interpretations of Paul's letters, including my own, and some of the reasons to
proceed with the help of postcolonial feminist interpretation.

To be sure, feminist critiques preceded and in some ways opened some
practical and disciplinary spaces for postcolonial analysis. At the same
time, we should avoid being overly triumphant about this precedence,
given the complicated historical interconnections between feminism, religious power, and colonialism.[44] For example, Spivak has analyzed some of
the ways Western or First World feminists have appropriated the history
of Two/Thirds World women. By claiming the authority to speak for their
"others," feminists like Kristeva, then, mimic the role of the imperialist.[45]
Unfortunately, this is not a new role for women of the West, as studies of
"colonial feminism" have since made clear.[46] Women's roles as missionaries
highlight this especially fraught territory. Kwok, for example, makes the
disturbing point: "Judging from the magnitude of women's participation

in mission and the amount of money raised to support such activities, the women's missionary movement must be regarded as the largest women's movement in the nineteenth and early twentieth centuries."[47]

Thus, even when using helpful analytic concepts like *kyriarchy*, we must be careful with how they are used.[48] Such a concept is instructive for our purposes, as it underscores how colonialism and sexism intersect. However, both Dube and Kwok have raised concerns about some situations where kyriarchy has been used to conflate dominating structures, with the result of "bracketing" or downplaying imperialism.[49] Their analysis coincides with Laura Donaldson's critique of the homology "man = colonizer, woman = colonized."[50] Challenging this homology should make clear the difference between identifying forms of oppression and treating all forms as identical.[51] Thus, in the following analysis, we should attempt to recognize how imperialism and sexism intersect with each other, as well as heterosexism, ethnocentrism, racism, anti-Judaism, poverty, nationalism, and militarism (among others).[52] Yet, even as gender is foregrounded in the following analysis of colonialism, these structures also should be comprehended in their distinct functions.

Procedure and Precedent

Having briefly contextualized this study in some of the intersecting dynamics between different segments of our field(s), we still must establish a mode of procedure that will address these dynamics as part of a feminist, postcolonial analysis of Pauline studies. Indeed, as the preceding comments should make clear, there are already a number of rich resources for decolonizing or postcolonial feminist work, and biblical scholars already have and could still further draw upon the insights of Spivak, Donaldson, Mohanty, McClintock, or Trinh T. Minh-ha, among many others.[53] In many cases, biblical scholars like Gale Yee, Judith McKinlay, Jean K. Kim, Hisako Kinukawa, Sharon H. Ringe, and Kathleen O'Brien Wicker are instructive pioneers and predecessors to this project.[54] However, due to the exigencies of time and space, this overview of procedure primarily draws upon the work of Dube and Kwok for a number of reasons. First, both were among the first to write in these areas, and they have done so widely and effectively.[55] Second, both have examined Second Testament texts, with at least some allusions to Paul's letters.[56] Third, and most importantly for the purpose of this section, both provide some structures or plans on how to proceed with such an analysis.

There is no single way to engage in this task, as Dube makes clear by introducing us to at least eleven different procedures for a postcolonial feminist interpretation.[57] Kwok is also careful to delineate that there is no one overarching method or approach for feminists who engage with postcolonial criticism (just as there is no singular feminist method). However, Kwok helpfully sketches five areas of "common concerns," most of which this study seeks to address (if only initially).[58]

Kwok highlights first the concern to "investigate how the symbolization of women and deployment of gender in the text relate to class interests, modes of production, concentration of state power, and colonial domination."[59] The interrelation of imperialism(s) and sexism(s) plays a foundational role in articulating postcolonial or transnational feminisms,[60] a point that already was mentioned and to which we will return. This could prove particularly relevant, as at least some Pauline interpreters have failed to recognize such interconnections when positing an "anti-imperial Paul."[61] Second, Kwok explains that "postcolonial feminist critics pay special attention to the biblical women in the contact zone and present reconstructive readings as counternarrative."[62] Thus, the analysis should address the role of women in the community as well as the context of the communities in ancient cities like Philippi and Corinth, as they fit Kwok's articulation of a contact zone as "the space of colonial encounters where people of different geographical and historical backgrounds are brought into contact with each other, usually shaped by inequality and conflictual relations."[63] Although this should be a concern throughout, it will be most evident in the analysis of the fourth chapter.

In some ways, the immediately preceding section initiated a consideration of the third area of concern, as it began to "scrutinize metropolitan interpretations, including those offered by both male and feminist scholars, to see if their readings support the colonizing ideology by glossing over the imperial context and agenda, or contribute to decolonizing the imperializing texts for the sake of liberation."[64] It should be noted that simply identifying the imperial context does not necessarily lead to decolonization.[65] Due to a lack of time and a certain degree of training and access, this study will not take up Kwok's fourth task, that is, "in order to subvert the dominant Western patriarchal interpretations, postcolonial feminist critics, especially those in Africa, emphasize the roles and contributions of ordinary readers."[66] The resulting gap in this work should, in turn, be critically engaged so that its results can be tested and measured against its import for "flesh and blood readers."[67] It is the genuine hope and goal of this work to prove to be a useful resource, whether by reactions of inter-connection or interrogation, for these or any readers engaging the multi-plicative forces and forms of domination. (Ultimately its success should be judged accordingly.) Finally, Kwok highlights the importance of "what Mary Ann Tolbert has called the politics and poetics of location."[68] Bibli-cal scholars must recognize the central shaping role of our complex social backgrounds in terms of gender, race, status, and sexual orientation among other factors (politics), while striving to assess our texts and interpretive results for their ethical or theological impact (poetics). Although this vol-ume often might focus more on one of these elements than on others, we should expect these other areas to influence this inquiry and any others that might, in turn, develop from it.

Perhaps the most direct way to begin to address the first two areas of concern sketched by Kwok (especially in the next chapter) would be to assess Paul's letters through some of the more pointed questions raised by Dube. On more than one occasion, Dube lists four questions that can be used to evaluate ancient texts on their literary-rhetorical grounds:

1. Does this text have a clear stance against the political imperialism of its time?
2. Does this text encourage travel to distant and inhabited lands, and how does it justify itself?
3. How does this text construct difference: is there dialogue and liber-ating interdependence or condemnation of all that is foreign?
4. Does this text employ gender and divine representations to con-struct relationships of subordination and domination?[69]

These questions address a central question for the study of Pauline let-ters, in general, that of Paul's relationship to and/or against imperialism. However, it does so by raising a number of other, affiliated issues that most Pauline scholars do not consider. In the analysis still to come, then, these questions will prove to be particularly useful for an assessment of Paul and some of the scholarly observations about his letters.[70]

While all four questions will be addressed in the following chapter, the latter two questions should prove most relevant in considering a still-evolving approach to Pauline interpretation in the second half of this chapter.

People's Possibilities: Subaltern History and Problems of Perspective

People's History and Pauline Studies

Having surveyed the recent past of Pauline scholars engaging issues of gender and empire, there is still one more horizon to consider, as it is still developing its own procedure and perspective. More recently, there has been a move toward thinking about a "people's history" approach within Pauline studies. This is, indeed, part of a wider movement and publication agenda, as indicated by the production of a whole series of volumes on people's history spanning centuries of Christian developments.[71] Following on the heels of these collections is a slightly more focused effort to examine the import of such an approach for the study of the communities to which Paul wrote his letters. So, on a smaller, more intensive scale, a number of scholars have begun gathering in working groups to conceive of alternative approaches to the history of the assemblies at Corinth, Galatia, and Philippi.

As a member and organizer of the last of these working groups (on Philippi), I argue that there might be some potential to such an evolving approach. Yet, I am also advocating (here and on previous occasions) for a mode of analysis more attuned to the intersecting dynamics of gender, sexuality, ethnicity, and empire. What place (if any) is there for feminist, postcolonial analyses of Pauline materials in such a people's history project? If many of these scholars are among those who have yet to take up the challenge to be accountable to such ethical-political issues (as described above), why and how will *this* approach be any different? Under what conditions could people's history decolonize the sexist, racist, and imperialist history of Pauline interpretation? It is precisely those questions that this study seeks to address now by highlighting the potential problems and the still manifest possibilities for "people's history."

First, one must detail how this orientation toward historical work differs from that before it, particularly in the context of Second Testament and early Christian studies. Perhaps the easiest way to enter into such descriptive (re)considerations is to examine how Richard Horsley explains this approach. As the editor of the first People's History of Christianity volume, focused upon Christian origins, Horsley introduces the volume with a helpful overview of the import and the difference a people's history approach makes.[72] People's history departs from standard history in a number of ways, not the least of which is the focus on people besides the elite, the so-called "great men," who were the shapers of human history.[73] This change in focus contests the idea that the non-elite are insignificant in history, leading to a reexamination of the scope and the sources for historiography. With one's historical perspective shifted to one "from below," the scholar must consider all aspects of life and look in interdisciplinary ways at a wider range of source materials.[74] From the outset, then, there appears to be little in the wider goals or perspectives of a people's history that is inconsistent or at least incompatible with the goals of feminist, postcolonial analysis. Both are looking to rearrange our perspectives on these materials to highlight or discover views of the world besides the normalizing elite imperial pale malestream.

The biblical scholar's adaptation of this move in historiography seems especially apt to Horsley: "For in the period of their origins, the communities and movements that were later called Christianity consisted of nothing but people's history."[75] Yet, given the influence of later Christian traditions and authorities, these materials and figures were seldom treated as belonging with the people. Debaters like Paul became saints, small assembled communities were churches, their leaders bishops, and their debates centered on doctrine. Aside from the potential for anachronism, this strategy of reading the early history obscured the frequently popular settings of these developing communities. The content and impact of their ideas and practices were not simply theological, but had wider social and political ramifications, particularly as they developed within the context of Roman imperial rule.[76] Instead of assimilating first-century contentions and expressions to the dominant frame provided by the later Eurocentric clerical male version of high culture, they might be more appropriately contextualized as the "little tradition" of the non-elite peasantry.[77] To do so, Horsley acknowledges that we must read elite sources critically and "against the grain," much as feminist historians have practiced such techniques.[78]

In this manner, Horsley's charting of people's history recognizes that there is some role for considering women and empire in adopting a new perspective on the history of these developing communities.[79] Yet, as previous interrogations of Pauline studies have shown, it is not simply a matter of *whether* gendered and colonizing dynamics are addressed, but *how* they are approached. As Horsley concludes his introductory survey of people's history and Christian origins, he gives no indication as to how and why this particular umbrella term is particularly adept at recognizing and resisting such power relations in history or in interpretation, aside from raising them as topics for our awareness. As an orientation toward the project of history, there is little that might specifically ensure the relevance and accountability for which we aim in feminist, postcolonial analyses. In stressing the "eclectically multidisciplinary" agenda of the project, Horsley unwittingly highlights the ambiguous status of people's history relative to the aims of feminist, postcolonial analysis.[80] Although such a description could broadly fit the manner with which feminist, postcolonial work necessarily draws upon a range of insights and approaches that reside in between or across traditional disciplines, it does not specify exactly how and why people's history is multidisciplinary. Which methods or disciplines "count" as appropriate or useful? On what basis is this decided and to what ends are we mixing or crossing the disciplines?

A people's history of Christian origins may not have reached a point where it can vigorously outline answers to such questions. Hence, we have an opportunity to help to shape the contours of this wider set of approaches and calibrate them so that they are more attuned to feminist, postcolonial goals. To determine if and how people's historians can be allies and conversation partners, then, we must more widely evaluate the development of what has alternately been called the new history, people's history, and/or history from below. Reconsidering the sources for Horsley's and others' constructions of this new kind of historiography should prove to be useful in this regard.

Genealogies, Genders, Gaps, and Geopolitics in People's History

There have been a number of cautions, concerns, and critiques raised with the development of these newer perspectives on the construction of history.[81] First among them are all those issues related to the naming and initial definition of this perspective on people's history or history from below. As mentioned above, these forms of historiography developed as responses to the way history had been written; it represented an attempt to do the opposite of Rankean history.[82] Thus, as it was based upon the logic of inversion or negation, it also manages to reaffirm and reinscribe the founding dichotomization (above/below or elite/people) that it purports to resist.[83] This way of organizing the approach resonates with the Orientalist rhetorics of history that constructed the rest as opposed to the West.[84] This underscores a range of other difficulties with the ideas that follow.

Even if one were to conceptualize the people in a non-oppositional fashion that manages not to reinscribe a problematic definition from the start, the term *the people* is itself plagued by its own vague indeterminacy. After all, to which people is it referring and whose people are they? Who counts as the people? Are the people: everyone, everyone besides the elite, the poor, the uneducated, the subordinate, and/or the subaltern?[85] These groups are far from identical. In discussing these people, a range of differentiating factors must be weighed and considered for their import and then the lines drawn must somehow be defended as legitimate. How poor does one have to be in order to be considered among "the poor" people? The placement of such an identificatory dividing line is highly unstable and ambiguous. Using the related terms *popular* or *below* does not lessen the definitional difficulty. As Jim Sharpe explains:

> As far as I can see, apart from regarding it as some sort of residual category, no historian has yet come up with a fully comprehensive definition of what popular culture in that period actually was. The fundamental reason for this is that "the people," as far back as the sixteenth century at least, were a rather varied group, divided by economic stratification, occupational cultures and gender. Such considerations render invalid any simplistic notion of what "below" might mean in most historical contexts.[86]

Each of these differentiating definitions has the potential to be so variedly vague that in specifying the term, scholars often erase significant factors, including gender, sexuality, and placement in imperial or colonial relations (among a range of others). Furthermore, the concept of a people often draws upon distinctions based on ethnicities and purported nationalities, those differentiations that have so often been deployed in colonized and colonizing rhetorics.[87] Even a concept so seemingly straightforward as "below" bears the marks of its hierarchical use: from the uncivilized races below the European on the chain of human progress, to the way the imperial male resides on the sexualized top of the world (with the passive virgin territories quaking below the military penetration and control).

Given the history of the development of this concept, though, perhaps it should be no surprise that historians of the people have not adroitly asked, "Are women among the people?" This approach to historiography traces a particularly British Marxist lineage to and through scholars like Eric J. Hobsbawm and Edward P. Thompson.[88] Feminists have long struggled over the relative utilities and problems of implementing Marxist theories or resources, given the historical erasure or even blindness to women and gender in Marxist works.[89] Unfortunately, the development of people's history approaches continues in a similarly problematic trajectory, particularly for those historians focused on women's history and/or the study of the subaltern.[90]

To elaborate upon these dynamics and difficulties in the history of history-writing, one could attend to the impact of and response to E. P. Thompson's work as emblematic of feminist and postcolonial concerns with history from below. After all, it was Thompson who viewed his task as rescuing the history of the people "from the enormous condescension of posterity."[91] Furthermore, Thompson's work *The Making of the English Working Class* has been widely acknowledged for developing the mode of social history later adopted and adapted by many feminist historians.[92] Yet, as indicated in the reflections above, the engagement with Thompson is not at all unproblematic. Once again, the main issue is not *whether* specific women are examined in this landmark work, but *how* Thompson chose to do so. Indeed, women are featured among the eighteenth- and nineteenth-century activists covered by Thompson, yet the normative, Marxist class identity is still defined by masculinity:

> [C]lass happens when some men, as a result of common experiences (inherited or shared), feel and articulate the identity of their interests as between themselves, and as against other men whose interests are different from (and usually opposed to) theirs. The class experience

is largely determined by the productive relations into which men are born—or enter involuntarily.[93]

One might apologize for Thompson's definitional efforts by attempting to explain the historical conventionality of androcentric terms ("men") for the general in the 1960s. However, this would only blind our analysis to how Thompson's work is itself developing a supposedly gender-blind, but essentially male definition of the "working man."[94]

Joan Scott argues that this kind of definition imposes an ahistorical unity upon working class movements in England, a unity which is plagued by the clumsy way in which women are placed as both internal and external to the historical subject constructed as masculine, rational, and properly political.[95] The first, universalizing gesture occurs in Thompson, as he tends to see the collectivity in terms analogous to the individualist, semi-biographical mode of "life history."[96] Thus, women like Mary Wollstonecraft *could* be included in this universalist category, yet their gendered particularities function to disrupt the seeming transparency of a united, coherent, and self-identical group. Simultaneously, a second, oppositional gesture recurs in Thompson, as he frequently posits certain women as negative foils to such masculinity-emphasized figures like Thomas Paine.[97] The tasks of the people are constructed as over against the feminine, specifically constructed as expressive, hysterical, and irrational, demonstrating how not only gender, but also sexuality and religiosity are mutually defined by and intertwined with class.[98]

Thus, to ask the question, "Are women included in the history of the people?" is likely to garner the complicated answer, "Yes ... maybe ... but how?" According to Scott, following in the footsteps of Thompson has been an ambiguous project for feminist historians. To include women in this kind of historical project cannot simply be a matter of adding evidence about women into the mix (the recurrent, reformist "add women and stir" formula). Rather than their incorporation into history, "[i]nstead, women either continue to be excluded from working-class history, or to be awkwardly included as special examples of the general (male) experience, or to be treated entirely separately."[99] The undesirability of all three outcomes indicates that the very nature of these pursuits have been structured in such a manner that requires the interrogation of their operating premises. The analysis of feminist historians highlights the need to identify and delineate how class is not isolated from, but is mutually constructed alongside gender, sexuality, and religion (among other dynamics) in both historical developments *and* in the work of historians.

The need for this kind of analysis as an accompaniment, adaptation, and/ or continuing critique of history from below is made all the more clear after turning toward its use and negotiation in the case of subaltern studies. Since the 1980s, a group of scholars began focusing on what can be known about the history of India from the perspective of the non-elite and offered a series of publications on these topics, titled *Subaltern Studies*.[100] Indeed, there are many reasons to connect the work of Ranajit Guha (and others), at least initially, with Thompson and Hobsbawm.[101] Guha and other historians of India and South Asia were interested in confronting the elitist tendencies of historians who had repeatedly failed to see how various subordinated groups acted differently from and independently of the elite. In this vein, both sets of historians were inspired by Marx and particularly for the historians of the subaltern, Gramsci, from whom the concept of the subaltern originally developed.[102] Yet, in the face of the claims made by scholars like Arif Dirlik, Dipesh Chakrabarty argues carefully for how the scholars of the subaltern studies made some substantial departures from and specific critiques of the British Marxists who preceded them.[103]

One particular locale for critique and departure in Guha's work involves the articulation of "political" subjectivity. Hobsbawm, for instance, had previously classified certain forms of peasant uprisings as "pre-political" if they were organized on bases different from class consciousness.[104] Both Hobsbawm's and Thompson's work evince a historicist, stagist view of what could qualify for revolutionary action, proceeding from "primitive" to more developed, conscious, and organized modes of protest. In such a view, the peasant must be transformed into a political actor, whereas Guha's work challenges such notions by insisting on the various participatory forms of the "politics of the people," especially as it differs from the elite and institutionally-focused means of delineating political action.[105] The creation of subaltern studies highlights, then, the distinctly Eurocentric tenor of even Marxist historical work, if it is left unexamined.[106] As with the Marxist evaluation of some women's subjectivity above, the Indian peasants' "primitive" rebellion is contrasted negatively with the working men's revolution by means of its association with the "religious," or *dharma*.[107] Furthermore, the historical process whereby working-class men (and sometimes also women) developed as a class was worked out in opposition to colonized peoples. All classes were educated into their participation with British imperialism, so much so that the working-class constituted themselves as a group "close to home."[108]

Indeed, the key difference between Guha and Thompson or Hobsbawm is the manner in which Guha treats differences like these. The universalizing trend observed by women's historians also has come under scrutiny by historians of the subaltern, as the stress of Guha's work relies less on identifying an overarching and generalized consciousness (in which all revolting Indian peasants share) than on examining the specific differences in insurgent practices.[109] This examination is crucial given the particular and continuing dynamics of colonialist, nationalist, and capitalist formations in South Asia. The more stagist, evolutionist paradigms of the European Marxists, for example, could be easily adapted to the nationalist (and possibly neocolonial) narrative of the elite guiding the peasants out of their pre-capitalist/pre-political phase into modernity and stable nationhood. Yet, it is exactly these kinds of elitist historical narratives that subaltern studies seek to resist and displace.[110] The expansion in the subjects of history involves a post-nationalist interrogation of how scholarship and the state both construct and erase certain forms of difference. (This lack of engagement with the specifics of colonizing and nationalizing practices is all the more remarkable in the case of Thompson, as his father Edward John Thompson himself had argued liberally against the British Empire and for Indian independence.[111])

Of course, closer examination of gender and the role of women is missing from not only the British Marxist forms of history from below, but also these South Asian, postcolonial studies of the subaltern. As a participant in some of the dialogues of the subaltern studies group, Spivak has made some of the strongest criticisms of Guha and others' work.[112] Given the strategic and often complicated ways in which Spivak writes in terms of feminist, Marxist, deconstructionist, and decolonizing techniques, her work is uniquely situated relative to the three historiographic trajectories considered here.[113] Aside from commenting upon the generalized absence of women in subaltern studies, Spivak notes how the figure of the woman is both necessary for, yet marginalized within, the concept of the subaltern.[114] Concepts of gender and sexuality function as carriers of territorial meaning and communal power, yet these scholars obscure the structuring role of these concepts.[115]

In her justifiably (in)famous article "Can the Subaltern Speak?" Spi-vak's interrogations range over the import of feminist, Marxist, and subal-tern forms of theorization. The masculinist bent of Marxism, for example, is signaled by its failure to examine the role of the family. As Scott and others have indicated above, Spivak also argues, "[n]or does the solution lie in the positivist inclusion of a monolithic collectivity of 'women' in the list of the oppressed whose unfractured subjectivity allows them to speak for themselves against an equally monolithic 'same system.'"[116] One cannot simply "add women" to the people nor assume the univocity of any such group (like women). Spivak similarly troubles Guha's delineation of the subaltern over and against the indigenous elite. Guha introduces not just two indigenous groupings (the dominating, client elite and the people/subaltern), but a third indigenous group that could have been dominant at regional or local levels.[117] Ironically, in an effort to be taxonomic (and even essentialist), Guha reintroduced heterogeneities and contradictions within the groups defined alternately as subaltern or elite.[118] Like "the people" in Thompson and Hobsbawm, "the subaltern" of Guha is frac-tured and ambiguously applied.

Finally, Spivak questions how gender is rendered in subalterneity and modernity. The figure of woman has been used in particular ways by both the colonizer and the colonized (both formerly and continuously):

> both as object of colonialist historiography and as subject of insur-gency, the ideological construction of gender keeps the male domi-nant. If, in the context of colonial production, the subaltern has no history and cannot speak, the subaltern as female is even more deeply in shadow.[119]

Spivak here elaborates on the monolithic construction of the "third world woman," a phenomenon noted by Chandra Mohanty and Uma Narayan, among others.[120] When approached through Eurocentric, patriarchal, and colonizing practices, the subjectivity of women in and after empire(s) is con-structed within a system that preserves rather than resists domination.[121]

These dynamics make it difficult to hear those voices to which E. P. Thompson believed historians could simply "listen."[122] This has meant, at times, that even feminists have unwittingly repeated colonizing narra-tives, especially in relation to colonized women. Feminist scholars ironi-cally, then, find themselves in the company of the elder Edward (John)

Thompson, whose imperializing "love of India" represents Indian women in need of his enlightened rescue.[123] Spivak sounds, then, a most powerful cautionary note about our use of such resources. To proceed in terms of a feminist, postcolonial analysis, we will need to attend to the effects of subject-construction from within *any* kind of history from below. Though he is disciplined by a more Marxist view of the world and its historical progressions, E. P. Thompson's mind-set of "rescuing" the people "from the enormous condescension of posterity" might share more than a passing family resemblance to the saving civilizing mission of empire.

Back to the Biblical: Antiquity and Feminist, Postcolonial Approaches

Returning to the field of Pauline studies, the questions must be asked again: can there be a history from below that traces women in empire? How do we write a people's history of the gendered and imperial dynamics of antiquity in the Roman era? The preceding analyses evoke some significant concerns for such a project. The tendency to universalize certain empowered identities and to whitewash differences of gender, sexuality, class, ethnicity, and imperial-colonial status have recurred in a great deal of historical scholarship. Moreover, dynamics like nationalism, capitalism, and (neo)colonialism have often been treated as if they were not constructed together with, and mutually reinforced by, normalizing dynamics of gender, sexuality, and religion.

These critiques, concerns, and contextualizations suggest that if there is a path for a women's history from below and a postcolonial people's history, it will require greater critical attention to these dynamics and differentials of power. If the people's history approach to Pauline materials is to be consistent with the ethical-political goals of feminist, postcolonial analysis, then it must demonstrate that it can and will interrogate this interpretive history alongside the variegated contexts of these early assemblies in Corinth, Galatia, and Philippi. Echoing Joan Scott's assessment of the fate of women in working-class history, the place of women subjects of the empire cannot be ignored or treated as a separate "special topic" to the "main task" of people's history.[124] Furthermore, this kind of analysis cannot be awkwardly included around the interpretive margins, nor should it be even more problematically inserted into the heart of the currently

kyriarchical viewpoints and approaches of malestream Pauline scholarship. It must begin elsewhere, starting with a critique of our approaches in
order to develop a procedure that will address these dynamics and assess
the structures of domination in the historical past and the historiogra-
pher's work. (The opening portion of this chapter attempts just such a
critical beginning.)

Though the potential for a feminist, postcolonial solidarity or partner-
ing with these efforts might still persist, it remains yet to question *why*
this particular umbrella term (people's history) is introduced and *how* it
might be suited to the task that it sets out for itself and that this study
has attempted to adapt. One might wonder what rhetorical appeal there
is in building upon the work of Peter Burke, E. P. Thompson, or E. J.
Hobsbawm. For a scholar of religion, the recourse to historiography could
be viewed as a grounding gesture, shifting one's position away from the
confessional or the spiritual and suggesting a certain more rigorous and
academic tradition. Yet, given the intersecting role of religiously styled
claims in much of what was described above, such a shift could distract
from the specific workings of sexist, racist, and colonialist structures.[125]
Rather, this tendency seems to call for closer attention and a heightened
vigilance for scholarship that is not only geared toward the historical or the
political, but also to their various intersections with and in the religious.

Recalling the recurrent historical scenes of the Other (working-class
woman, Indian primitive, devoted colonized native wife) constructed
simultaneously with some mode of religiosity should also remind us of
its co-construction on specifically gendered terms. Is part of the appeal of
people's history, then, in avoiding the troubles that gender makes for history? It is hard to ignore that the roots of this history from below go back
to *before* historians were confronted by the critiques of those attempting
to write women's history. E. P. Thompson wrote *The Making of the English
Working Class* at a time more tolerant of its uniform and masculine class
consciousness. It must be asked whether particular allusions to this type
of book or this period in scholarship constitute an attempted nostalgic
return, especially because, as Keith McClelland notes, "[t]he question of
gender has been the single most important challenge to existing historiography since the book was written."[126] If the answer were to come back in
the affirmative, this would suggest that there is no place for feminist, postcolonial analysis in this kind of people's history. Not only must a feminist,

postcolonial analysis be cautious of such nostalgia, but it must also remain attentive to the function of claims to be doing something "new." As Peter Burke so savvily explicated in terms of labeling this kind of social history as "new history," historians since the time of Polybius have continuously claimed innovation for themselves.[127] Given the current context of a globalized, neocolonial economic system, one must also be on guard for how claims to newness fit into narratives of market progress and capitalist comprehensiveness, whatever the "new" form of scholarship being touted.

Regardless of the future direction of these projects on the people's history of Pauline assemblies, this study not only refuses to avoid this "most important challenge," but also seeks to complicate it by greater critical attention to the imperializing and colonizing trajectories that coincide with rhetorical and historical work on women, gender, and sexuality in antiquity. These issues are not marginal, but central to this project (if not to all practitioners of people's history). As indicated at the start of this discussion, these tasks are not incompatible with some of the initial ways Horsley, for example, describes the goals and approaches of a people's history of Christian origins. Indeed, for the last two to three decades, feminist biblical scholars have been developing and refining just such critical approaches to interpreting problematic source materials like the letters of Paul.[128] Recognizing that these letters are not transparent windows to the past, Elisabeth Schüssler Fiorenza, in particular, has repeatedly argued for a critical "reading against the grain" of the kyriarchical texts of this time period. To practice historical remembrance of women, one must recognize that these texts are not descriptive of a first-century reality but are attempts to be prescriptive of a reality they are seeking to construct.

Thus, for interested participants in the search for a people's history of Pauline assemblies, the work of feminist interpreters should prove themselves to be instructive examples of the approaches already available for such a task. Though feminist scholars have attended to the dynamics of empire, in text and interpretation (hence the kyriarchy as opposed to patriarchy in Schüssler Fiorenza's work), the critical questions and the evaluative reflections of postcolonial feminist scholars, like Dube and Kwok, should aid in recognizing and assessing the intersecting and mutually constructing dynamics of empire with gender, sexuality, and ethnicity. Furthermore, feminist, postcolonial, and most especially queer theoretical work could also stress a continuously critical disposition toward the potential for universalization that persistently plagues projects like a people's history. Any efforts to determine the ordinary, the typical, or the normative view of a group (especially one so poorly delineated as the people or those below) must be treated with special suspicion, given the ways norms have functioned to reinforce (rather than resist) the status quo. The normative so often leads to normalization, particularly of the perspective of the elite pale malestream that holds a certain prized status or performance of gender, sexuality, ethnicity, age, ability, and imperial-colonial placement. Queer theoretical perspectives, in particular, demand that we inspect the functioning of such norms.

Once more, the resources are already at the disposal of people's history projects; the question remains as to whether one should and/or how one could aspire to reconstruct the typical view of the peasant or the poor woman in the assemblies at Corinth, Galatia, or Philippi. In constructing the common people, commonalities are likely reinforced and reinscribed, erasing the differences within and among these people and whitewashing a complex picture into a monochromatic representation. Such a potential goal in people's history likely also marginalizes the particular, the challenging, the fascinating, and even the queer within these communities, dulling the rich possibilities of historical reconstructive efforts.

In the end, the people's history projects could be one productive venue for the development of feminist, postcolonial analyses of Pauline history and interpretation. In his reflections on a people's history of Christian origins, Horsley reflects on the need for eclectically multidisciplinary approaches to these materials. It is the argument of this chapter that what Pauline studies now requires are the specific, transdisciplinary insights of feminist, postcolonial analysis. We can remain cautiously optimistic, but still vigilantly critical about people's historians as potential allies and conversation partners in this process.[129]

A Hymn Within and a Heavenly Politeuma

Introduction

As described in the previous chapter, a paradigm shift is under way for Pauline studies. Through a series of conferences and collections, the Paul and Politics group has sought to demonstrate how it is better to situate the letters of Paul within their political context than within either a religious individualist or an anti-Jewish antagonist framework.[1] This contextualization has produced a significant body of work that highlights Paul's use of imperial language in his efforts to communicate with a number of audiences: in Galatia, Corinth, Thessalonica, Rome, as well as Philippi. This is, indeed, a commendable trend and one that provides openings for feminist, postcolonial analysis. A thorough analysis of this context and Paul's use of images and language in the Roman imperial world, however, involves more than identifying such images. The question that must be asked is *how* Paul argues with and through imperial language. What dynamics are reflected in Paul's letters when such terminology is used? What kind of power relations are founded or reinforced in his letters?

Asking such questions aids in qualifying and polishing both the explication of Pauline politics and the analysis of the letter's rhetoric. Far too frequently, rhetorical criticism has focused only on identification over considerations of the function and import of Paul's letters. Doing this stalls the "critical" component of a rhetorical-critical analysis.[2] In a related fashion, noting the power dynamics of the argumentation ensures that the efforts at political contextualization expand to the politics inscribed in the letter itself. This interpretive practice would demonstrate the continuing relevance of diagnosing imperial relations as an aid to contemporary resistance and as a resource for the prevention of our own collusion within or reinscription of oppressive dynamics.[3] As outlined previously, these are important goals for feminist, postcolonial analyses in Pauline studies.

As a result, the selection of a procedure for reading the rhetorics of Paul's letters must have a clear sense of its goals from the beginning. If the priority rests on maintaining a critical, political interpretation (as suggested above), then it seems especially important to attend to the dynamics of Paul's arguments and how they do or do not intersect with the Roman Empire. A better way to grapple with the function of imperial images involves placing them in the overarching argumentation of the whole, rather than isolating certain passages or phrases. What follows is a partial attempt to do so for a couple of passages that are frequently cited for their political resonance. This will be partial, in at least three senses of the word: (1) by analyzing what place some of these arguments have in the whole, rather than by analyzing the whole from the beginning; (2) by recognizing how I read for particular goals (as all do), compatible with feminist and postcolonial interpretation (as most do not); and (3) by highlighting how the letter represents Paul's own prescriptive attempt to argue for particular actions. Tracing the repetitive rhetorics should not only facilitate the assessment of such arguments (the task for this chapter), but it could also help in reconstructions of the audience for the letter (one potential goal for the fourth chapter).

So it is in this chapter that the analysis turns to the rhetoric of the text of Paul's letter to the Philippians, while considering the priorities certain scholars have placed in their interpretations. A great deal of focus has been directed on the Christ hymn (Phil 2:6-11) and some of the language on the *politeuma* (3:18-21). By reexamining these passages and the scholarship that claims they carry an anti-imperial resonance (Horsley, Wright, Cassidy, Agosto, Oakes, and Heen, among others), the chapter demonstrates the need for a feminist, postcolonial analysis that attends to the many directions in which the power dynamics in the text run. It also addresses the question about the stance of the text vis-à-vis the imperialism of its time by answering four guiding questions from the work of Musa Dube (raised in the previous chapter), expanding the analysis of the text beyond these two passages.

——— **A Heavenly *Politeuma* and a Hymn Within** ———

When scholars have cited the letter to the Philippians as an indication of Paul's political view of the Roman Empire, they have typically alluded to either 3:18-21 or 2:6-11. Though they are certainly not the only ones to do so, Richard Horsley, N. T. Wright, Richard Cassidy, Efraín Agosto, Peter Oakes, and Erik Heen each represent some of the better and more recent efforts at explicating these passages often in isolation from the whole letter. Thus, as a precursor to the following analysis of the overarching argumentation and as an indication of why a feminist, postcolonial analysis is needed, this study examines their claims about these specific passages.

For example, when Horsley presents an entire section on "Paul's Counter-Imperial Gospel," he does so by quoting 3:20-21 in the introduction's epigraph.[4] Here Horsley highlights how this passage evokes the ruling ideology and interconnected cultic thought of the Romans. Translating *politeuma* (3:20) as "government" makes clear that Paul's opponent in this passage is the current government, that of the Romans.[5] Horsley argues that Paul is proposing an alternative form of rule, which in turn leads to an alternative society.[6] Paul achieves this by offering the genuine *sōtēr* (3:20), over against Roman claims to provide safety (*sōtēria*) and peace.[7] Horsley explains that Paul is in direct competition with the imperial cult when he uses such terms.[8] Thus, when the letter alludes to how Paul's *sōtēr* can "subject all things" (3:21), it most certainly includes the imperial authorities.[9] Rather than casting Paul as arguing over against Judaism(s),[10] Paul's perspective and the expected reversals of the *parousia* seems especially at home in apocalyptic thinking.[11] The explication of this part of Philippians, then, becomes a key part of describing Paul's counter-imperial agenda.

N. T. Wright's perspective builds upon that of Horsley and the *Paul and Empire* volume, even as it describes Paul's argument in a slightly different fashion. Though his examination of 3:20-21 also notes the interconnections between political and cultic systems, Wright seems to suggest that Paul is not proposing an alternative to empire. For example, Wright maintains:

Paul, in other words, was not opposed to Caesar's empire primarily because it was an empire, with all the unpleasant things we have learned to associate with that word, but because it was Caesar's, and because Caesar was claiming divine status and honors which belonged only to God.[12]

The empire offends not by its form of rule, but because of its claim to something that was exclusively God's. By his redeployment of terms like *sōtēr* and *kyrios*, both commonly used titles for Caesar, Paul exposes how the Roman Empire is the parody of the "real thing," God's empire.[13] When viewed alongside Paul's arguments in the beginning of the chapter, the climactic appeal of 3:17-21 is cast as a matter of having the appropriate loyalty (*pistis*).[14] For Wright, this is primarily a religious or cultic problem: Paul shows how he changed his allegiance in Judaism to demonstrate how the audience should alter their allegiance in "paganism."[15] The injustice or exploitation of the empire is never the problem, so much so that Wright argues that neither Paul nor the Philippians need renounce their Roman colonial citizenship (3:20), which he assumes they have.[16]

Richard Cassidy claims that further understanding of Paul's attitude to the empire in Philippians must begin in a different place than in Horsley's work.[17] By investigating the timing and conditions of Paul's imprisonment, Cassidy seeks to explain why he believes Paul's position has shifted so significantly since he wrote Romans 13:1-7.[18] From this viewpoint, then, he suggests Paul's arguments in 3:18-19 are commenting on "Neronian sexual depravity"[19] as one way to relativize the benefits of Roman imperial authority.[20] Cassidy maintains that references to the "enemies of the cross" within these verses could also be indicators of Paul's own experiences of the persecution of believers in Rome.[21] Like Wright before him, Cassidy believes the audience at Philippi is comprised mostly (or even entirely?) of Roman citizens, making Paul's claims to another, better kind of citizenship (*politeuma*, 3:20) a further indication of the relativization of Roman power.[22] Noting (as Horsley did before) that Paul uses imperial titles for Jesus, Cassidy especially stresses the unsurpassed sovereignty of a lord who can "subject all things" (3:21).[23] To Cassidy, such claims are significantly less subtle than previous lines, comments sure to be deemed as treasonous in the Roman Empire.

In beginning to discern "aspects of a postcolonial reading" of Philippians,[24] Efraín Agosto briefly treats this passage as one of four key topics. The language of "heavenly citizenship" in 3:20 is explained in terms of the opposition the Philippian community likely was facing.[25] Agosto's interest in the possible persecution is, like Cassidy's, also primed by his treatment of Paul's imprisonment[26] and fueled by Philippi's status as a *colonia* of the Roman Empire.[27] At Philippi, then, Roman citizenship was not only attainable, but desirable. However, the community's recognition of a previously crucified *sōtēr* and *kyrios* challenges the idea of such earthly honor (see 3:19, although Agosto does not cite it).[28] Although this is viewed as a "radical" challenge, it is not the end of such privileges. In Philippians, now, "imperial Roman citizenship must take second place."[29]

Finally, Peter Oakes builds upon the social-historical work in his dissertation and of some of the aforementioned scholars to stress that the predominant theme in this passage is God's sovereignty over Rome.[30] In Philippians, Paul "remaps" the universe, thereby reconfiguring the setting of life in the Philippian community.[31] For Oakes, this entails the experience of suffering, one which Paul and the audience at Philippi hold in common. Of all the passages in the letter, including especially the hymn, 3:20-21 is "still more sharply political" because it is attempting to relocate allegiance away from Rome and colonial authorities at Philippi to Jesus and God.[32] The language evokes Roman citizenship, but this state will be "elsewhere."[33] For Oakes, Jesus' role in this state parallels, and in the end, outstrips the central tasks of the emperor:

> If the emperor's key function towards the *provinces* was the bringing of universal submission to a single head, his key function towards the *Roman people* was to be the one who would save them from their enemies and from internal trouble.[34]

Upon Jesus' *parousia*, he can and will achieve both for just one, new community: universal submission (in 3:21) and a salvation that rescues them from their enemies (in 3:18-20). On Oakes' assessment, the Philippians now have a different citizenship, with a different saving emperor reigning from some distance.

Although they differ on matters of background and points of significance, each of these scholars stresses the political and distinctly imperial valence of Paul's arguments in this section of the letter.

Turning to the considerations of the hymn in 2:6-11, an overview must begin again with the key role played by Horsley's studies.[35] Here, the accent is on the end of the hymn (vv. 9-11). Horsley maintains that Paul teaches an important part of his anti-imperial gospel through the hymn.

The exaltation of Jesus (2:9) and the reverence or obeisance shown to him (2:10-11) are in opposition to another divinized *kyrios*, "already enthroned in Rome."[36] Building off of Dieter Georgi's work on theocratic thought in Paul, the hymn could also be echoing common cultic views of the death and divinized ascension of an emperor.[37] Though not elaborated upon here in Horsley's argument, the pattern of reversal in the hymn and its claims about the "real" divine kyriarch could also fit with Horsley's arguments for Paul's apocalyptic mind-set, particularly in 1 Corinthians.[38]

Although Cassidy's study also tends to focus on the latter half of the hymn, it also stressed the specification of Jesus' death on a cross (2:8c): "in emphasizing that Jesus suffered death by crucifixion, Paul is inevitably drawing attention to the fact that Jesus was put to death by Roman authorities."[39] Despite this ultimate expression of Roman authority, the end of the hymn shows how Roman power is limited and even dissolved.[40] God's exaltation of Jesus demonstrates that a different kind of subjecting power is, in fact, decisive on the cosmic, rather than the earthly, level. With a name above all names (2:9), and a sovereign status for which every knee must bend (2:10), Jesus is owed the allegiance that the emperor receives.[41] Cassidy explicates that this would be particularly problematic to teach as a prisoner in Rome, because such lines could also be read as: "at the name of Jesus, *Nero's* knee should bow . . . and *Nero's* tongue confess that Jesus Christ is Lord . . ."[42] Any such claims to Jesus' unsurpassed sovereignty would be a challenge and affront to the emperor's authority and would likely be met with a death sentence.[43] These are definitive signs to Cassidy that Paul has adopted a stance of opposition to Roman rule.

Oakes also stresses the new kind of divine sovereignty expressed in the latter part of the hymn, only here he suggests that Paul himself composed the last three verses.[44] In doing so, Paul crafted a passage that rewrote Isaiah 45 and thus not only displaced the imperial authority, but also replaced God with Jesus as the one to whom reverent bowing is due.[45] This reverence is due to Jesus because he has achieved universal sovereignty, not simply over all the nations (as an empire could claim), but over all three planes of existence, that is, the entire universe.[46] This sovereignty shows that Jesus is like the emperor, only better. In a similar fashion, Oakes alludes briefly to the first half of the hymn as a mode of moral legitimation for his imperial-style authority: like the emperor, he does it all for the good of others.[47] Like Horsley before, Oakes can make these claims because of the ground-breaking work of Georgi, yet he differs from both of these scholars in key areas. Whereas Horsley tends to stress that these claims would recall the imperial cult, Oakes asserts that such arguments are mostly social and these kinds of allusions need not carry a cultic resonance.[48] Furthermore, contrary to Georgi's work, Oakes views the scene in the hymn as more reminiscent of an enthronement than the apotheosis of an emperor upon his death. In the time described by Paul in the hymn, Jesus is currently ruling; it is not an acclamation coming after his reign.[49] On Oakes' reading, the hymn is meant to be a comfort to suffering Philippians now, not in the future.

Unlike Horsley and others' emphasis on the latter half of the hymn, Erik Heen's analysis stresses the first half, particularly the very first verse. Heen contextualizes the language of *isa theō* (one like or equal to God, 2:6c) in the ruler cult of the Greeks and Romans, as well as in the competition for civic honors in the empire.[50] If a person displayed significant enough benefaction, then they could be paid honors similar to those of the gods.[51] Given the service Jesus paid in the first half of the hymn, he is not dissimilar from legendary heroes and deified emperors when he is given the great rewards of the latter half.[52] As a result, Heen argues that the hymn functions as a critique of the emperor and the patronal abuse in cities of the east.[53]

Both Agosto and Wright briefly comment upon the political significance of the hymn. In fact, like either Horsley or Heen, each of them stresses one part of the hymn over the other. Like Heen, Agosto notes how Paul depicts Jesus as a model leader because of his "servant" attitude (*doulou*, 2:7).[54] The hymn fits with larger patterns in Paul's commendations of other examples willing to sacrifice, showing how different Paul's pattern of leadership was.[55] Like Horsley, Wright focuses on the conclusion of the hymn in its expression of Jesus' lordship. Paul has, then, "a very high Christology"[56] that claims Jesus as the real *kyrios*, rather than Caesar. Linking the two passages briefly examined, Wright maintains that the hymn explains why people should have this new allegiance, because Jesus is "Lord of the whole world."[57] Unlike Agosto, though, Wright notices how Paul attempts to model himself (3:7-11) as similar to the Christ hymn.[58]

This brief overview suggests how topical an analysis of these passages might be for any seeking to examine imperial dynamics in Paul's letters. As some of these scholars have indicated, there are some interesting connections between 3:18-21 and 2:6-11. The final observations of Wright also highlight how much is to be gained by understanding these passages by further contextualizing them in the wider rhetorical tendencies of the whole letter. What follows is a more explicit attempt to do so, focusing particularly on the function of Paul's arguments. However, for the purposes of a feminist, postcolonial analysis, this wider rhetorical contextualization is, on its own, not nuanced enough to attend to the intersecting power relations of and within Pauline rhetorics. Certainly, none of the preceding interpretations adopt a feminist analytic perspective, and only one attempts to articulate aspects of a postcolonial reading.

Thus, the questions that drive this part of the study are derived from the procedural overview of the previous chapter. Having contextualized feminist, postcolonial analysis in terms of several areas of concern enumerated by Kwok Pui-lan, this overview concluded with a list of four key questions, provided by Musa Dube, that can be used to evaluate ancient texts on their literary-rhetorical grounds:

1. Does this text have a clear stance against the political imperialism of its time?
2. Does this text encourage travel to distant and inhabited lands and how does it justify itself?
3. How does this text construct difference: is there dialogue and liberating interdependence or condemnation of all that is foreign?
4. Does this text employ gender and divine representations to construct relationships of subordination and domination?[59]

In the analysis of the next section of this chapter, these questions will prove to be particularly useful for an assessment of Philippians and some of the scholarly observations about the letter.[60]

In offering answers to these questions, this study seeks to build off of, but also respond to, the observations made by Horsley, Wright, Cassidy, Agosto, Oakes, and Heen. Whereas it now seems clear that Paul implements imperial-political terminology in these passages within Philippians, it is still not entirely clear how he does so. In an attempt to clarify this matter, this study interrogates how these images function within the larger arguments Paul is making in the letter. Yet, as the arguments and overviews in the previous chapter illustrated, too often the roles of women, gender, and sexuality have been elided, downplayed, or simply ignored in the study of Paul's letters. This failure to make the connections between gendered and imperializing dynamics is particularly problematic given the current geopolitical order and the place of biblical rhetoric in this order. As a result, some feminist, postcolonial analysis of the rhetorics of Paul's letters now seems well past due.

Rhetorical Interactions and Pauline Interpretation: A Postcolonial Paul?

Engaging with and implementing postcolonial feminist work can provide a new perspective on the question of Paul's place in the Roman imperial world. Indeed, in comparison to most analyses of Paul by scholars interested in Roman imperialism (the section above) or engaged with postcolonialism,[61] this set of questions should provide a rather different sense of the arguments presented in letters like Philippians. For many reading Paul's letters in the light of Roman imperialism, the answer to Dube's first question ("Does this text have a clear stance against the political imperialism of its time?") seems already decided. Yet, given the history of interpretation sketched in the previous chapter, there are plenty of reasons to be cautious, even suspicious, of any interpretation that might prematurely valorize Paul as arguing against empire. Thus, one discerns a tension between a mostly malestream confidence and a feminist, postcolonial suspicion. Perhaps the best way to resolve the first, disputed question regarding Paul's stance vis-à-vis imperialism is to examine the rhetoric of the letter through the other three questions in an effort to discern an answer to the first.

"Does this text encourage travel to distant and inhabited lands and how does it justify itself?"

By working through Dube's second question, we address a topic rarely covered in those studies placing Paul in his Roman imperial context: Paul's justification for his movement in the empire.[62] In fact, the conditions for Paul's letters all involve traveling across some distance to address an audience in often densely inhabited, colonized locales. Paul always writes from some distance, and the letter to the Philippians is no exception. In fact, this letter reflects upon this matter with some regularity. From early in the letter, Paul seeks to clarify for his Philippian audience that his imprisonment ("my chains," 1:13) somewhere else does not prevent his success.[63] Rather, he has advanced or made "progress" (1:12) even from within the confines of Roman imperial power, the praetorian guard (1:13). Perhaps contrary to expectation, the message that travels to Philippi is that Paul has traveled somewhere else and has successfully won many for Christ.

This message precedes Paul's next journey to Philippi, a return anticipated and echoed throughout the letter. Though he considers being with Christ to be a better option (1:20-23), Paul maintains that the Philippian community needs him: it is "more necessary because of you (pl.)" (1:24). This action should bring "progress and joy" (1:25) for the community, as the letter explicitly connects this benefit to Paul's *parousia* (1:26). That Paul twice justifies his travels in the name of progress echoes the historical rationale for colonization: empire is for the good of the subjects, a paternalistic, civilizing force of advancement. The imperial resonance of Paul's *parousia*, the term used for the arrival of a victorious emperor or the visit of an imperial administrator, then, may not be entirely coincidental.[64] This resonance would be especially striking for an audience at Philippi, given the city's prominence in the history of Rome's civil wars, its subsequent establishment as a *colonia* in the Roman Empire, and the accompanying development of the colony's imperial cult.[65]

The issue of Paul's continuing absence and the possibility of his return shape a number of the appeals in the letter. The immediately following instructions of how to live properly as citizens (1:27) are given with an emphasis upon pleasing Paul. What Paul hears about them should be sufficient reason for their action, "whether coming and seeing you or being away" (1:27). The obedient attitude he extols later in the letter, as an application of the hymn treated as anti-imperial by many scholars, is also expected whether he is absent or among them ("my presence [*parousia*]," 2:12). When Paul cannot be present, he discusses his plans to send emissaries, like Timothy and Epaphroditus, in his place (2:19-30). One of the conditions of Paul's work, in general, seems to be his ability to commission people to travel across some distance to other locations. Yet, even when Paul explains whom he is sending to Philippi and why, the topic of his presence and his desire to travel also crops up (2:24). In each of these instances, whether Paul travels to see them or not, he still expects certain reactions from the audience. The persistence of this topic[66] indicates that Paul seeks to position their acceptance according to the recurrent possibility of his arrival/return. That all of these travel contingencies involve divine approval ("gospel of Christ," 1:27; "this from God," 1:28; "on behalf of God's approval," 2:13; "in the Lord," 2:24) is a topic that will be examined below.

As already mentioned, this letter does not just discuss travel, but it also presupposes travel to distant, inhabited, and colonized locales. Grappling with the significance of the circulation of the letter could still be a fruitful avenue to consider given the colonized settings of these communities in the Roman Empire, in general, and the particulars for the community in the colonized context of Philippi (a major concern for the more historically oriented fourth chapter). Beyond discussion of the mode of ancient letters, though, it must also be recognized that the message of the particular letters travels as well. By writing, Paul seeks to transfer his way of thinking or acting from one location to another. Nowhere might this be clearer (in Philippians and other letters) than when Paul argues from his own model.[67] Though it is most explicit in 3:14-17 and 4:8-9, Paul uses model argumentation throughout the letter, typically to highlight his own prominence.[68] Indeed, the "progress" that Paul brings with him wherever he goes demonstrates his model quality, as does his close association with the divine. Paul's call for the Philippians to imitate him resonates with the colonizing practice of mimicry, a topic that one scholar has applied to the Gospel of Mark, but has yet to be considered for its impact on these exhortations.[69] Such calls to imitate are ambivalent, however, as Paul's argument mimes imperial discourse by claiming its supreme authority as model, while opening the possibilities for resistance to the claims made by either Paul or the empire.[70] The rhetorics of imitation are themselves such a complex phenomenon in the colonized scene that they will require their own, fuller analysis in the following chapter.

Thus, an initial survey finds that Paul not only depends upon, but also explicitly argues from, the practice of traveling to a distant place. Dube and Kwok's suspicion of the "mission to the Gentiles" as a justification for imperial travel seems well founded here.[71] The letter depicts Paul as the bringer of "progress" to the communities he visits, while casting the audience as in need of his unique authority and model. This, indeed, suggests that one could be far more hesitant in evaluating how Paul argues in terms of politics or empire than most of the preceding malestream interpretations. Though there are clear indications of how this travel is justified in the letter, such justification can be easily explicated by addressing Dube's next two questions.

"How does this text construct difference: Is there dialogue and liberating interdependence or condemnation of all that is foreign?"

When asking how Paul constructs difference in Philippians, the oppositional tenor of these arguments comes squarely into view. Paul's attitude toward difference frames how he justified his activity and the specific contents of the letter.[72] Just as he argued from his own model, one of the key ways Paul shapes his view of difference is to argue from a series of antimodels. When people think differently from him at the site of his imprisonment, they are depicted as envious and divisive (1:15-17). To make clear how the Philippian audience should be unified, acting according to Paul's own model, he highlights some "opponents" ("those who stand against you," in 1:28), who will meet with destruction. If the community should follow Paul's argument, they will act in unity, unlike those others who "seek their own things" (2:21), "according to divisiveness" (*eritheian*, 2:3; cf. 1:15, 17).

   Some might object that Paul's stance of violent opposition to those "outside" the community can still be suitably anti-imperial, especially if Paul is cast in the apocalyptic mode.[73] Though there are many reasons to have reservations about such an objection, Paul's arguments indicate that he is far from dialogue and interdependence, even among those who seem to "belong" in the community. As mentioned above, Paul seeks obedience from the community, with "fear and trembling," no less (2:12). This obedience is no qualified "love command," but is to be enacted "without grumbling or questioning" (*dialogismōn*, 2:14).[74] In Paul's argument, the lesson of the Christ hymn (in 2:6-11) is one that specifically rules out arguing, questioning, or dialogue between the community and Paul. The purpose of this prohibition is so that the audience "might be blameless and pure, children of God without fault, in the midst of a crooked and twisted generation" (2:15). The dualistic trajectory of Paul's argument and application of the hymn is once again compatible with the colonizer's narrative of "civilization." The community can become one with the pure "lights in the world" (2:15) by becoming silent, compliant, obedient subjects in opposition to the base, perverted, and savage surrounding world.[75]

Such strong language for those outside or "foreign" to his community is not an isolated instance for Paul, but a persistent feature of his argument. To develop a contrast with his own model status (3:2-11), Paul famously and viciously warns the Philippians of those who are dogs, evil-doers, and mutilators (3:2).[76] Paul continues this dualistic and violently condemnatory argument, even within 3:18-21, the passage explicated above as a favorite for those who find an anti-imperial, or postcolonial Paul.[77] Those who disagree with Paul are described as "enemies" (3:18), doomed to destruction since their minds are on the wrong (earthly) things (3:19). That safety and destruction are doled out along absolutist lines of obedience and loyalty makes this letter compatible with, rather than contrary to, imperial thinking. Even in the final section of the letter (4:10-20), Paul works prodigiously to show how he is neither dependent upon nor "interdependent" with the Philippians. Unlike the community, who are depicted as in need of Paul's presence and the accompanying progress, Paul received aid, but is still "self-sufficient," because he did not "speak according to need" (4:11). Attending closely to how Paul frames both unity and difference throughout the letter clues in the interpreter to the exclusive, hierarchical, and dominating manner in which Paul expresses his claims, in 3:18-21 and in the whole.

Far from encouraging dialogue and interdependence, Paul regularly argues violently and oppositionally about those who are deemed "outside" the community. An even greater challenge for the recuperation of an anti-imperial or postcolonial Paul, though, is his attitude toward the Philippian community. The letter argues that the community can only attain the right kind of unity through obedience and fear: not by questioning or considering their roles, but by acknowledging authority and adhering purely to Paul's exclusive, absolutist vision. Though Paul implies that there are other stances and responses that differ from the arguments he presents here, the tenor of the letter's arguments highlights the perils of some modes of resistance and the specific need for interdependence in decolonization, as highlighted in Dube's work.[78] Rather than replicating the form of interconnectedness of global capital, or valorizing the disconnectedness of nativist independence movements or early Western feminism, liberating interdependence seeks to theorize solidarity apart from exploitatively colonial and gendered foundations.[79] Too often, the experience of "independence" after colonization belies the continuation of economic dependence and the preservation of the colonial thinking on nationalism and sexism.[80] It was precisely these kinds of dynamics that were not recognized or taken up as part of the malestream analysis that preceded this study. Thus, these interpretations were unable to develop a more cautiously critical stance to the political rhetorics of Paul; a stance necessary to feminist, postcolonial analyses in Pauline studies.

Does this text employ gender and divine representations to construct relationships of subordination and domination?

Finally, following Dube's fourth query, the deployment of gender and divine representations should be examined. As the preceding reflections on the hymn indicate (and as one might expect), Paul refers to the divine with regularity in this letter. However, the pertinent issue is not whether but how he does so. The letter works to affiliate Paul with the authority of the divine, often using God as a "witness" (1:8) or guarantor of his argument (1:28; 2:13; 3:9, 15; 4:7-9, 13).[81] Frequently, Paul places himself in between the community and the divine, so that any possible benefit they might receive from the divine is because of Paul, their intermediary (1:26; 2:17-18; 3:17-21; 4:7, 9). Recognizing such a dynamic alters the significance of the hymn's seemingly anti-imperial terminology. Recall that N. T. Wright has argued, "Paul, in other words, was not opposed to Caesar's empire primarily because it was an empire, with all the unpleasant things we have learned to associate with that word, but because it was Caesar's."[82] If Paul is arguing in terms of a divine empire, then it seems that he is positioning himself as a provincial governor or colonial administrator for the divine *imperator*. Another related possibility, highlighted by Kittredge's analysis of 1 Corinthians, is that Paul is reshaping Roman patronage language in his attempt to establish interconnected hierarchies of patrons and clients.[83]

Many who argued for Paul's anti-imperial stance also stress that he uses specifically political language in this letter (as in 3:20-21), often to explain the relation of the community to the divine. The letter exhorts its audience to "live as citizens (*politeuesthe*) worthy of the gospel of Christ" (1:27). Unlike the aforementioned enemies, those who join Paul will be part of our *politeuma* (a commonwealth,[84] citizenship, government, or polity; 3:20), from which Jesus as *kyrios* and *sōtēr* will come.[85] However, missing from most previous interpretations is the observation that the opposed fates of destruction and safety are also emphasized (1:28; 3:19-20) on both occasions where Paul uses terms with this Greek political root (*politeu-*). Furthermore, in both cases this violence comes from a divine source. Paul represents the divine as ruling through the threat of destruction and the dominating power of violence. To the extent that the divine is linked to the dense use of military language in this letter[86] or to patronage,[87] the representation is particularly gendered, as these institutions were maintained by and for elite, imperial males. In fact, patronage and the military were densely intertwined in the Roman Empire and were among the more effective means the empire found for social control of subjects.[88]

Again, to some scholars, the divine use of threat might be *somewhat* mitigated as a dominating argument if it can be shown that such relations are meant only for those "outside" the community. Yet, these same passages (and a few others) show that what characterizes the divine is the power of subjection. The community shows their unified spirit when they accept that they are meant to "suffer on his (Christ's) behalf" (1:29). The community is in a debased position in this *politeuma* (*to sōma tēs tapeinōseōs hēmōn*, 3:21), whereas Christ's body is one of glory (*tēs doxēs*, 3:21). Even if they can somehow become transformed by the divine, it is only achieved because Christ has the power "to subject all things to himself" (3:21). This order of subjection coincides with the terminology of unequal power relations not only in political contexts, but also in the realm of household management. As Kittredge has already shown, this language of subordination is specifically gendered, as it defines elite male authority over wives, children, and slaves.[89] Even the celebrated Christ hymn emphasizes God's power to "exceedingly exalt" Christ with a "name over *all* names" (2:9), so that "*every* knee might bend" (2:10).[90] Since the unity Paul describes in this letter involves the subservience of all to a kyriarch (*kyrios*, 2:11; 3:20), the universalism expressed in the letter is enlisted in an order of domination. Given the role of universalist claims in the racialist discourse of European colonialism, this confluence of domination, universalism, and violently enforced boundaries should trouble our engagement with Paul's letters.

The subordinationist rhetoric of the letter highlights Christ's power in the latter half of the hymn and elsewhere, but the first part of the hymn is also put to effective argumentative use. The exhortation immediately following the hymn makes clear that Paul wants the community to apply the first half to their own lives. Just as Jesus adopted a stance of obedience (*hypēkoos*, 2:8) and humility, they should respond in a similarly obedient fashion (*hypēkousate*, 2:12) to Paul.[91] If this obedience is to follow from Christ's "taking the form of a slave" (2:7), then it also clearly participates in establishing a dominating order. The communal obedience is compulsory, with "fear and trembling," as in a slave/master relationship.[92] Paul is again in the intermediate authoritative position: they should obey him whether he is present or not (2:12), and the establishment or continuation of this hierarchical relationship is meant for God's own pleasure (*hyper tēs eudokias*, 2:13). The rhetoric of the hymn and the way its effect is powerfully evoked in the repetitive dynamics of the letter as a whole should also give pause to those persuaded by the work of much malestream interpretation of the text.

Though Paul is in the intermediate place in a hierarchy of authority in this letter, the argumentative use of himself as a model predominates (1:3-11, 12-14, 24-26; 2:16-18; 3:7-11, 14-17; 4:2, 8-9). Some of these model rhetorics draw their authority from the way Paul depicts his actions as echoing the pattern presented in the hymn. He is a model because he is willing to suffer or give up status to gain something greater (1:12-14, 23-26; 3:7-11).[93] Timothy, Epaphroditus, and the hymn are each used once as models in the letter, as argumentative support of the primary model of Paul. In all of these cases, the model's actions involve neither leveling nor participatory dynamics, but an effort to ascend in a hierarchical arrangement. Because all of these models are male, these arguments likely also reflect hierarchical gender dynamics. Furthermore, the terminology used to describe the community is itself phallocentric, since Paul insists: "we ourselves are the circumcision" (3:3).[94] The "we" of Paul's discourse is not only masculine, but is also someone with status. If the pattern extolled by Paul (and his supporting models) is to give up some kind of status to gain something greater, the argument is geared toward those who have status to spare. The question remains, What about most people, who have rather low status in the Roman Empire? Because Paul is a man with relatively higher status (3:4-6), he casts the paradigm of belonging on his own terms. To accept his view would require those members of the community, unlike Paul in the imperial and kyriarchal system, to identify with a task they cannot complete: voluntary loss of status.[95] This highlights that Paul's position and point of view are not the only options available to the community receiving the letter, stressing how there were other possibilities for resistance to the empire and/or Paul. (These possibilities will receive further consideration in the chapters that follow.)

If the exhortation to Euodia and Syntyche (4:2-3) is not an afterthought, as scholars are increasingly willing to admit, it becomes easier to recognize the continuation of these gendered, hierarchical arguments. Paul's argument for these two women leaders to "think the same thing in the Lord" (4:2) builds upon the letter's dualistic and subordinationist tendencies. The appropriate state of mind is one of the model qualities Paul claims to demonstrate (1:7; 3:14-17) and attempts to establish in the community (2:1-5), over against others (2:3; 3:18-19). Those who accept Paul's mindset ("think this," 3:15) and authoritative model ("become coimitators of me," 3:17) are "mature" (3:15) and will gain safety (from a *sōtēr* and *kyrios*, 3:20). Those who "think anything other" (3:15) receive a foreboding divine *apokalypsis* (3:15) and are enemies doomed to destruction (3:18-19). Paul argues that safety is gained through loyalty to a *kyrios* who has the power to subject all (3:21). In Philippians, Paul's authority is strongly linked to divine authority, explaining why he feels he can call the community his "crown" (*stephanos*, 4:1). Given these immediately preceding claims, the argument directed to Euodia and Syntyche is most likely Paul's effort to convince them to adopt his imperially gendered mind-set, accept his authority within a subordinating chain of models, and be on the "right" side of this *kyrios*.[96] Further interrogation of these imperially gendered arguments, of Euodia and Syntyche's roles within them, and the historical possibilities of reconstructing these roles in the contact zone will be developed in the fourth chapter of this study.[97]

Throughout Philippians, then, Paul develops and intertwines gendered and divine representations in order to establish relations of subordination and domination. These arguments ensure an elevated position for Paul in an imperial and patriarchal hierarchy. According to the letter, the only way to gain safety and peace is by obeying Paul as an expression of loyalty to a divine lord (see also 4:9, where doing what Paul does earns the presence of the "God of peace").[98] Even Paul's closing greetings, highlighting "Caesar's household" (4:22), indicate his place in this order of domination. However this allusion is interpreted in terms of personnel or geography,

the terms are unmistakably located in the nexus of imperial and patriarchal power: the household, where effective emperors learn to claim their
mastery over all realms in their role of "father" over all.[99]

———— Initial Connections and Conclusions ————

By examining the letters of Paul, like Philippians, through these three
questions, this kind of feminist, postcolonial analysis can develop a
nuanced answer to the first: "Does this text have a clear stance against
the political imperialism of its time?" Indeed, the answer produced by
this analysis proves rather different from the opening assessment of the
heavenly political texts by malestream interpreters. Paul argues for and
from his ability to travel, along with his message, model, and others who
support these. The letter is Paul's opportunity to characterize the community as in need of his authority and the progress it can bring to them. This
attitude is justified in light of the violently dualistic way he conceives of
difference in the letter. Enemies are condemned and those who "belong"
are required to be obedient. Paul casts the community in the dependent,
subordinate role of a hierarchical system, a system explained and maintained by reference to particularly gendered power dynamics endorsed
by the divine. Even if one can argue that Paul makes these claims over
against the empire of his time, as several scholars in the opening section
of this chapter did, it is not significantly different from the imperialism
of his time. In Philippians, Paul argues and thinks imperialistically, possibly so that he might "both subvert and reinscribe the imperial system."[100]
These patterns indicate that, even if this is an effort to subvert the Roman
Empire, this letter can be easily re-assimilated or co-opted to an imperialist or colonialist agenda.[101] Though Kwok might locate this tendency
to the period of Constantine and Nicaea, her words aptly describe Paul's
efforts in Philippians "to maintain its symbolic unity and to marginalize
ambiguous and polarized differences."[102]

Significant portions of this analysis would have been more difficult to
develop if the role of gender in colonized/ing discourse were not recognized, the activities of women in colonial and anti-colonial movements
not considered, or feminist approaches not engaged. In fact, the gendered dynamics might further explain why Paul makes such arguments
in (imperialesque) competition with the Roman Empire. Contributions

from feminist, postcolonial, and queer theory all highlight how conflicts that are depicted as contests between men or male-coded entities implement women as the site of exchange, interaction, and/or battle.[103] When conquered space is figured as female,[104] it is not surprising that Paul's exertion over against other imperial contenders carries an interwoven gender resonance. Paul strains to code the community as colonized and feminine, in need of his divinely approved model and authority. To prove his elevated position, like the emperor who proves his mettle in his household, though, he must also demonstrate how he can command obedient responses and control the women in his community. Thus, Paul's specific argument for Euodia and Syntyche to "think the same thing" is not only a patriarchal gesture, but it is also an attempt to prove his imperial manhood.[105]

This analysis suggests that Paul reinscribes and mimics the imperialism of his time in the letter to the Philippians. A more comprehensive feminist, postcolonial analysis would require an assessment of these imitation rhetorics in light of the elusive colonizing strategy of mimicry.[106] Paul's imitation, then, may be at least partially similar to the surge of nationalism experienced by peoples striving to throw off colonial governments and mentalities.[107] This should cause at least some suspicion, as Dube argues:

> Because the imitation or reversal models hardly offer liberative alternatives, the literature of both groups tend to be characterized by sharp dualisms, rigid cultural boundaries, vicious racisms, heightened nationalisms, and hierarchical structures that would license any power to victimize other nations.[108]

Even still, the pains taken to extol colonial mimicry underscore its fundamental instability ("almost the same, but not quite white . . .") and the distinct potential for seditious resistance.[109] These possibilities and the relative utility of Bhabha will be further considered in the following chapter on the rhetorics of imitation in Paul.

This might prove an important point when considering the role of women and/or the colonized peoples in and around Philippi, an ancient imperial "contact zone." As a *colonia* of the Roman Empire on an important route for travel, Philippi brought people of disparate ethnic, cultic, political, and geographical origins together. Given the Roman imperial control of the city, their mixing, like the argumentation in Philippians, would have been "shaped by inequality and conflictual relations."[110] Like the colonial attempts to enforce cultural mimicry, though, the conditions of a contact zone would also have provided possibilities besides fearful obedience. These possibilities provide fruitful avenues for how this study might construct the potential historical situation for this letter and the roles of women in this community (the task for the fourth chapter).

Previously, an argument has been made that Christ's rule (2:9-11; 3:20-21) is being favorably compared here to the unjust Roman one and thus is a positive political distinction for modern readers (and possibly also for Paul's audience at Philippi). However, the terms of this contrast remain in the domain of rule as hierarchical, exclusive, and subordinating (*hyperypsōsen, kyrios, politeuma, sōtēr, hypotaxai*). What *most* links these two favorite passages for the political contextualization of Philippians is the way they both conclude and collude with a comprehensive order of subjugation (every knee bowing, every tongue confessing, all things subject). The argumentation does not seem to pose Christ and this community (as defined by Paul in unity with his version of Christ) as separate from, or as an alternative to, this kind of domination. Since Paul's arguments do not challenge this notion of rule, it is problematic for any feminist, postcolonial interpreter concerned with an analysis of kyriarchal images and social arrangements.[111]

A higher level of suspicion about Paul's role in the overarching argumentation also tempers claims about how anti-imperial the message of the letter is. Though Paul uses political terminology in letters like Philippians, he does so to establish imperial and kyriarchal power dynamics. Horsley's proposal that Paul is competing with the empire might prove correct, and Cassidy's inferences about the conditions of the imprisonment are provocative in the face of Roman authority, but Philippians does not seem to provide an alternative form of rule. Agosto and Oakes were correct to identify sacrifice, servitude, suffering, and sovereignty as themes in the letter, but they are mostly deployed to reinforce Paul's exclusive claims to authority (in a fashion not wholly dissimilar from the empire). Heen's analysis of the hymn perceptively notes how it paralleled encomia to divinized heroes like the emperor, but neither the arc of the hymn nor its place in the argumentation of the letter seem to critique the hierarchical mentality common in empires. Finally, Wright's blunt observation about God's empire rings true for this letter, yet it fails to recognize how ardently Paul labored to run the imperial relations through his own model and authority.

Thus, Paul is not just repeating imperial images in his letters; he is also mimicking imperial-style power arrangements in an effort to consolidate his own authority. Though he might be competing with the Roman Empire, or qualifying some of the particulars (such as whose rule it is and his place within it), ultimately his arguments mark his attempts to reinscribe imperial relations.[112] The arrangements are neither leveling nor inclusive, but hierarchical and exclusive. That difference, dissent, and nonconformity are met with violence accentuates how Paul's order would not be opposed to terrorizing threats of violence, a mode of control common for the Romans. When Paul presents his own model in a hierarchy of authority with a select number of male supporting figures, the exclusive space replicates, instead of challenges, the insulation of power and privilege sought by elite colonial males. In the end, even if one can manage to argue that all this time Paul is working to overthrow the exploitative Roman Empire, it becomes hard to deny how easily adaptable Paul's rhetorical methods are to an imperial agenda. Unfortunately, this kind of accommodation or collusion will be a significant part of the history for those who claim Paul's texts as their own.

In learning to recognize and assess how Pauline rhetorics function, then, feminist, postcolonial interpreters cannot adopt a hermeneutics of trust and transparency with regard to the text. It is imperative that one attempts to read against the grain of such arguments and to become savvier to the multiplicative effects of these rhetorics, especially if one is also seeking to engage historical reconstructive work. As a result, then, this chapter attempted to delineate and interrogate how a focus on Roman imperialism in Pauline studies has left a number of rhetorical-political dynamics obscured, whereas the following chapter will attempt to do the same for the potential applications of Bhabha-inspired forms of postcolonial analysis. Although both should ultimately stand on their own, they should also perform the necessary preliminary functions for the historical reconstructive reconsiderations of the Pauline contact zone that follow.

CHAPTER THREE

The Rhetorics of Imitation and Postcolonial Theories of Mimicry

"Become co-imitators of me," Paul writes in his letter to the Philippians (3:17). This is one of several argumentative moments where Paul makes explicit what seems to be running throughout many of his letters: various dynamics of imitation. Furthermore, he does so as a subject of the Roman Empire, writing to other subjects—both women and men—in the *colonia* setting of Philippi. Although many Pauline scholars have noted the former (how imitation is a recurring topic in these letters), very few have taken the latter (the imperial context) as an opportunity to engage with postcolonial or feminist, postcolonial work. This is particularly unfortunate for the topic at hand, given a number of postcolonial explorations of the phenomenon alternately called mimicry, mimesis, or mimeticism, from the likes of Homi Bhabha, Rey Chow, Meyda Yeğenoğlu, and Anne McClintock (among others). Such an engagement should supplement the increasing emphasis on Roman imperialism as a vital context for these first-century works and, more specifically, aid in developing a feminist, postcolonial analysis of Pauline studies. This kind of analysis could prove to be productive for a reconception of the colonial and communal dynamics in the city of Philippi and within the potential audience of the letter. Opening the analysis of imitation rhetorics in this manner allows for a more complicated picture with regard to agency, resistance, and/or co-optation (among other issues), while decentering and reconfiguring the predominant focus of scholarship on the role of Paul.

Imitation Rhetorics in Paul and in Pauline Scholarship

The arguments Paul presents to communities like the Philippians, Corinthians, Thessalonians, and Galatians represent his efforts to get them to imitate him and think the same things he does. Though Paul makes use of a term with the mimesis root only once within the letter to the Philippians (*symmimētai*, in 3:17, cited above), this argumentative effort is by no means limited to this term, this section, or even this letter.[1] The efforts to extol certain kinds of imitation are evident from the beginning of Philippians, where Paul seeks to establish his own model status by showing that he has the appropriate attitude toward the Philippian community: "it is right for me to think/feel this on behalf of all of you (pl.)" (1:7, but see all of 1:3-11). The right mind-set—and that Paul "thinks this" (*touto phronein* 1:7)—is a repetitive element of the model argumentation of the letter. Paul displays his model quality not only by showing that what he has already done is "progress" (1:12), because "most of the brothers have become more confident in the Lord because of my chains" (1:14), but also by "remaining in the flesh" for the present and future good of the community (1:24; including their progress, joy, and boasting in 1:25-26). As a result, Paul argues that the community should share or adapt to his mind-set and be engaged in "the same fight" as Paul's (emphasized by the phrase "in me" twice in 1:30). Thus, even before leaving the first chapter of this brief letter, we have a distinct indication that Paul is seeking to establish himself as a model, in order that his audience at Philippi might imitate him in some way.

As the letter proceeds, Paul displays exemplary service (2:17), while expecting the Philippians to obediently conform to the right path (2:12, 14-16). Their actions are due to Paul so that he might be able to boast and not have done his work "in vain" (twice in 2:16). This should also mean that the Philippians share the same sense of joy that Paul has ("in the same way you (pl.) yourselves should also rejoice and rejoice with me," 2:18). As mentioned above, the audience should become "co-imitators" of Paul (3:17) as a demonstration of their proper frame of mind ("those who are mature, let us think this" in 3:15), a frame of mind that two women—Euodia and Syntyche—are also called to share with Paul (4:2). Finally, Paul exhorts the Philippians to do "the things you have learned and received and heard and seen in me" (4:9). Evident from the start, the calls to imitate Paul become more explicit the further Paul argues. The community should have the same struggle, the same attitude, the same joy, and in the end do the same things as Paul. This sameness is even stressed in the act of imitation: they should become *co*-imitators of Paul.

Though these arguments are persistently and predominantly deployed to posit the primacy of Paul's model status, this is not the only way Philippians implements the rhetorics of imitation. These arguments establish the imitation of Paul first, before turning to other, more truncated arguments using supporting models. Thus, the Philippians can show they have the same mind (2:2-5) by following the model presented in the hymn Paul quotes in 2:6-11. Paul makes clear how the audience is meant to follow the hymn by stressing the element of obedience immediately after its citation (2:12). In this instance the best way to imitate Christ is to act out of obedience (*hypēkousate*, 2:12), just as Christ did (see especially 2:8, *hypēkoos*).[2] However, since the obedience is framed in terms of Paul's absence or presence, it seems that it is due to Paul. The argument to imitate Christ's obedience, then, feeds the more frequent calls to imitate Paul and do and think the same things as he.[3]

The letter turns to two other supporting models, Timothy and Epaphroditus, in a similar fashion. Both of these figures echo certain qualities the letter highlights as part of Paul's exemplary status. Not only is Timothy like Paul ("I have no one of similar mind," 2:20), but this similar mind also involves being one "who will truly care" about the Philippians (2:20). Epaphroditus has shown a willingness to suffer to fulfill a service to the community and to Paul, as the letter twice notes how close he came to dying (2:27, 30). Paul describes him as his "brother and co-worker and co-soldier" (2:25), and as a supporting model, Epaphroditus shows that he is concerned about the community on the occasion of receiving the bad news of his illness (2:26). Like Paul before them (1:7, 12, 14, 24-26; 2:17), Timothy and Epaphroditus have the proper frame of mind and do the right things with regard for the Philippian community. Pointing to them at this point in the letter seems to be implicitly building the appeals to imitation. To Paul's mind, they are both meritorious, and he plans to send both of them to the community, only strengthening the impression that Paul is seeking for the Philippians to imitate him through the imitation of these intermediaries. Yet, Paul's elevated status is never far removed even when laying out other models, as he is reintroduced in both sections. As Timothy's arrival is just a precursor to Paul's own imminent return (2:24), so Epaphroditus's tasks involve serving Paul (2:25, 30), while surviving and returning for the relief of Paul's anxieties (2:27-28). So, when Paul exhorts the community to "hold such people as honored" (2:29), it seems that he has these supporting figures, as well as *himself*, in mind. Likewise, when he argues for the audience to become "co-imitators of me," he also quickly connects the call to look to the ones "as you have a type in us" (3:17). Timothy and Epaphroditus mimic Paul's model, while a collective "us" is shaped to reinforce the arguments for Pauline imitation.[4]

Besides these other models nestled into the middle of a series of arguments for imitating him, Paul further develops these communal "us" rhetorics through two other kinds of argument. Throughout the letter, those worthy of imitation are contrasted with those who are not. These anti-models work out of envy, rivalry, and divisiveness (1:15-17; cf. 2:3) and "seek their own things" (2:21; cf. 2:4). They are labeled a "crooked and twisted generation" (2:15), dogs, evil-workers, and the mutilation (3:2), as well as enemies (3:18; cf. 1:28). In addition, the model and anti-model argumentation build upon each other to create a potent claim about community belonging: the Philippians should be characterized by their unity and sameness (a very specific sort of "us" rhetorics). The calls to imitate Paul and a few others are intertwined with ones to "think the same thing" (2:2), unlike those who are divided and divisive. The letter crafts a message that if the community remains united in a proper mind-set ("stand in one spirit," 1:27; "those who are mature, let us think this," 3:15; to "stay in line in the same way," 3:16), they will gain safety and avoid the destruction of those who are not ("a sign to them of their destruction and your [pl.] safety," [1:28]; "their end is destruction . . . having their minds on earthly things," 3:19; cf. 2:12; 3:1, 15). If the audience follows Paul's arguments here, their community identity will be defined by whom they imitate, as well as if and how they specifically do so in unity and sameness. Framed as a matter of life and death, proper imitation is crucial in order to belong in the "us" constructed by this letter. From Paul's point of view, the Philippians need to be like "me" to be one of "us."[5]

It seems almost inevitable that any analysis of such arguments for imitation would involve questions of social formation, power networks, and authority dynamics. Yet, it is precisely these issues that most biblical scholars previously and almost continuously avoid or in Elizabeth Castelli's apt assessment, "skirt."[6] Thus far, the exception to this rule has been Castelli's study, which attempts to adapt a Foucauldian analytic for examining and interrogating scholarly and Pauline arguments about imitation.[7] Castelli's analysis grew out of a lack of attention by Pauline scholars to the issue of power in imitation, but also in Paul's letters in general. Scholars tend to either spiritualize Paul's call to imitation or simply reinscribe it as already authoritative, instead of contextualizing such arguments in terms of Paul's attempt (or even his need) to convince his audience.[8] From the beginning, Castelli characterizes most interpreters as holding that:

> imitating Paul has nothing to do with power relations, and everything to do with social expediency or the benign observation that Paul was obviously a special figure to the early churches [sic], so why should one not attempt to align oneself with his position?[9]

This tendency led Castelli to reevaluate the discourse of imitation in ancient classical sources as well as Paul's letters.

This reevaluation of scholarship on and the backgrounds for the study of Paul resulted in a different starting point for making meaning out of the rhetorics of imitation. Castelli notes that there is something inherently hierarchical about arguing through imitation.[10] Imitation is based on the superiority of the model in the element to be imitated and proceeds from the assumption that the imitators are inferior or somehow lacking the trait or practice the model provides. Yet, the imitators can never quite measure up to the original model, thus reinforcing both the hierarchical nature of the power dynamic (the copy or imitator will always be lower, subordinate, or less perfected or advanced than the model) and the authoritative quality of the model (the relationship is asymmetrical with the imitated one remaining superior).[11] Thus, upon turning to the moments where Paul argues using variations of the Greek word *mimētēs*, Castelli's study is able to address such power dynamics and explicate the hierarchical nature of Paul's demands for imitation.[12] Her analysis includes a brief treatment of the "co-imitators" passage noted above (3:15-21), discerning the hierarchically privileged place Paul secures for himself through such argumentation.[13]

Despite these efforts, in most ways, scholarship on the imitation passages in Paul has not been drastically altered. A recent commentary by

Markus Bockmuehl will be sufficient to demonstrate certain continuing tendencies in Pauline interpretation.[14] Bockmuehl's commentary confirms the position maintained in this chapter that imitation is important for the argument of the letter by asserting that "the theme of imitation recurs as an integrating focus on every major section of Philippians."[15] Bockmuehl's ability for tracing some of the same dynamics as Castelli's study is constrained, however, by his effusive enthusiasm for Paul and this particular letter. Here is "Paul at his most mature," and reading the letter, "we find a man whose faith in Christ has not merely survived but aged with grace and wisdom, refined and true as gold."[16] Turning to the same passage where Castelli finds hierarchical privilege (3:17), Bockmuehl sees a rather practical, normal (rather than normalizing) appeal to discipleship, as Paul is merely transferring "the essence of the relationship between Jesus and his disciples."[17] According to Bockmuehl, the Philippian community needs Paul in this role: "Only his own apostolic example can vouchsafe for his Gentile churches [sic] an authentic and personal expression of the life of Christ."[18]

In a fascinating turn, Bockmuehl himself mimes the scholarly tradition Castelli has critiqued while rather clearly identifying with Paul as a pre-eminent authority and model. The rapturously sentimental view of Paul encourages him to repeat many of the dynamics that can be found in the calls for imitation of the letter, as well as in Castelli's analysis of ancient mimetic discourse.[19] Bockmuehl's commentary elevates Paul to the prominent position he hopes to attain by insisting on his exclusive authority ("only his own apostolic example"). Rather than interrogating these social dynamics, Bockmuehl maintains that the community needs Paul to function in this manner, implicitly juxtaposing the "authenticity" of Paul's claims to other, less effective paths for belonging. Furthermore, he spiritualizes Paul's argument and generalizes it to the point where it is seen as identical or continuous with quite different traditions.[20]

The difference between Castelli's and Bockmuehl's approaches to the rhetorics of imitation highlights the need to further examine the hermeneutics and the politics of scholarly identification. As Elisabeth Schüssler Fiorenza has argued, most interpreters of Paul tend to identify with him, while assuming his views were identical with those of "his" communities.[21] There should be a difference between identifying Paul's imitation rhetorics and identifying *with* Paul as a model to be imitated by the interpreter.[22]

Even if one can assume for the moment that the meaning of Paul's argument in Philippians is transparent to the twentieth or twenty-first-century scholar, Bockmuehl never pauses to evaluate *whether* the Paul presented in the letter is an entirely unproblematic model. Instead, he works in terms of polarized dichotomies when he labels Castelli's possibly helpful analysis as a "politically deconstructionist" reading "into" the text of "almost exactly the opposite of what is said."[23] By erasing the political valence of his own act of reading, Bockmuehl also passes over the hierarchical elements to Pauline imitation, which might be especially relevant to engage for one, like himself, who seems to identify with and imitate Paul's model. Such a reading would not have to ignore the rhetorical elements of sacrifice, service, and the common good, which he highlights as a difference between his and Castelli's interpretation. However, it might want to integrate apparently "opposite" takes on the text that attend to such power dynamics (like Castelli's), as arguments on these terms have often been used as paternalistic explanations or imperialistic apologies. At times, Paul's arguments sound structurally similar to colonialist rationales like the "anti-conquest" narratives, which detail the colonizers' selfless "protection of women" or their beneficent "duty to the natives."[24]

Nevertheless, Bockmuehl's commentary does quite a few things that Castelli's study does not. Whereas Castelli's examination of Pauline texts is limited to those passages that have a *mimētēs* term in them, thus treating only one section of Philippians, Bockmuehl recognizes the importance of imitation to the whole argument of the letter. Similar to Bockmuehl, then, this study attempts to highlight imitation rhetorics even where certain terms are not explicitly implemented. Beyond these stylistic qualms there are considerable concerns about Castelli's admittedly pioneering work on imitation. Unlike Bockmuehl and other malestream evaluations that seek to "rein in" Castelli's study, this study maintains that perhaps Castelli's analysis of imitation rhetorics does not go far enough.

This suggestion about Castelli's study is prompted by the dissonance between her introduction of Foucauldian analytics and the analysis of biblical texts that follows it. In her analysis of some of the Pauline passages on imitation, Castelli rightfully and repeatedly stresses the hierarchical and authoritative tenor of these arguments. Indeed, this is one of the primary ways that Castelli's interpretation is unique and helpful. In the face of the bulk of Pauline commentary, it was and is important to show how imitation arguments are not merely pragmatic, inevitable, expedient, or neutral.[25] However, in her efforts to explicate the power dynamics of such argumentation, Castelli misses an opportunity by overwhelmingly emphasizing their dominating or repressive effects.[26] This is surprising considering her choice of Foucault's conception of power to analyze this discourse.

Throughout his work, Foucault has attempted to avoid, as well as provide an alternative to, the notion that power primarily operates in a repressive or prohibiting form.[27] For Foucault, power is more often defined by what it is not: it is not a power-over, it is not something one has, and it is not a matter of some force governing from above. Rather, power relations can be found in the interstices, or are better seen as "capillary," as Castelli notes; diffuse, interconnected, and spread throughout the social body.[28] According to this view, power would not be effective if it only ever said "no." Power is not prohibitive, but productive: it produces relations and induces a series of "yeses" to certain knowledge forms (hence the combination *pouvoir-savoir*, or power-knowledge, in Foucauldian lingo). Power works by producing a whole series of effects that are multiple, diffuse, and ambiguous. Thus, power is not exercised by a subject or constrained by the subject who intends certain effects. In fact, the operation of power-knowledge relations can run counter to what might be expected, prompting a variety of effects that might include resistance to certain dynamics.

Given this view of power, Castelli's interpretations of a few Pauline *mimesis* passages seem to be a bit too uniform for her chosen analytic. Her readings have a strong tendency to conceive of the power relations in only one manner, as hierarchical and authoritative. Certainly, Paul does seem to argue for imitation practices that move toward these forms of social control; yet, these are not the only interpretive possibilities. Even as Castelli commendably attempts to avoid a focus on Paul's intention in her analysis,[29] her (admittedly overdue) emphasis on how Paul might be trying to secure a dominant, authoritative position for himself, in a way, reinscribes this as the only imitative option. However, if a Foucauldian analytic can be of use here, it might suggest that there are a variety of possible effects of such argumentation. Subjects (such as those members in the community that some still anachronistically call "Christians") are produced in relation to such power-knowledge formations, but they are not determined by them. In a similar fashion, imitation need not mean only one thing in either the first or the twenty-first century. Yet, Castelli's exegetical stress on the dominating effects of Paul's discourse leans toward giving the Paul presented in these letters too much definitional "power," thus, in a sense, repeating and reproducing it without further interruption or interrogation. This is a different kind of mimicry than Bockmuehl's, but it is still conditioned by the rhetorical dynamics of Paul's self-inscribed place in his letters.

Is this the only way to make meaning out of these Pauline calls to imitation? How might further reflection on Foucault or recent rhetorical theory expand some of the interpretive possibilities for such fraught argumentation?[30] Certainly, one must pay close attention to the dominating elements of these arguments, but in doing so a feminist, postcolonial analysis cannot afford to surrender the possibilities of an alternate history then or a resistant practice today. If the analysis were to stop at Castelli's initial investigations into Pauline imitation, it could foreclose a number of options in terms of the Philippian community's view of and uses for imitative practices, both before and after receiving this letter. By ruminating on just such possibilities, this study might also be able to generate strategies relevant to our own current struggles.

Pursuing such a route allows the answering of questions, not of whether and how to follow Paul's calls to imitation, but of whether and how such calls can be the occasion to formulate the possibilities of feminist and/or postcolonial forms of imitation. The former path keeps the queries at the impasse of either accepting this oppressive exhortation and the authority it grants or rejecting it. At least implicitly, these two scholars seem to take the opposing sides in this impasse; Bockmuehl finds a friendly Paul whose authority he can accept, whereas Castelli works to catalogue this problematic Paul so that we can begin "trying to think differences differently."[31] So, taking up the latter path (and Castelli's concluding words), how might an analysis of imitation function differently? Are there possibilities for resistance or an ambivalent agency in an imperial situation, either today or in the recent and distant past?

—— The Promise and Perils of Postcolonial Mimicry ——

The opposed options of acceptance or rejection frames the question of "what to do with Paul's calls to imitate?" in ways similar to any study

that asks: "what did Paul think about _____?" Such queries prioritize
discovering Paul's point of view, with the often implicit assumption that
finding this should help determine one's views now. Paul's place as authority is left unquestioned and intact. To proceed differently, though, this
study attempts to pick up the traces of other options, while decentering
this predominant focus on Paul. Besides these two rather limited options,
how else could these imitation rhetorics function? Posing this question
should also help to elucidate the possibilities for the audience of this letter:
the Philippian community.

Castelli was correct when she notes how the process of imitation
can never be completed.[32] The tension of imitation involves a difference
between model and copy. Yet, it is precisely the potential differences
between Paul (the primary model in his arguments) and the audience (his
sought-after copies) that has gone under-examined in most malestream
Pauline scholarship. The exception to this general rule has been the feminist rhetorical work of scholars like Schüssler Fiorenza, Anne Wire, and
Cynthia Kittredge. These scholars recognize that, since the letters attempt
to address their arguments to particular audiences toward particular ends,
one might be able to "read against the grain" of such argumentation to
look for the possible views of these communities. The letters are conceived
not as isolated pearls of wisdom, but as one part of an ongoing exchange
and struggle. Thus, the letters (and not just the calls to imitation) begin
already from a place of difference. In fact, this might be one of the main
reasons that the letters are written: that some think, say, or do things differently from how Paul wishes (or at least he worries that they might).
Realizing this, particularly in light of Paul's persistent calls for imitation,
allows one to wonder how, what, or whom else the community might
have been imitating. This provides an opportunity to think about others'
agency, most especially in the fraught situation of a colonized context, like
that of Philippi under the Roman Empire.

Here various critical theories of interpretation can be of use.[33] Some
of the resources developed in the study of colonialism and postcolonialism are particularly relevant for an approach to Philippians because, by
the mid-first century C.E., Philippi was under the authority of the Roman
Empire and designated a *colonia iuris Italicum*.[34] Not only was the setting
of this particular letter that of a colonized context, but the biblical com-
pendium in which it will eventually be included also became an imperial

document. As Kwok Pui-lan forcefully reminds, the Bible "must also be seen as a political text written, collected, and redacted by male colonial elites."[35] Furthermore, since their creation, biblical texts have been used in ancient as well as more contemporary forms of colonization.[36] Indeed, colonialism is by no means a thing of the past, as neocolonialism and the accompanying persistent and pernicious conditions of globalized injustice demonstrate the urgency of seeking postcolonial, anti-imperial, and/or decolonizing approaches to biblical interpretation.

The utility of engaging postcolonial theory becomes all the more clear, though, upon turning to the topic of this chapter: the call to imitate. Mimicry, mimesis, or mimeticism have been explored by postcolonial critics because often this is precisely what imperial powers have sought from those they colonized. The British, for example, called rather overtly for mimicry of British topics and standards in the educational system of India.[37] The goal of programs such as these is a more effective cultural management of the colonized people(s). For India, it meant the development of a class of "mimic men," those who are "Indian in blood and colour, but English in tastes, in opinions, in morals and in intellect."[38] Despite the traditional British classicist attempt to do so, one should be careful not to collapse British and more contemporary imperialisms with Roman and more ancient forms of imperialisms.[39] Nevertheless, contemporary postcolonial theory might still prove useful since one can observe that calls to imitate aspects of the colonizers' culture are a recurrent part of imperialism. The required cultic obeisance to Roman deities and emperors or the enforcement of graduated forms of Roman law throughout the empire, for example, demonstrate how this tendency was also operational for colonized locales like Philippi.[40] Furthermore, when the question is raised, "What can be done with such hierarchical and imperial calls for imitation?" postcolonial work offers a number of strategies for recognizing and negotiating the oppressive dynamics of such arguments so that alternative understandings can be implemented.

The most well known postcolonial theorist to do so is Homi Bhabha, whose conceptual apparatus prizes mimicry, ambivalence, and hybridity.[41] In his work "mimicry emerges as one of the most elusive and effective strategies of colonial power and knowledge."[42] Bhabha's work recognizes that the colonizers' call for imitation involves a claim to difference, a difference explained in dualistic terms of the savage, uncivilized, or undeveloped status of the colonized versus the masterful, civilized, and superior place of the colonizer. However, the call to become like the colonizer is the undoing of this hierarchical dynamic. Since the mimicry of the colonized demands and creates a hybridized version of the apparently superior and pure colonial culture, the colonized do not become like the colonizer, but inhabit a third "in-between" space. This hybrid phenomenon fractures the basis of colonial authority: the founding dualism that asserts inherent difference and the stability of identity for both groups. Indeed, if the colonizer calls for the inferior colonized (often classed so in terms of race or ethnicity) to imitate, the colonizer's argument implies that the inferior race can become like the supposedly superior race. Colonizing discourse is contradictory to or incoherent within itself as this call conflicts with the notion of inherent ethnic, racial, or class status. Thus, the call for imitation is an ambivalent argument: a demand that seeks to display authority but destabilizes itself in the process.

Here, Bhabha highlights something missing from Castelli's analysis of the hierarchical dynamics of the model-copy relationship: how unstable the model's authority is. If imitation is meant to be a demonstration of the model's superiority, then, in a sense the model's authority is not evident or natural without the imitation by the copy. It is an anxious request. The authoritative status of the colonizer/model must be repeatedly enacted or performed to show its authoritative status. If it is not repeated, then it seems the colonizer/model does not actually have the authority claimed. The definition of the colonizer depends upon the colonized. Here is the "paranoia of power," as Bhabha explains: "The colonialist demand for narrative carries, within it, its threatening reversal: *Tell us why we are here.*"[43] Just as one cannot be a model without someone imitating the model, one cannot be an empire if one does not have imperial subjects. Both pairs are mutually constituted.

This suggests something of a conflicted agency for the colonized: their imitation of the colonizer can become a form of resistance or mockery.[44] The *appearance* of their obedient imitation is a resemblance, or "sly civility."[45] If read in between the lines, such mimicry is both a resemblance of and a disrupting menace to the colonizer.[46] The inexact replication troubles the idea of the "original" as the imitator is "almost the same, but not quite," that is, "almost the same, but not white."[47] If the colonized inhabit this ambivalent place of neither the one nor the other by conforming neither to the image of the savage or the civilized, they are something else entirely, while contesting the territories and terms of the two previous identities.[48] The uncertain identity exposes how uncertain the colonizer's control of the colonized is. Colonial mimicry highlights the potential for the agency of the colonized: it denotes a productive ambivalence where transgressive resistance becomes possible.

Before conceiving of how Bhabha's work on mimicry might help develop alternative interpretations of biblical imitation, it is important to reflect upon the possible foci of this inquiry. Mimicry becomes more complicated if one wants to think about the potential rhetorical utility for the Philippian or current, postcolonial contexts. The focus could be on Paul's possible mimicry of the Roman Empire or on other parties mentioned in Paul's letters and their relation to imitation arguments. Mimicry might support the conceptualization of various communal responses from the Philippians, for example, allowing for their own forms of agency. These inquiries also call to mind the role of the interpreter as possible mimic. Finally, given all of these potential foci (Paul, others in the letter and/or the community, interpreters), it still remains to reflect on what relation these various foci have relative to empire(s) and the efforts against imperialism(s).

So, the question remains, what to do with these arguments? As argued above, most scholars have focused predominantly on the role of Paul, to the detriment of a more vital engagement with these imitation rhetorics. Instead of apologizing for or recuperating him, it can be noted how the arguments in Paul's letters reflect the colonizer's discursive tendency toward dichotomization. Whereas "opponents" have a prominent place in the scholarship on letters like Galatians or 2 Corinthians, throughout Philippians, models are contrasted with anti-models: some are unified in thought and spirit and display good will, whereas others are envious and divisive (1:15-17; 2:1-3). Some can be "blameless and pure, children of God" (2:15), who obediently refuse to question Paul (2:12-14), whereas others are a "crooked and twisted generation," who lack this appropriate attitude (2:15). The true circumcision are juxtaposed to the dogs, evil workers, and mutilators (3:2-3). There are ones who are mature and think the correct things, whereas enemies think about other, earthly things (3:15, 18-19). Again and again, the former are promised safety, whereas the latter are described as doomed to destruction (1:28; 2:12; 3:1, 15, 19-20).

Through Bhabha, though, it could be remarked how unstable and
ambivalent this definitive-sounding, all-or-nothing scenario is. Instead
of adopting Paul's point of view, one can recognize that there are several,
more ambivalent responses to these arguments, getting beyond the problem of isolating Paul the author/model/colonizer's intent. Yet, ironically,
at least one recent treatment of his letters in light of Bhabhan hybridity
kept the focus squarely upon Paul.[49] Appealing to Daniel Boyarin's own
hybrid description of Paul as "Jewgreek" or "Greekjew,"[50] Robert Seesengood attempts to problematize the question of whether the sources of
Paul's thinking are Hellenic or Hebraic.[51] In doing so, though, Seesengood misses an opportunity to decenter the role of Paul and investigate
the possibilities for the audience's ambivalent agency.

In the case of Paul's imitation arguments, Bhabha's work could highlight how Paul, the prospective model and authority, *needs* members of the
community to achieve this role. This observation might, in turn, shift some
of Castelli's observations about the power relations in the model-copy relationship. Paul's authority, like the colonizer's, is unstable and fractured,
particularly upon making such calls for imitation. After all, if members
of the Philippian, Corinthian, Thessalonian, or Galatian communities
(either before or after the reception of the letter) do not "properly" imitate Paul, his claims to distinct authority would be significantly problema-
tized. For Castelli, the inability to achieve sameness with a model is the
sign of the impossibly impregnable authority of a model.[52] But to Bhabha,
this same inability is the sign of the model/colonizer's lack of definitive
control over the copy/colonized. Indeed, in these letters, the sending of
such a message seems to imply an anxious concern that people are not imitating Paul, or at least not imitating him in the way he would like. Despite
the attempts to display a divinely endorsed authority, the power of Paul's
calls for imitation are far from conclusive. Such argumentation provides
an opportunity for resistance and even could have been preceded by other,
transgressive forms of imitation (of Paul or of other figures or standards
taken as models). Control over agency, identity, and subjectivity resides
less in the hands of a monolithically dominating force than in the ambivalent interstices where colonized subjects can both mimic and menace such
attempts at domination.

The rhetorics that fashion these calls to imitation are further undone
by the dynamics of sameness and difference. In Philippians, the arguments

work to elevate Paul above all other figures as worthy of the community's imitation. To show this, Paul attempts to argue that the audience needs him for a number of benefits: progress (1:12, 25), joy (1:25; 2:18), glory (1:26), safety/security (1:29; 2:12; 3:1, 20), and peace (4:7, 9). The sheer number of times the text attempts to explicate Paul's model authority makes it a central or, as Bockmuehl observes, an integrating theme for the letter.[53] Yet, of course, the repeated argument also implies that the members of the community can and should try to be like Paul. If this is possible, then the unique place of his authority seems minimized. If so, why would the community accept such an argument? What, in the end, makes Paul so different? That someone can be Paul-like is further highlighted by the supporting figures of Timothy and Epaphroditus (2:19-30). Since there are these intermediates, these "mimic men," the difference between Paul and others seems not to be so great after all. Yet, this weakens the very foundations of the repetitive calls for imitation: Paul's claim to be a discernibly superior model.[54] It is not so difficult to conceive of others' agency upon their hearing of such ambivalent, insecure, and internally incoherent arguments.

Reading through these rhetorics, it is hard to imagine how biblical scholars fail to consider that there could have been and likely were competing discourses in the communities to which Paul writes. Yet, it is precisely these possibilities that most malestream Pauline scholars miss when they align their interpretive point of view with Paul's. By repeating or mimicking Paul's arguments or assuming that the ancient audiences univocally and unproblematically did so, scholars seem to be misunderstanding the particularly rhetorical character of the letters. As Wire convincingly demonstrates, by preemptively reinscribing Paul's point of view as the normative model (in the first or twenty-first century), Pauline interpretation creates another ambivalent paradox. "Because an argument Paul makes cannot be rejected as unconvincing, it also cannot convince. In this way the authority we attribute to Paul prevents him from persuading us."[55] The reception and meaning made out of such arguments are not a foregone conclusion.

What biblical interpretation needs is a healthy appreciation of its own conflicted, unstable, and ambivalent processes of identification with and through biblical materials. Following Bhabha, the act of interpretation is by no means a self-evident or straightforward repetition of those one imbues with "authority," whether it be Paul or Prisca, Luther in Witten-berg or "Lawrence of Arabia," the British Lord Macaulay or the American president. Where biblical argumentation has been used in various forms of domination and control, processes of resistance can begin with unex-pected imitations.[56] Where the same argumentation has fed the struggle against imperialism, colonialism, or neocolonialism, though, it also can-not be assumed to have a univocally positive function for our futures.

Post-Poning Any Undue Celebrations: ──────── Criticisms, Cautions, and Calibrations ──────── of Postcolonial Mimicry

Before recuperating the letter to the Philippians as an ideal occasion to reevaluate the effects of imitation rhetorics, it seems necessary to consider the other ways mimicry might function in colonial and postcolonial con-tact zones. On more than one occasion, for example, Rey Chow has raised a few cautions about Bhabha's valorization of mimicry, ambivalence, and hybridity. Chow points out that the terms of the resistance Bhabha theo-rizes begin with and remain rooted in the colonizer's point of view:

> But what kind of an argument is it to say that the subaltern's 'voice' can be found in the ambivalence of the imperialist's speech? It is an argument which ultimately makes it unnecessary to come to terms with the subaltern since she has already 'spoken,' as it were in the system's gaps. All we would need to do would be to continue to study—to deconstruct—the rich and ambivalent language of the imperialist![57]

For Chow, such a strategy reinforces the centrality imperial argumenta-tion claims for itself and is a sign of assimilation or reconsolidation rather than resistance.[58] Chow expands on this critique in her more recent work, *The Protestant Ethnic and the Spirit of Capitalism*.[59] Since hybridized iden-tity facilitates a proliferation of meaning and a drive for continual pro-duction, it is also consonant with the dynamics of incessant capitalism.[60] While instructively demonstrating how colonial power is much more than a towering monolith or univocity, Bhabha's mimicry also reads like only one more strategy in the multiple forms of colonial production.[61] In accordance with a Foucauldian analytic of power, colonialism is successful because it takes multiple, diffuse, various, and even contradictory forms in order to secure its authority. The fractures Bhabha finds are more often signs of colonialism's subtle vitality than its undoing.

Nevertheless, Chow holds "that mimeticism is, perhaps, the central problematic of cross-ethnic representation in the postcolonial world."[62] Because it is so central to an analysis of the Philippian and the postcolonial contexts, it is vital to reassess mimicry or mimeticism. One way to do so is to examine Chow's proposition that there are three levels of mimeticism.[63] The first level involves the white man's claim to be the original model, founding the imperative for the colonized and racialized other to attempt to become like the ruler.[64] This level should be familiar, by now, as it closely corresponds to Castelli's analysis summarized above. It echoes Trinh T. Minh-ha's observations of the European call to the natives: "'Be like *us*.'... Don't be us, this self-explanatory motto warns. Just be 'like.'"[65] The colonized is in an impossible situation here, as the imitator can always only be a "bad copy" relative to the standard of authenticity set by the imperialist model. Yet, this is the only access the copy has to the "superior" culture and language.

The omnipresent inferiority complex of the first level is qualified by a second kind of mimicry that corresponds mostly to what Bhabha describes.[66] Rather than remaining always already inadequate, the copy has a more complicated position within the space provided by the incomplete and ambivalent form of the colonizer's call for imitation. Aside from the cautions raised above, Chow also stresses how this second kind of mimicry still begins with the white man/colonizer and in failing to unseat his priority, is not necessarily dissimilar from the first form.[67]

In light of these first two kinds of imitation, Chow proposes a third form defined as "coercive mimeticism."[68] Coercive mimeticism works not by demanding the imitation of a "better" party, but by expecting the ethnic to perform or mime what is most recognizable as ethnic.[69] Unlike Frantz Fanon's analysis, where "For the black man there is only one destiny. And it is white,"[70] the only destiny in coercive mimeticism is to be ethnic. Here, Chow's emphasis on the visual nature of mimicry comes clearly to the surface: the ethnic subject must be recognized or seen as conforming to the stereotype of their ethnicity. In conforming to this notion of "Africanness" or "Asianness," though, it seems likely that there was no original to which an African or Asian can conform.[71] Thus, the ethnic develops a kind of self-mimicry, where certain images are affirmed as a process of containment. They are "to resemble and replicate the very banal preconceptions that have been appended to them."[72] Such internal policing of group boundaries becomes a way to attack or shame others as disloyal for not being properly "authentic," leading to lateral violence within or across ethnic groups rather than resistance.

Chow describes these kinds of mimeticism in three levels not because they are arranged in terms of hierarchical elevation or historical order, but because they overlap and coexist with each other.[73] The three levels are never entirely separate from or mutually exclusive of each other. In fact, Chow again and again demonstrates that the very effectiveness of concepts like mimeticism, ethnicity, or woman is dependent upon their flexible overlap and contradictory instability.[74]

Chow's analysis of the three levels of mimeticism proves useful to an understanding of the argumentation in Paul's letters, especially as the letters seem to be developing and appealing to a sense of communal identity. As Denise Kimber Buell and Caroline Johnson Hodge have argued, Paul implements "ethnic reasoning" in his letters, particularly in the cases of Galatians and Romans.[75] In ways similar to Chow, Buell and Johnson Hodge note the interplay between particular and universal in the concept of ethnicity, since this form of reasoning can move between the poles of fixity and fluidity.[76] This might, in turn, explain some of the ambivalence of imitation rhetorics. On the one hand, Paul's model status is set throughout these arguments and reinforced by his "confidence in the flesh" (Phil 3:4). Despite the impressive catalog of his particular, fixed ethnic credentials that follow (3:5-6), Paul also is able to claim that he counts them and "all things" as loss or "dung" (3:7-8). Granted, Paul still "has" (3:4) these qualities (his fixed identity), but he can give them up to gain something else (3:7-11) (his fluid identity).

Furthermore, the "us" crafted throughout the letter are distinctly opposed to and differentiated from the selfish, disobedient, twisted enemies. These distinctions are also marked in terms of ethnic difference. The "us" who follow Paul's model will be the "circumcision" (3:3) (just like Paul, who asserts his own proper circumcision in 3:5). Paul is "like a father" to Timothy (2:22), a supporting model whom the community should also imitate. The anti-models are slurred as "dogs" and "the mutilation" (3:3), whereas an alternate translation for the "generation" (*genea*) that is "crooked and twisted" (2:15) is a race or people. In a move common to ethnic reasoning, Paul presents these totalized dichotomies and reinforces them in terms of the opposed fates of safety and destruction (1:28; 2:12; 3:1, 15, 19-20).[77] Both groups are characterized by a totalized, fixed, and absolute sameness: all of them will be destroyed, whereas all of "us" should be the same in order to be safe and secure.

However, it is the "should" part of that argument that deserves additional attention. Once more, Paul needs the community to respond in unity and sameness ("us") to prove his fixed definition of the communal belonging.[78] The implicit premise of making such claims and calls to form this "us" through imitation is that the community has not done so. This does not seem wholly unlikely. Because Paul is arguing in terms analogous to the founding of an *ethnos*, it should be remembered that the people in the community at Philippi likely were not of the same *ethnos* as Paul (hence, Paul's famous moniker: "apostle to the Gentiles"). Seeing Paul argue cross-ethnically in and to a colonized context (from somewhere in the Roman Empire to the Roman *colonia* Philippi), one can appreciate Chow's view "that mimeticism is, perhaps, the central problematic of cross-ethnic representation in the postcolonial world."[79] So, for those who were not previously convinced of this course of action to imitate Paul and become "us," the identity of "us" must be fluid enough to include them. The potential for inclusion or exclusion is stressed when Paul notes efforts to move or continue in the same direction: "from the first day up to now" (1:5), "holding on to the word of life" (2:16), so to "stay in line in the same way" (3:16; cf. 1:27-28; 2:12; 4:5, 14-16). The danger of this fluid situation and not making it in the end is underlined by how they should seek "safety with fear and trembling" (2:12). The contradiction of ethnic/communal identity as both fixed and fluid is not a sign of the argument's fracture and failure, but its adaptive efficacy. This is precisely the reason one (particularly in an imperial situation) would use a category like ethnicity to argue in the first place: its unstable utility.

Thus, strangely, to the extent that the parties are both fixed and fluid relative to an identity, Paul and those members of the community who potentially agree with the argumentative claims in Philippians are quite similar. Yet, it is a unity with considerable distinctions within it, as made

plain by the analysis of preceding sections:[80] Paul argues hierarchically for
his own model status, with additional models in supporting, subordinate
roles. The community can differentiate themselves positively in this hierarchy by becoming like these models or negatively by becoming like the
anti-models. As Chow also stresses, the significant difference of this mimicry is visual: what Paul can see the Philippians do. As the letter stresses
Paul's return several times (1:26; 2:12, 24), it also stresses the element of
Paul seeing how they follow his imperatives upon his return (1:27). The
imitation of Paul must be recognizably "Paul-ish:" they should engage in
the same fight they saw in Paul (1:30) and do the things they have seen in
him (4:9). This will mean that they look different from the crooked and
twisted as they "appear as lights" (2:15). In turn, how they appear is shaped
by how and to whom they look: to others' interests (2:4), rejoicing when
they see Epaphroditus (2:28), looking out for those dogs, and looking to
other models as they imitate Paul (3:17). Thus, even the visual component
to the calls for unity and sameness reflect how these arguments are "ethni-
cally complex *and* asymmetrical."[81]

Bearing in mind those who might not assent to such arguments, the
rhetorics of imitation coincide with Chow's sense of coercive mimeticism.
The argumentation in Philippians structures and polices certain boundaries of communal identity, often in terms of ethnicity. In the imperial
context of the Roman *colonia* at Philippi, these acts and arguments for violent exclusion seem to be directed less at the ruling administration than
at other people and perspectives in the prospective community. The spec-
ter of safety gained and withdrawn recalls instances of lateral violence in
colonized contact zones, rather than resistance.[82] In this way, Paul's arguments coincide with and reinforce imperial power: the common strategy
of divide-and-conquer. Even if they are aimed against the empire of the
time, they are easily misdirected, co-opted, and reassimilated to the imperial agenda. A second kind of coercive mimeticism is evident upon turning
to the role of biblical interpretation in previous imperial situations. The
demand for biblical figures and later "biblical" believers to conform to certain stable identities marks the complicity of scholarship with the nationalism, ethnocentrism, anti-Semitism, Orientalism, and racialization that
accompanied various European imperialisms.[83]

These readings of the mimicry rhetorics, however, are not the limit of
what they might mean in the first, eighteenth, twentieth, or twenty-first

centuries. It seems vital to still think more creatively about communal or ethnic identity, either for today's struggles or from the perspective of others at Philippi. The question still remains whether others in the communities at places like Corinth or Philippi conceived of ethnicity and community in the same fashion. What did those who fall outside of the boundary demarcated by Paul think? Chow's work helps to elucidate both the coerciveness and the simultaneous ambi- or even multi-valence of such arguments. Castelli and Bhabha are not necessarily "wrong" to accentuate the hierarchical and the subversively ambivalent elements, respectively, of mimicry. It is just that imitation could contain both of these meanings and more. Though the path of imitation holds possibilities for conflicted agency and resistance, it is also fraught with the perils of coercion and hierarchical authority. The imitation in Paul's letters means different things to different parties at different times. Although this pries open the possibility for perspectives in the assemblies besides Paul's, it is also not prematurely certain of the anti-imperial resonance of this difference. A difference in conception or practice does not mean that those holding or exercising certain positions relative to imitation in the empire are not also being shaped, co-opted, or even assimilated into the empire. Considering that not only Paul's letter to the Philippians but also biblical scholarship in general is increasingly engaged in cross-ethnic representation, there may be no one correct place to arrive. The three levels of mimeticism explain how there could be many, simultaneous understandings, yet there has been only minimal treatment of how this same set of imitation arguments are also simultaneously gendered.[84]

Resistance, Risks, and Replications: —— On the Limits of Mimicry for a Feminist, —— Postcolonial Analysis

Both Meyda Yeğenoğlu and Anne McClintock examine Bhabha's notion of colonial mimicry, but they do so to further problematize how the dynamics of race, ethnicity, and empire all critically intersect with gender. Both profitably complicate questions of whether and how there might be feminist and/or decolonizing forms of imitation. As McClintock quite pointedly observes, this complication seems especially necessary for

utilizing Bhabha's conceptual apparatus, since he writes only "Of Mimicry and Man."[85] Indeed, by either ignoring women, gender, and sexuality, appending them after the fact, or treating them as peripheral to the
"main" task, postcolonial theory runs the risk of replicating the colonialism it seeks to upend.[86]

Yeğenoğlu, for example, reconsiders the utility of mimicry for the specific context of Algerian women's roles in colonial representation and anti-
colonial resistance. In doing so, Yeğenoğlu revisits Fanon's analysis of the
French colonialist focus on veiled women.[87] The aspect of visual control
is central in this dynamic, as the colonizers "must first of all conquer the
women."[88] The imperial agenda again signifies a certain kind of coercive
mimeticism, not just in terms of ethnicity, but rather, in the places where
ethnicity, colonialism, and gender intersect. One's relationship to "the
veil" now characterizes the colonized Muslim or Arab.[89] Algerian women
were not called to mime the colonizer, but mime the imperially gendered
role the colonizer put upon them. Like Bhabha, Yeğenoğlu highlights
how this Orientalist focus displays the anxiety of the colonizing males'
representation of woman as "masquerade."[90] Unlike Bhabha, though, in
focusing also on gender, Yeğenoğlu is less assured about the possibilities of
resistance stemming from the colonial anxiety, because "both the closure
of the subject's identity and the resistance of the other is never final, but
always partial and relative."[91]

The gendered dynamics are crucial, as the colonized culture itself is por-
trayed as feminine and both the colonial male and female remain fixated
on the colonized woman's body.[92] Despite the partiality of its possibilities,
women's agency is not completely constrained by colonialism's coercion.
Following Fanon and Malek Alloula's analysis, Algerian women's veiling
actions become a kind of refusal or frustration to the scopic demands of
colonial power.[93] In a way, the colonized women mimic the male colonialist discourses of woman as masquerade and of foreign Muslim as exoti-
cally concealed. But by doing so, they threaten the colonizer's ability to see
and, in turn, control the colonial subjects: a veiled woman can see without
being "seen."[94]

In asserting women's agency in response to colonialism, Yeğenoğlu
implements Luce Irigaray's explication of women's mimicry as subversion.[95] Similar to Bhabha's focus on a third, in-between space (only preceding his work by several years), Irigaray argues that women's mimicry

does not place them in either the masculine or the feminine role but in an effective "elsewhere."[96] The key to Yeğenoğlu's reuse of Irigaray's own playful repetition, though, is a stress on "purposeful but distorted imitation."[97] Since she is concerned with what actually makes imitation subversive, Yeğenoğlu cautions: "However, repetition of the dominant norms in and of itself may not be enough to displace them, for there is risk involved in it. The trap here is becoming complicit by receding back into the old definitions that one seeks to combat."[98] More complex than Bhabha and more deliberate than Irigaray, Yeğenoğlu carefully delineates the *risks* of mimicry as a strategy, especially when one invests it with an almost automatically seditious quality.

Given specific historical conditions and critical reflection, the miming of certain veil practices can be an anti-hegemonic disruption and parody.[99] Even so, continued assertions of this subversive quality run the risk of ignoring oppressive adaptations to the strategy, as when the post-independence Algerian nationalists showed their own specific patriarchal tendencies.[100] Yeğenoğlu's work, then, is a kind of elaboration upon Chow's coercive mimeticism. It suggests that even the coercive intra-communal form of mimicry that plays upon gendered, ethnic, and colonialist stereotypes can be turned into a form of resistance. Still, unlike Irigaray or Bhabha, Yeğenoğlu stresses the risks and limits in trying to effect a different kind of imitation. The persistent question becomes what makes an imitation *different enough* from the coercive call that it troubles the dynamic. Purpose and continued critical reflection begin to answer the question for Yeğenoğlu's analysis of this particular situation.

Anne McClintock also addresses certain aspects of Bhabha's and Irigaray's work on mimicry. McClintock persistently critiques elements of postcolonial theory, since: "Seeking only the fissures of colonial ambivalence (hybridity, ambiguity, undecidability, and so on) cannot, in my view, explain the rise to dominance of certain groups or cultures, nor the dereliction and obliteration of others."[101] With Bhabha's work clearly in mind, McClintock also wonders what makes certain forms of mimicry or ambivalence different enough to be resistant.[102] Queries such as these become especially important when considering the practice of mimicry and the apparent multiplicity of meanings attributed to it (see Chow above). For McClintock and others, explaining the origins of colonial domination or the potential for mimicry has been made more difficult by scholars such as Bhabha, as "male theorists of imperialism and postcolonialism have seldom felt moved to explore the gendered dynamics of the subject."[103] This gap in scholarship is typified by Bhabha's elision of gender and class in his conceptualization of postcolonial mimicry.[104]

The omission of certain questions of domination, difference, and gender has deleterious effects on the analysis of various imitation practices. Aside from the hopefully now obvious shortcomings in terms of gender, Bhabha's focus on the ambivalently hybrid "mimic man" may not be nearly as seditious as originally hoped. For example, on the African scene of colonialism, a native with apparently "in-between" characteristics does not disrupt the categories of savage and civilized, but reinforces an argument for imperial supremacy: linear progress.[105] When empires stress their cultural forward progress and their primitive subjects' degeneration, discovering an "improved" colonized subject is not menacing but "indispensable to the narrative of the historical belatedness of the native."[106] Similar to at least one of Chow's critiques of Bhabha, McClintock shows how colonialism works by finding ways to include and contain ambivalence, in this case by the narrative of progress. Attention to the material conditions of colonization demonstrates how not all types of mimicry, ambivalence, and hybridity are the same. A "hybridity" executed by massive militarized sexual assault or a "mimicry" enforced as cultural assimilation are not always opportunities for resistance.[107] Rather, these are some of the more successful forms of colonial domination, demonstrating McClintock's assertion that concepts like mimicry are less useful if they are reduced to only one social category.[108]

Whereas Bhabha reduces mimicry to race/ethnicity, Irigaray ties mimicry most directly to women.[109] Both gestures make certain forms of imperial power possible. McClintock delineates at least one problem for Irigaray's imitation:

> for Irigaray herself runs the risk of privileging mimicry as an essentially female strategy and thus paradoxically reinscribes precisely those gender binaries that she so brilliantly challenges. In the process, Irigaray also elides the theatrical and strategic possibilities of male masquerade: camp, voguing, drag, passing, transvestism, and so on.[110]

As also highlighted in Yeğenoğlu's analysis above, imitations risk reinscribing problematic dynamics through their repetitions. Failure to grapple with and unseat gender binaries haunts postcolonialism, because "gender dynamics were, from the outset, fundamental to the securing and maintenance of the imperial enterprise."[111] As both McClintock and Yeğenoğlu's work shows, women are quite frequently figured as the site of the colonial contest. Furthermore, the colonial imagination can be characterized as "porno-tropic," as it sexualized and gendered peoples and locations in accordance with the rationales and fantasies of colonialism.[112]

For McClintock, neither Bhabha's nor Irigaray's theory alone can explain how mimicry often functions in colonial situations. This is evident when one considers the various roles a "white" male can adopt in colonized locales like British-controlled India (a common locale for Bhabha's conceptualizations). In the colonial imagination, the title character from Rudyard Kipling's *Kim* can adroitly pass as whatever race or class he prefers, whereas other lower-classed native mimics are seen as unfortunate monsters.[113] As McClintock notes: "Evidently, passing 'down' the cultural hierarchy is permissible; passing 'up' is not."[114] In both their gendered and imperial aspects, males' racial or ethnic transvestism needs to be examined as "the colonial who passes as Other the better to govern."[115] Gayatri Chakravorty Spivak worries about a separate though parallel phenomenon in some current postcolonial aspirations to U.S. class power that hold "upward class mobility—mimicry and masquerade—is unmediated resistance."[116] Both mimicking moves repeat or prize a primary privilege of elite pale males.

Colonization is also thoroughly gendered in its implementation of arguments about family and sexuality. By invoking the analogy of family, empires have found a way to both domesticate and naturalize their claims to authority.[117] Because the subordination of women and children within the familial order were and often still are seen as natural and self-evident, the nation or empire that mimes "family" can extend its authoritative reach with paternalistic beneficence.[118] In such an argument for authority, it becomes especially important to show how women's sexual roles fulfill certain constrained expectations. Colonized women (particularly in Africa) are classed as degenerate and primitive by virtue of their apparently aberrant bodies and sexuality, whereas the "good" woman bears

the responsibility of properly reproducing racial, ethnic, national, and/or
imperial difference.[119]

These arguments continue even in anti-colonial struggles, as exempli-
fied by Fanon's explanation for Algerian women's roles in armed struggle.
From Fanon's point of view, women join the revolution primarily through
the men to whom they are tied domestically, typically as wives or widows.[120]
Though these women show an agency by mimicking colonial expectations
for revolutionary purposes (as Yeğenoğlu demonstrated above), they are
but the military males' "women-arsenal."[121] Women's militancy is reduced
to the males' effective implementation of the heterosexual family, in which
women are subsumed in the post-independence nation-state. Thus, gendered arguments about family and sexuality conveniently legitimate both
colonialist and nationalist claims for a "hierarchy within unity,"[122] replicating and reinforcing elite imperial male power, rather than resisting it.

McClintock's work provides an important proviso for the theorization
of mimicry, given its pluriform functions for, rather than against, empire.
Nevertheless, even as she denies the universal success of resistant imitations, as styled by either Bhabha or Irigaray, McClintock does not simply
assume the reverse: that all forms of mimicry secure the maintenance of
imperial power.[123] To do so would be to grant the colonizing argumentation the power it claims. Rather, McClintock suggests seeking not a perfect or seamless imitation but "that delicious impersonation that belies
complete disguise."[124] Such a mimicry produces a dissonance and refuses
the erasure of difference required for absolute sameness. These dissonances
are more easily comprehended when the analysis is fine-tuned to the collaborations and juxtapositions of mimetic practices in and through gender, sexuality, race/ethnicity, class, nation, and empire. Looking to only
one social category in mimicry often prevents those opportunities for
mimicry to be recognized as resistance, while reinscribing what it might
otherwise aim to subvert.

McClintock and Yeğenoğlu's reflections on mimicry stress the importance of perceiving multiple intersecting categories of analysis, particularly
when arguments like the calls to imitate in Paul's letters have multiple
interpretive possibilities.[125] This is also stressed by a number of feminist
and postcolonial feminist biblical scholars, including Elisabeth Schüssler
Fiorenza, Musa Dube, and Kwok Pui-lan.[126] Such work should elucidate
that Paul's letters are not only cross-ethnic in argumentation, but they are

also cross-gendered: Paul's imitation rhetorics are directed to communities with both women and men. Although the presence of Euodia and Syntyche, for example, at a key moment in the argumentation of Philippians (4:2-3) makes this plain, it also should be a starting assumption for this developing movement.[127] To work against the androcentric tendency to erase them, "we must assume that wo/men were present and active in history until proven otherwise" (even, or perhaps especially, in letters where women are not explicitly mentioned).[128] Thus, when Paul delivers these arguments for imitation and the development of a particular kind of "us," he does so to women in the community, both named and unnamed.

Yeğenoğlu's and McClintock's work is also useful for an analysis of Philippians, given the military rhetorics of the letter.[129] Once one notes the general allusions to opponents, suffering, and staying in place in light of the more specific references to the *praetorium* (1:13), fighting (1:30), and fellow combatants (2:25; 4:3); the larger arguments for obedience and conformity begin to sound more like calls to imitate an absent, but exemplary, general.[130] This kind of rhetorical practice would be especially striking at Philippi considering Roman military and imperial history: the Romans founded a *colonia* and settled veterans there after a key battle in their civil wars was fought just outside the city limits. Such arguments are also notable for an analysis that includes gender, because the military, as an institution, was maintained by and for elite, imperial males. In the case of Philippians, they are even more striking since Paul describes the two women, Euodia and Syntyche, as his co-combatants, those "who struggled alongside me" (4:3) in the past.[131]

Just as postcolonial theory and anti-colonial struggles often ignored or constrained the agency of militant women, biblical scholars have mostly minimized or passed over the impact of these women in the community at Philippi. Yet, Paul's imitation rhetorics are also specifically directed to these "militant" women. Because Paul argues throughout for adopting his own mind-set (thinking the right way in 1:7; 3:14-17), his call for Euodia and Syntyche to "think the same thing" should be read as a directed argument for the two of them to "become co-imitators of me" (3:17).[132] This concerted effort on Paul's part implies that these women are either not already imitating him or are doing so in an unexpected and unappreciated fashion (at least for Paul). As a result, the letter to the Philippians can also be read as a cross-gendered, cross-ethnic argument for imitation within an imperially militarized zone. The relevance of such intersecting social dynamics requires further cautious and careful evaluation.

The letter is gendered not only as it addresses women (both in general and in particular), but also as it develops arguments in terms of maleness, ethnicity, and "familial" sexuality. Paul's supporting models—specific versions of Christ, Timothy, and Epaphroditus—are all described in distinctly masculine roles: kyriarch (2:11), son (2:22), and co-soldier (2:25). As good "soldiers," they also display the appropriate qualities of obedience and conformity to the will of the rhetor that marshals them for his purposes. As already highlighted above, Paul and these other figures claim to represent the ethnic identity that should be imitated. Of course, ethnicity is not easily separated from gender, a point key to McClintock's engagement with colonialism. This point is further underlined for Philippians by the gendered, ethnic, and sexualized terms "circumcision" and "mutilation" for the audience and their opponents (3:2-3). The phallic communal rhetorics attempt to construct and constrict the shape of the audience's densely woven mimicry. Paul is both the "father" (2:22) and authoritative model for a community who are addressed as "children" (2:15) and "brothers" (or more optimistically "siblings," 1:12, 14; 2:25; 3:1, 13, 17; 4:1, 8, 21).[133]

Where does the responsibility lie to produce (or reproduce) these children and brothers? It depends upon whether and how the community follows Paul's call to imitation. They achieve their status as children, making Paul the papa proud (2:16; 3:3), by obediently refusing to "talk back" or question Paul, as one might expect from a "crooked and twisted generation" (2:12-16). Only these children can become "mature" (3:15) by thinking the right things with Paul. This type of argument clearly coincides with the colonial rationales of degeneration and progress. While the fault for potential degeneration lies with the community, Paul claims an ability to bring "progress" to the community twice in the letter (1:12, 25). Progress is the paternalistic power's privilege and imperial gift.[134]

Philippians, then, operates in analogous fashion to colonizing argumentation by coding the community in a feminine or maternal role. "Good" women/Philippians help the father reproduce the innocent children through subordination and obedience; "bad" women/Philippians become perverse, primitive, or twisted by virtue of their disobedience.[135] The credit goes to Paul, whereas the burden to properly reproduce a particularly gendered, ethnic, sexual, and imperial difference is the audience's. Parallel to the Roman emperor's claims to be a father to his colonized family, Paul mimes the emperor's authoritative gender while exhorting the community to perform an imitation similar to that demanded of Rome's subjects.[136] Furthermore, for the women in the community at Philippi, these arguments for mimicry might have been refined to have very precise effects. Calls to imitate this dynamic could be an effective way to circumscribe all but the most limited, "maternally" reproductive role for women (if not physically, at least conceptually). In 1 Corinthians, Paul combines explicit calls to imitate (4:6; 11:1) with targeted prescriptions of behavior in terms of appropriately gendered and/or erotic roles (5:1-5; 6:9-20; 7:1-40; 11:2-16; 14:26-40). Like Fanon's consideration of other militant women, such arguments and those interpreters who uncritically follow them naturalize and domesticate the women in these communities, denying or erasing their potential agency.

Instead of being undone by degrees of difference, arguments appealing to notions of family or progress demonstrate how the letter can contain ambiguity within its set boundaries. A progress and degeneration narrative explains how Paul can have a descending arrangement of supporting models and potential followers without decreasing his prominence. In a related manner, McClintock suggested that using "family" as a concept justified hierarchy within a unity as an extension of other common or "natural" arrangements. The various levels promoted by such mimetic practices problematize Castelli's view of absolutized differences in mimicry. Likewise, the presence of intermediate "mimic men," various in-betweens, or parties in a third space, as highlighted in both Bhabha and Irigaray's work, dovetail with the hierarchical order without threatening its unity or authority.

Imperial patriarchal power adapts such apparently confining strictures to expand and multiply its modes of mastery. As a result, even Paul's claims to humble or lower himself (Phil 3:7-11; 1 Cor 2:1-5; 4:9-13) can be seen as an extension of authoritative imitation rhetorics. After all, as McClintock shows, the ability to "pass down" the status scale is permitted to the privileged on the colonial scene. Paul is another possible example of "the colonial who passes as Other the better to govern."[137] In the other direction, though, given the hierarchical tendency of the letter and Paul's predominant position throughout it, there are limits to whether and how much others can "pass upward" in their imitation of Paul. Even if a member should manage to properly mimic Paul the model, their "success" can always be attributed to the progress that Paul brings. The letter effectively frames an imperially gendered set of reactions to whatever response the community enacts: refusal or failure is yet another sign of their primitivism, whereas obedient acceptance and a conforming mimicry are indications of Paul's progressive, enlightening effect on them.

Reading the rhetorics in this way suggests that Paul's letters enact a version of coercive mimeticism vis-à-vis gender, as well as ethnicity, sexuality, and empire. But how does one explain Paul's conspicuously explicit efforts to convince Euodia and Syntyche to imitate him, or his linking of imitation with calls for women's covering? One option is to explain it in terms of the imperial strategy to "first of all conquer the women."[138] It might be especially important for Paul to convince women, especially these important women, to don the "Paul-ish" clothing of mimicry. To do so would be a recognizable sign of Paul's authority and an immense aid for convincing others of his legitimacy. In the cross-ethnic context of this argument, the women could also signify the communal/ethnic identity, because women are commonly conceived as the reproducers of ethnic/national difference. The more well-known Euodia, Syntyche, or the Corinthian women prophets were in their communities, the more likely their conformity would also encourage wider assimilation to such calls for imitation. The important role these women seemed to have played in these communities does not assure their actions were seditious or subversive (as Irigaray might hope). Rather, as the history of empires has repeatedly shown, women with status were more often imperial assistants and alibis than anti-imperial allies.[139]

There are still other possibilities for conceptualizing the rhetorical exchange between Paul and community members. Some scholars assert that Paul's letters are labors against the Roman Empire, even in the face of various critiques of how Paul argues in terms of gender and empire.[140] If so, Paul's treatment of female colleagues in the movement(s) might be attributed to what Musa Dube labels the "first things first" attitude of men towards women in struggles for decolonization.[141] Indeed, the label also seems to fit any postcolonial or anti-imperial biblical interpreter who continues to ignore the role of women, gender, and/or sexuality in their work. Ironically, adopting an apologetic stance with regard to the gender politics of an anti-imperial Paul runs the considerable risk of sustaining the very imperial dynamics one seeks to upend. In this light they are like most scholars, who tend to see women, or indeed any other figure, mentioned in Paul's letters as part of Paul's mission. Women co-workers are reduced to implements of a Pauline "women-arsenal."[142]

Like Fanon's analysis of Algeria before them, though, these scholars erase the resistant colonized women's agency and obscure the possibilities for alternative histories of decolonization. Though the letters might insist on a certain form of imitation, or construe practice as indicative of degeneracy or progress, these are not the only potential forms and practices. Throughout this chapter, a number of theorists have suggested the utility and vitality of some kind of imitation with a difference. If Paul repetitively develops and then selectively targets his argument for mimicry to Euodia and Syntyche, to Corinthian women prophets, or to other colonized women still obscured, this could have been a response to what these co-workers, prophets, and assembly members were doing. Instead of assuming the point of view of Paul's arguments, then, scholars could posit that it was other members of the communities who initiated or engaged in imitation practices. Euodia and Syntyche, for example, could have been the initial advocates of this other sort of mimicry. Given Paul's attention, they would have *at least* been prominent practitioners of this, other model.

This imitative practice could also have involved some form of resistance or subversion. As McClintock and Yeğenoğlu suggested above, it is not the perfect imitations that are satisfying and effective, but those imitations that purposefully and recognizably distort. An imitation with some kind of difference cannot be received seamlessly but registers as a dissonant practice that refuses to erase the different agency of the imitator. Paul's directed calls to women like Euodia and Syntyche, or indeed even whole letters of his (like Philippians or 1 Corinthians), could be an indication that Paul has seen such a dissonant imitation by these women and/or other members of the communities. By following another model, or following Paul's in ways even he did not expect or approve, they likely demonstrated a refusal to assimilate to Paul's, or quite possibly, the empire's arguments. Otherwise, how else could Paul recognize it from afar? The emphasis on Paul seeing the outcome he wants underscores the insecurity of his authority. However, in light of the distance between them, this demand to be "seen" in a particular way could have been refused or frustrated prior to, in response to, or throughout this rhetorical interaction.[143] In a militant atmosphere of struggle within an empire, it seems unlikely that subordinated subjects would easily give up such a fight.

Considering such possibilities prepares the way, then, for further reflections on the potential historical roles of women in the colonized contact zone.

CHAPTER FOUR

Women in the Contact Zone

—— Contact Zone and Transcultural Interactions ——

When Kwok Pui-lan described some of the most common concerns shared by feminist scholars interested in postcolonial criticism, she noted that they "pay special attention to the biblical women in the contact zone and present reconstructive readings as counternarrative."[1] This concept of "contact zone" plays a prominent role in Musa Dube's postcolonial feminist work (among others), especially as it is concerned with the dynamics of space, place, and land possession as key components to both the historical and rhetorical functions of colonialism(s).[2] It seems, then, that the concept of contact zone could be useful for embarking upon a feminist, postcolonial analysis of Pauline letters (and of Pauline interpretation). This might be most relevant as the analysis shifts in an attempt to reconstruct some of the potential historical roles of women in the communities to which Paul wrote in the first century. Indeed, foregrounding a concept like contact zone could help to remap one's approaches to the contexts of cities like Philippi, Thessalonica, or Corinth.

This might especially be the case given the conditions of travel that help to determine the creation and reception of Paul's letters, as well as the various communities' interactions with the traveling stranger Paul. An initial examination of this issue in answering Dube's question ("Does this text encourage travel to distant and inhabited lands and how does it justify itself?" above in chapter 2) determined its preliminary relevance, but it is a dynamic in need of further examination. This should be one of the utilities in looking to concepts and theories from the study of colonial argumentation, especially as the practices and representations of travel figure prominently in the mutual constructions of center and periphery, colonizer and colonized, self and other, and home and away.[3] Critical attention to how gender, sexuality,

community, nation, ethnicity, and empire intersect in these representations aids in remapping Pauline scholars' perspectives on historical reconstructive processes.

In her work analyzing the uses of travel writing in European imperialism,
Mary Louise Pratt coined the term *contact zone* to describe "social spaces
where disparate cultures meet, clash, and grapple with each other, often
in highly asymmetrical relations of domination and subordination—like
colonialism, slavery, or their aftermath as they are lived out across the globe
today."[4] Pratt's definition highlights not only the dimension of space, but
also the dimension of time, as these relations continue to shape the world
"after" colonialism, even in current events. The relations in a colonized contact zone are not the result of one, cataclysmic, all-determining event (a key
battle or the arrival of a dominating force) but are established and maintained by multiple, prolonged, and ongoing contact between peoples who
were previously seen as geographically and historically separate.[5] Here, Pratt
is borrowing and adapting the term *contact language* from linguistics, where
it is used to explain the necessarily improvised forms of communication that
typically result when users of different languages meet in the contexts of
trade. The term is not meant to indicate a happy or uncomplicated exchange
between equals; rather, it involves "conditions of coercion, radical inequality, and intractable conflict."[6]

Upon reading such a description, one might believe contact zone to be
just another way to describe the edges or peripheries of an empire. Yet,
Pratt envisions the term to be both a synonym for and an analytic corrective to an emphasis on "the frontier" of a colonial power. The term frontier
primarily orders one's point of view in line with the perspective of the
colonizer, the traveling explorer, and the European expansionist. But, in
Pratt's own words,

> "contact zone" is an attempt to invoke the spatial and temporal
> copresence of subjects previously separated by geographic and his-
> torical disjunctures, and whose trajectories now intersect. By using
> the term "contact," I aim to foreground the interactive, improvisa-
> tional dimensions of colonial encounters so easily ignored or sup-
> pressed by diffusionist accounts of conquest and domination.[7]

Though the conditions of empires involve oppression and domination,
Pratt stresses that these conditions do not foreclose the possibilities of

others' agency, nor negate the opportunities for conceptualizing the historical copresence of oppressed subjects in a colonized context. The colonizer's point of view may be dominant in most of our sources (whether ancient or modern) and thus script the way we look at the period, but their version is not the "whole story." Rather, this version was shaped in a process of interaction with those subjugated; thus, if analyzed carefully, one might be able to find gaps woven into these scripts, gaps indicative of other concepts of space and time.[8]

Inderpal Grewal adapts and then reuses Pratt's notion of the contact zone to apply critical insights to domains besides the genre of travel narratives as practiced by Europeans. This is possible because the rhetorics of imperial travel help to shape representations and cultural reproductions in ways untethered to the Orientalist literature so often examined in postcolonial studies.[9] One can discern the influence of such ideas on speech-acts not immediately identifiable as "travel literature." In this formulation, the dispersion indicates that the concept of the contact zone can also be implemented in contexts besides the peripheries; its spatial and communal constructions of home and away, inside and outside are also key to the colonizers' metropolitan locales.[10] Grewal further qualifies Pratt's work by stressing that this occurs "at various sites in the colonial period through gendered bodies" and "that the 'contact zones' are everywhere and are contained in particular discursive spaces that embody and control the narratives of encounters with difference."[11] These reformulations indicate the potential relevance for examining a *colonia* (like Philippi) in neither the periphery nor the center, as well as the ways in which gender factors into such imperial dynamics.

Implementing such a conceptualization allows feminist, postcolonial analysis to resist the often imperially gendered narratives of innocent possession and rightful ownership presented in colonized/ing texts. The task of the critic, then, involves more than simply redescribing the situation from the point of view of the elite colonial pale male, especially as such a task only repeats and hence, reinscribes a dominating authority. Rather, this process can resist such oppressive dynamics by focusing on the interactive copresence of subjects from a variety of positions. A number of these key ideas have rather clear connections to the starting points of feminist historiography as practiced both within and outside of biblical studies. Feminist scholars insist that women and other oppressed groups were always there, even as they were "written out" of history (hence the favorite aphorism, "women hold up half the sky"). One method held in common includes the strategy of "reading against the grain" of the dominant, pre-scriptive text to articulate a history of those oppressed by such texts.[12]

However, the mode and motivation of this process must further artic-ulate its accountability, especially as it involves considerable time and energy focusing on the already dominant representations from "the mas-ter's text(s)." Such a focus could easily lead to a reification of the author-ity and priority of these imperially gendered frameworks. Furthermore, interpreters must be vigilantly, continuously, reflexively, and suspiciously critical about our own aspirations to scholarly authority, careful not to be (in Spivak's words), "the first-world intellectual masquerading as the absent nonrepresenter who lets the oppressed speak for themselves."[13] Given my own specific position as an elite educated pale male from the heart of the world's latest empire, I must be especially aware of these com-plicated histories of complicity.[14] Pratt herself has noted that in previous eras, "hyphenated white men are principal architects of the often imperi-alist internal critique of empire."[15] Meanwhile, closer to "home" in biblical studies, Laura Donaldson has similarly warned of "neocolonial anticolo-nialist" (or neo-anti-colonial) readings of biblical texts.[16]

Nevertheless, an awareness of these cautions and the potential for one's work to be consolidated back into a kyriarchal, imperial, or neocolonial system makes the efforts all the more important, because feminist, post-colonial analysis cannot leave such adaptive and lingering systems unchal-lenged. On ethical-political grounds, this study can and must engage such master texts as the Bible precisely because of its historical and continu-ing uses against those suffering under the intersecting structures of sex-ism, imperialism, colonialism, racism, nationalism, heterosexism, and poverty.[17] This analysis is certainly dangerous, difficult, and conflicted, because these texts and their uses have been and are still a danger to a great many. Yet, it is a necessary risk, particularly given the effective manner in which these structures have constrained and contained alternate views of the past. In dealing with such a dangerous, but still cited, authorita-tive, historical tradition (as is the case with the biblical heritage), Schüssler Fiorenza explains: "If it is a sign of oppression when a people does not have a written history, then feminist and other subaltern scholars cannot afford to eschew such rhetorical and historical re-constructive work."[18] In a related manner, Sara Mills has argued that in postcolonial feminist analysis of spatial relations, "the paucity of material produced by colonised [*sic*] subjects, itself symptomatic of colonial relations, forces us to examine a range of other textual and theoretical options in order to construe a range of spatial frameworks existing in conflict within colonial space."[19] A feminist, postcolonial analysis of Pauline studies, then, should not forego reflections on the historical horizon, even if and as the resources for reconstructing women's lives in imperially gendered contact zones are limited (often only to traditional sources like Paul's letters).

Although sometimes it might seem like biblical studies does not have many resources for the task of presenting "reconstructive readings as counternarrative," concepts like contact zone and transculturation are useful avenues for engagement with the problematic heritage of biblical arguments and interpretations. Both concepts emphasize the mutual and interactive involvement of colonizer and colonized. Whereas colonial cultural forms are typically viewed as imposed "from above" by the imperial or metropolitan center, Pratt's adaptation of "transculturation" questions such a monolithic, "one-way-only" flow of argumentation.[20] Materials and concepts circulate back and forth: from the periphery to the center and back again. Their subjectivities are in many ways mutually constituted, as marginalized groups adapt and creatively reuse the dominant culture, while the dominant culture constructs its own notions of itself and "others" from the encounters with those it attempts to marginalize. The metropolis does not just create the periphery (despite the dominant claim otherwise), but the margins determine the center.[21]

It is this transcultural process, characteristic of the contact zone, that makes possible reconstructive claims about the subordinated others. As scholars like Spivak and Inderpal Grewal so persistently formulate it, this process can be neither a naive valorization of those silenced nor an undue celebration of the hybridly multicultural foundations of imperial cultural identity.[22] Rather, feminist, postcolonial analysis should be on guard against such conclusions when it is reminded of the hierarchical conditions of this contact: contact shaped by violent conflict, continuous coercion, and asymmetrical power relations. Such conditions cannot and must not be obscured, else the efforts to analyze those occupants of one contact zone will be prone to fall into the patterns of the aforementioned "imperialist internal critique of empire," and ironically limit one's abilities to recognize and engage other, contemporary contact zones.

Pauline Travels and the
Philippian Contact Zone

Having explicated some of the theory and analytic practices first offered in the study of women, imperialism, and travel conditions (if not always writing), it becomes imperative to demonstrate further how this might apply to biblical studies or more specifically, to the interpretation of a Pauline letter. This study maintains that such a reflective turn was an important practical measure, because the anti-imperial and feminist scholarship on travel and the contact zone is both relevant and useful. Although many possible connections and applications can and will be noted (in this study and, I hope, after), there are striking similarities in terms of the contours and the influence of certain collections of writing by Paul of Tarsus and Mary Kingsley, for example. As a late-nineteenth-century travel writer, Kingsley's role in colonial discourse is complicated by her gender, status, ethnicity, and inconsistent sympathies with the colonized peoples of west Africa.[23] Nevertheless, Kingsley's writings were used to help determine British imperial policy in terms of slavery and economic mode and remained an authoritative resource for a host of colonial discussions in terms of ethnic, class, national, imperial, sexual, and gendered identities.[24] Similarly, as a first-century traveler and writer, Paul's role in the Roman Empire is complicated by his gender, status, ethnicity, and inconsistent sympathies with others under imperial rule. Yet, eventually his letters were collected and used as an authoritative source by those exercising power in the Roman Empire (and later, other empires) for norms about the duties of slaves, women's communal roles, sexual behavior, and appropriate attitudes toward imperial figures. On at least this level, the scholarship on more recent colonial contexts is dealing with nearly the same range of issues that a feminist, postcolonial analysis of Paul attempts to negotiate.

Beyond these basic observations about two very different figures with two rather different histories of interaction in a series of contact zones, these concepts are an excellent analytic "fit" for this study, given the historical conditions of cities like Philippi and the rhetorical efforts of Paul's letter to the community there. In the four centuries prior to this letter, Philippi endured successive colonizations and became a colony of the Roman Empire in 42 B.C.E. when Octavian and Antony settled some of their veterans there.[25] The famous battle that preceded this first Roman settlement and the likely violent manner with which land was confiscated and consolidated into the hands of a few wealthy Roman colonists stress Liew and Wimbush's observation that the conditions of the contact zone also often make them "combat zones."[26] Rather than the traditional view that Philippi's status as a *colonia iuris Italicum* was a benefit to the local population (as often argued by scholars of this letter), a number of scholars more recently have argued that the conditions in this *colonia* would have further deprived the vast majority of its residents and would not be seen as "progress."[27] The accompanying exploitative economic conditions involved debt and foreclosure for most of the Roman and the "Greek" land-owning farmers.[28]

Furthermore, the history of Philippi and the conditions of this Roman *colonia* brought people from disparate ethnic, cultic, political, and geographical origins together. Several different ethnic groups resided in first-century Philippi. The Roman ruling minority lived among descendants of the Thasian and Macedonian colonizers of the past, the persistent Thracian tribes, and a growing number of migrant workers and slaves from the Greek east.[29] Greek would have been the main language in use, despite the large number of surviving material remains in Latin. What these predominantly Latin inscriptions at Philippi demonstrate is not the extreme "Romanization" of Philippi but the manner of expression preferred by the elite administrators of the empire. The inscriptions indicate the power of this colonial elite and their desire to impress the authorities at "home" in Rome.[30]

This meeting and mixing of various peoples and languages are also indicators of the differential access to power in this colonial contact zone. In the process of settling Romans at Philippi, the non-Romans' land would have been confiscated first, and according to social models developed by Peter Oakes, a good portion of these Romans in time likely lost these lands to their wealthier and more influential compatriots. The relative "benefits" of Philippi's status as a *colonia* in the Roman Empire would have been limited by these conditions of land ownership and would have depended upon one's status as a citizen. Such status was limited to certain free, elite, propertied, adult males of "proper" lineage and ethnicity. Access to the rights decreed by Roman law required citizenship, but even "average" Roman citizens had difficulties exercising such rights if they lacked extensive wealth, property, or a powerful patronage network.[31]

These privileges indicate significant stratification through an oligarchic and imperial political structure that was acquired through violent conflict and maintained by coercive possession and enforcement. As in Pratt's view of the contact zone, most residents of the colony would have been in a range of subordinate positions as a result of the multiple asymmetrical power dynamics. Subsistence-level poverty likely affected most of the population at Philippi, with a considerable group living in unhealthily sub-subsistence conditions.[32] Slaves were also a significant portion of the work force and of the measurable "wealth" or influence of the elite.[33] Within these dynamics, gender would also have been relevant, because women were barred from Roman imperial citizenship. This additional layer of dominating differentiation even affected relatively advantaged elite, propertied, adult, free Roman women, as they could work only vicariously and dependently through an elite, propertied, adult, free Roman male spouse or family member, who might also be a citizen. Even within these limits, though, such women would have benefited by their complicity in the dominating order, as the residents' experiences of gendered identity would have been complicated by ethnicity, class, imperial positioning, and free or slave status. Though it might not completely exclude a select few Roman women from these benefits, the kyriarchal dynamics of this structure would certainly have compounded the colonized conditions of poor, enslaved, peasant, and/or non-Roman women in a doubled, tripled, or even quadrupled/quintupled oppression.[34] One would likely find more women significantly (but also variously) subordinated in such a structure than those who might have benefited by their complicity and collusion in this arrangement.

Not only do the historical material conditions of this Roman *colonia* tend to reflect Pratt's and others' discussions of the contact zone, but Paul's letters, like Philippians, also seem to be expressions and negotiations of the colonized contact zone. Paul's role in these various communities depends upon his ability to travel and to write about his missionary travels.[35] His letters themselves travel, from one contact zone to another, and Paul reflects on this dynamic in several of his letters. In Philippians, for example, he locates himself spatially within his imprisoned setting (1:12), one indication of the asymmetry and coercion of the colonized contact zone.[36] Yet, he also shows his elevated influence or power as a result of his contact with imperial authorities, speaking about or even for the entire praetorian guard (1:13) and some from the household of Caesar (4:22).

His lingering presence or anticipated copresence with the Philippians is also repeatedly stressed (1:25-26, 27; 2:12, 24), as he hopes to return there and have what he considers the appropriate reception (of himself and his message).[37] Paul further locates himself in terms of his ethnic spatial status as one who should have considerably more confidence (3:4-6). This view of his elevated status might explain why a pattern of suffering-to-gain, or descend-in-order-to-ascend, structures Paul's view of himself and of communal identity (1:12-14, 23-26; 2:6-11; 3:4-11; cf. 1 Cor 1-4).[38] In fact, knowing the travel literature of more recent empires, these kinds of arguments might summon various tropes of the colonial adventure hero, who endures trials and tribulations only to bolster his or her imperially racialized and gendered authority.[39]

Paul's adventures in various Roman imperial contact zones could be contrasted by the constancy he seeks from his audience at Philippi. Speaking in terms reminiscent of military discipline and warfare formation, the hero-turned-general barks orders to stand firmly (1:27; 4:1) and stay in line (3:16).[40] Such rhetoric stresses that Paul seeks to speak spatially to the entire community, organizing obedient communal members in terms of opposition and separation.[41] Good subjects in this order are contrasted to a range of outsiders: divisive ones (1:15-17; 2:3), the perverse (2:15), the dogs (3:2), and enemies who focus on earthly things (3:18-19). The last of these contrasts highlights not only a hierarchical differentiation between people in Philippi, but also a spatial separation in mind-set and expectant outcome: the heavens (3:20). Here is where Paul seeks to be ("with Christ," 1:23), the highest of the three cosmic planes subordinate to a divine *kyrios* (2:9-11; 3:20-21). It is also what constitutes the community as a separate political space: a steadfastly obedient and thus heavenly *politeuma* (1:27; 3:20). The politics of heaven are shaped by imperial-spatial dynamics and transmitted in arguments to a colonized contact zone.

Though Paul's "mission" and message involve traveling to various contact zones and encountering and intermingling with those of different historical, cultic, political, or geographical origins, he repeatedly prioritizes a set of hierarchical differentiations and spatial separations. However, if this communal ethic and praxis of separation had held sway in the first place at Philippi (and elsewhere), it would have precluded the transcultural contact necessary for Paul to establish "his" communities. If people in these cities remained hierarchically differentiated and spatially separated in a constant fashion, then, Paul, a traveling stranger (with even stranger ideas that travel with him), would have encountered significant difficulties in attempting to interact with local populations. This tension recalls a similar ambivalence in colonial claims to enforce separation in terms of gender, sexuality, race/ethnicity, class, and imperial status in various colonized contact zones. In India, for example, the official imperial ideal was distance and separation between ruler and ruled, British and Indian, and especially British women and "native" space.[42] Yet, this ideal erases the prerequisite for and continuing historical material practices of British imperial presence: regular contact, interaction, and crossing of boundaries.[43] Though distinctly different from this colonial contact zone, the dynamics in a Roman *colonia* like Philippi would have been shaped by similar conditions of contact, crossing, and interaction.

Thus, this ambiguous dynamic is not only relevant for the colonial settings of the past three centuries, but also for the ancient imperial setting of the first century. As Jorunn Økland has recently demonstrated, the ancient discourses of gender and space also balance between an idealized gender separation and a hierarchical integration or co-presence.[44] Although traditionally this separation is equated with the lines between public (coded as male) and private (coded as female) spheres, scholars of both antiquity (Økland) and more modern colonial formations (Sara Mills) critique any simplistic deployment of this divide in gendered discourse.[45] One cannot reduce the roles of Paul and women like Euodia and Syntyche according to these codes. Mills's insights about one context is likely apt for the household assembly spaces in places like Philippi: "This idealised separation did not match the actual lived reality where the lack of privacy within the private sphere of the bungalow created a very public private space."[46] The conditions of contact and the spaces for gathering in such contexts likely mixed the intimate and the public.

If considered further, this alternating, ambiguous dynamic between hierarchical contact and separation could further enlighten the historical and rhetorical relations between Paul and his various "co-workers" in Philippi (Timothy, Epaphroditus, Euodia, and Syntyche) and elsewhere. As highlighted in the discussion of mimicry, such relations signal tensions between distance and closeness; between differentiation and similarity. Recognizing such tensions could help in remapping the historical reconstructive efforts of this chapter. Too many historical reconstructions of these interactions between Paul and the assemblies to which he wrote have constructed the audiences of the letters as passive and willingly obedient receptors, roles akin to the "proper natives" in the idealized travel narratives of colonizing Europeans.[47] In assuming that Paul's women co-workers hold unproblematically similar views to Paul, the malestream interpreter treats these historical figures instrumentally as just another weapon in Paul's "women-arsenal."[48] Furthermore, in projecting such static roles onto potentially locally based residents of Philippi, scholars repeat colonizing tropes of separation and civilization, where the colonized are depicted as timelessly backward, in need of imperial progress.

However, the latter discourse identified by Økland, hierarchical integration or co-presence, fits especially well with Pratt's notion of the contact zone and likely corresponds to many more practices in these imperially gendered spaces. These studies of gendered claims in various imperial-colonial spaces stress that one must not rely upon the idealized, patriarchally prescriptive narratives of colonized or colonizing discourse. Foregrounding these aspects of the contact zone enables a further analysis of potential colonial subjectivities, countering the narratives that are predominantly presented in order to reconstruct the roles of women (and others). Returning to first-century Philippi and Paul's letter to the community, renewed attention should be paid to the role of two women in the letter's argument, Euodia and Syntyche.

Euodia and Syntyche: Reconstructing Co-Workers in the Contact Zone

Given Schüssler Fiorenza's imperative for historical reconstructions and Kwok Pui-lan's descriptions of such reconstructions as counternarratives, a feminist, postcolonial analysis should attend to the place of Euodia and Syntyche in this site of transculturation, Philippi, a Roman imperial contact zone. In his letter to the assembly there, Paul describes these two women as those "who struggled alongside me" among the rest of his co-workers (4:3). The work in which they were engaged is not entirely clear from the argument in the letter. Mary Rose D'Angelo maintains that this description "portrays their earlier missionary endeavors with Paul in a heroic vein."[49] Their potential missionary task and heroic role recall the

way imperial women travel writers often adopted and adapted the conventions of colonizing heroism in their work.[50] This also reminds the contemporary interpreter that women often worked with men in colonizing
missions in Asia, Africa, and other colonized contact zones.[51] Adding to
D'Angelo's work, Cynthia Briggs Kittredge also considered whether Euodia and Syntyche might have been an independent missionary pair but
also speaks more generally of their leadership roles, quite possibly among
the *diakonoi* and *episkopoi* greeted at the start of the letter (1:1).[52] Contrary
to most malestream scholarship on the letter, the two women do seem to
be working together, not in a conflict with each other.[53]

If their potential leading roles cannot be further specified than this,
then perhaps this reconstruction should focus on their joint activity of
struggle. If Euodia and Syntyche not only are struggling together but also
along with Paul, what roles might this involve? Since Paul considers himself sent (*apostolos*) to deliver a message to the non-Judeans (including, for
example, most of the inhabitants of Philippi), the struggle likely involved
competing for local minds and hearts over and against both indigenous
and imperial cultic practices with all of their attendant social, economic,
and political resonance. If Paul's letters are reliable on this point (an
important "if"), then it seems Paul at least thinks Euodia and Syntyche
joined him in missionary activity in the Philippian contact zone, either by
traveling there or as already established residents. Yet, these three people's
ambivalent and at least semi-subordinate roles in the Roman Empire
also raise the distinct possibility that "the struggle" was against imperial
forces.[54] No matter how Paul seeks to depict himself, he is writing this
letter from prison (1:12), so he must have run afoul of some party with
imperial authority at the site of his imprisonment.[55]

It is possible, then, to view Euodia's and Syntyche's activities as somehow working against the empire. This past struggle to which this letter
refers could have also involved imperial threats or imprisonment for these
leading women. In the letter to the Philippians, Paul argued that another
co-worker, Epaphroditus, risked his life (2:25-30), just as two other
co-workers, Prisca and Aquila, "risked their necks" in efforts to reach
non-Judeans on another occasion (Rom 16:3-4). That same letter names
another female-male pair, Andronicus and Junia, as remarkable apostles
suffering imprisonment with Paul (Rom 16:7).[56] These other passages
indicate that Paul considered both females and males as his co-workers,

and this conjoined activity could involve imprisonment and mortal risk. Furthermore, it seemed like much of this work demanded travel and a sense of being sent (*apostellō*) on a mission. Thus, these figures manage to display *both* the dangers of contesting accepted beliefs in a contact zone *and* the self-assured authority of those who travel with claims of divine mandate.[57] The latter would have rather chilling implications for future colonial situations.

Though scholars lack any letters from Euodia and Syntyche, one can attempt to further locate them spatially within the dynamics of the colonized contact zone. Both Euodia and Syntyche have Greek names, which serve as potential indices of their status and ethnicity. The name Euodia comes from the term for a "good journey," as it is linked to the verb expressing freedom of passage, help along the way, or prosperity in a journey. Syntyche as a name describes one who is fortunate, or "with luck."[58] For an interpreter like myself, who bears a name with a rather clear military-imperial resonance (Marchal), the significance of such names provoke a number of questions.[59] I cannot help but read such names with suspicion about their connections to colonial travel, as they offer ideal conditions for unconstrained missions, plunderous fortunes, or any imperial intervention met with little resistance. Who is being helped along the way and whose good is served in these kinds of journeys? From whose perspective are such travels met with luck?

Yet, one's views of the names of these two women leaders can change upon further investigation. The social-historical modeling work of Craig de Vos and Peter Oakes both stress the servile origins of the women's names. De Vos maintains that both women were likely *liberta*, freed slaves, with relatively low status, highlighting two known inscriptional occurrences of freed slaves named Euodia.[60] Oakes is rather less committed about their slave or manumitted status, but recognizes that Syntyche "sounds like various slave names."[61] Euodia's and Syntyche's likely status as slaves (or former slaves) underscore their own experiences of the coercion and asymmetry of the kyriarchally colonized contact zone.[62] Indeed, their names may have been given to them because of their (former) masters' view of his own "good fortune." Their names are quite possibly the expression and commemoration of the masters' joy at their ability to acquire slaves (through military and/or economic ends). This raises questions about how those bearing such experiences would receive calls for obedience and subordination or metaphors of slavery (evident in several of Paul's letters) to explain communal membership.[63] One could assume that an enslaved or emancipated Greek woman in Philippi would view such arguments in a fashion quite different from a free Judean man from Tarsus. Indeed, it is precisely one potential basis for these differences, Euodia's and Syntyche's gender, that led to two different interpretive attempts to masculinize their names (a fate not uncommon for women in Pauline interpretation).[64]

It is often these kinds of differences that have been passed over in the interpretation of Pauline letters like Philippians. The letter's argumentation suggests that there was a conflict between Paul and these two women, or at least a difference in mind-set. Since Paul's view of communal unity has been continuously argued in the preceding chapters, his call for Euodia and Syntyche to "think the same thing" (4:2) is seeking for them to think the same thing as Paul. As argued in the previous chapter, Paul is making a cross-gendered, cross-ethnic argument for imitation within an imperially militarized zone. This view of the situation is bolstered by Paul's turning to a third party, someone called only a "true yokeperson," to "take hold" of the women (4:3). Such an argument reflects that Paul trusts someone as *better* yoked to his authority and/or more closely miming his point of view, not-too-subtly signifying that these two "are no longer truly yoked with him."[65] The interpretation of this situation is only further complicated by Paul's reference to another co-worker, Clement (4:3). His name is Latin in origin (from *Clemens*, meaning mercy), hearkening perhaps to the only authority that can grant clemency in this era: the Roman Empire. Although occasionally a scholar will argue the name indicates his military position or history,[66] the name more often designates a freeborn commoner.[67] As a free Roman plebeian male, Clement could have benefited from Roman imperial aggression and control, while simultaneously being exploited by the upper echelons of Roman society.[68]

Within a scant two verses of Paul's letter to the Philippians, then, there is a small interaction not entirely dissimilar from Pratt's concept of the contact zone. There are parties of different ethnic, cultic, geographic, political, *and gendered* origins[69]: Roman, Greek, and Judean; free, enslaved, or manumitted; women, males, and those who might "count" as *viri* by Roman imperial norms.[70] Evidently, there is conflict over the right way of thinking in the community. In the schema Paul presents in this letter, such views show one's place in a set of hierarchical differentiations.

There are some who are enough like Paul, like the one who is properly and truly yoked well to Paul's position and, by implication, there are those who are not. The rest of the letter presents those who are different (divisive, perverse, dogs, enemies) as belonging to a separate, demonized space, and threats of destruction often accompany such differences (1:28; 2:12; 3:1, 15, 19-20). Given the conditions of these hierarchical and asymmetrical differentiations, calls for those who disagree with Paul to "unify" could also be violently coercive in tenor.

Following the line of argumentation in the letter to the Philippians, Paul frames the situation in ways akin to what Dube has analyzed as "a type-scene of land possession."[71] Paul has come into contact with Greek (and possibly indigenous Philippian) women at Philippi. He writes on this occasion to convince the community to take his view and this section of the argument is particularly directed to garner Euodia's and Syntyche's conformity, showing how important they were in Paul's estimation. He has so shaped his arguments that if the two women do not accept his mind-set and the community does, they will be effectively written out of the community. However, if they assent to his mind-set, then it seems Paul believes the community will go along with them. Euodia and Syntyche (like Dido, Rahab, or Pocahontas) are the site of contestation, because they stand in for the people and the territory Paul would like to claim.[72] Such observations resonate with both Økland's work showing how women bear the boundaries and meanings of space on their bodies in Pauline discourse and the related postcolonial feminist work of Laura Donaldson and Anne McClintock, who stress the role of women, sexuality, and female-gendered territory in colonial argumentation.[73]

But to allow Paul's point of view to dominate one's view of the conditions of the contact zone is to accept common colonizing rationales. Assuming Euodia's and Syntyche's passivity or pliability in this scenario supports the view of Paul as the heroic male on a colonizing mission and Philippi/Philippians as the empty land waiting for enlightenment, civilization, or salvation.[74] Working this way involves forgetting a key element of Pratt's use of the contact zone, the interactive copresence of colonizer and colonized. The transcultural process of contact seriously grapples with the likelihood of information and arguments flowing the other direction.[75] Those considered peripheral or subordinate contributed to and helped shape the discourse that attempts to dominate one's view of this past. Too

often, because there are few resources besides Paul's letters to develop concepts of these first-century communities in various imperial cities, most
malestream Pauline scholars have rhetorically acquiesced and operated as
if there were no community outside of what Paul describes. When and if
other participants are considered, they are treated as "bit players" to our
main character, the missionary adventure hero Paul.[76]

Kittredge has recently offered a corrective to such a tendency by highlighting the feminist historical rethinking of the elements of "authorship"
and "theology" in Pauline letters. In keeping with the work of Schüssler
Fiorenza and Antoinette Clark Wire, Kittredge emphasizes that the ideas
and beliefs of these groups were formulated in community.[77] Thus, when
Paul writes in and to these groups, he has to learn and then use communally
shaped ideas to argue his points. In this historical scenario, it is possible
that those considered marginal (or those he is attempting to marginalize)
have actually contributed to the formulation of these letters' argumentation. In several cases, scholars have argued that Paul quotes traditions that
precede the letters, like the hymn in 2:6-11, using materials quite possibly
composed by others.[78]

If a feminist, postcolonial analysis recalls the reconsideration of mimicry in the preceding chapter, while recognizing the communal setting
and interactive copresence of these contact zones, it should emphasize that
there were other points of view than Paul's. Paul selects and shapes the
argumentative materials for his own purposes, but it seems almost inevitable that there was a range of different views about a number of ideas
and practices in the community at Philippi (and elsewhere). Lest we for-
get, Paul's targeted argument to Euodia and Syntyche strongly indicates
that there is disagreement between Paul and two leading members of the
Philippian community. As the analysis in the previous chapter suggests,
this could have involved a different praxis of mimicry for these women
and/or other members of the community. This imitative practice could
also have involved some form of resistance or subversion. As McClintock
and Yeğenoğlu suggested, it is not the perfect imitations that are satisfying and effective, but those imitations that purposefully and recognizably
distort. An imitation with some kind of difference cannot be received
seamlessly, but registers as a dissonant practice that refuses to erase the
different agency of the imitator. Because Paul's argument assumes a difference between Euodia and Syntyche and himself, the letter may be one

indication that they (and/or others) are enacting just such dissonant practices. Paul seems to have recognized this situation of difference, even as he attempts to squelch it for his own distinct form of authoritative difference and obedient sameness. Nevertheless, there is no reason to assume the letter settles the conflict or difference in mind-set between them.

This raises the historical possibilities that Euodia and Syntyche negotiated the Philippian contact zone differently than Paul, even after receiving the letter. Indeed, some of the key differences between them in terms of their locations in space and time might give some insight into how these two thought differently from the arguments of the letter. As Greek, potentially long-time residents of Philippi, enslaved or manumitted, low-status, and possibly poor females in a Roman *colonia*, Euodia and Syntyche were likely to see a life path conditioned by suffering in a manner less positively than Paul. Indeed, their potential positionality indicates that their experiences of suffering were caused by the interconnected structures of Roman kyriarchal occupation and oppression in terms of gender, geography, sexuality, ethnicity, slavery, status, and imperial stakes.[79]

Recognizing Euodia's and Syntyche's potential position(s) in the intersecting kyriarchal orders of first-century Philippi, though, should not simply lead to an unqualified valorization of them as decolonizing feminist subjects. Paul's willingness to recognize them as co-workers shows that their roles were likely also shaped by dynamics Paul accepted, including possibly missions to the "unconverted." Both colonial and "native" women's various roles in imperial missions throughout the centuries should give us pause en route to reclaiming Euodia and Syntyche as themselves heroes of anti-imperial or anti-kyriarchal liberation.[80] This also would fit with some of the more complicated models for how empires function in such contact zones. Empires are diffuse and improvisational in their practices, strategies, arguments, and ideologies; loyal often only to that which would keep their power consolidated.[81] Through these modes, colonial powers convince their colonized subjects to lessen resistance and encourage collaboration or a more active form of complicity. Thus, imperial authorities manage to negotiate, destabilize, override, or redirect any uniform sense of classed, ethnic, geographic, or gendered solidarity within and across the various colonized populations. These populations, however, should not only be figured as manipulated and passive in their conflicted positionality because collaboration gives subjects access to other, more intricate (and possibly more effective) forms of resistance (as the various forms of mimicry examined in the previous chapter indicate).

Therefore, one could potentially view women with some position in an albeit small community at Philippi as both resistant and complicit, both colonized and colonizing. In this manner, they likely could be little different from Paul, who seems to challenge imperially gendered dynamics only to reinscribe them to his own ends.[82] Yet, the analysis still comes back to this position of difference, in terms of mind-set in the letter and in terms of the communal space of Philippi. Paul anticipates or responds to conflict with these women; their different ethnic, class, geographic, and/or gender status could explain why they would adopt different positions on this or other matters. If they recall ancestral stories of various, and especially the recent Roman, invasions and colonizations, then perhaps Euodia and Syntyche were resisting an additional invasive attempt at possession of the land or people of Philippi. It is also distinctly possible that the problem is not *that* someone possesses this land/people, but it is the *someone* who is making this claim: Paul. This might remind the reader of N. T. Wright's arguments that the problem with Caesar's empire is not that it is an empire, but that it is Caesar's, instead of God's.[83] Since Paul expects the audience to understand the way he presents his argument to them, his argument expects that the community would also recognize Euodia and Syntyche in leading roles. Is Paul's argument an indication that he is competing with these two for the rightful "possession" of this land or people? Would this form of "taking hold" (4:3) of the community be significantly different in terms of kyriarchal relations in the contact zone? Are these arguments reflective of two different strategies of mimicry in use or under consideration in the assembly?

Euodia's and Syntyche's different positions in the letter and in the Philippian contact zone raise the possibilities that they were moved by efforts at resistance or at least a different form of complicity than Paul's. Their status as enslaved or manumitted women does not rule out continued loyal service and acquiescence to imperial orders, but it also provides an insight into why they might have "struggled" in the past Paul alludes to in the letter. Emphasizing such a potentially conflicted copresence in the contact zone resituates many claims about Paul's authority in the community and highlights the more interactive and mixed communal dynamics within communities like the Philippian one. This requires that one continue to investigate and formulate the full range of complicated roles women likely played within these communities.

In the end, this feminist, postcolonial analysis cannot, with confidence, proclaim members of these movements like Euodia and Syntyche as whole-hearted imperial resisters or as traveling missionaries, fully accommodated to the dictates of the Roman Empire. Yet, the consideration of these dynamics of travel and contact offers important new perspectives on the complicated historical dynamics that shaped, whether directly or indirectly, the literature that survives from this era. Attempting to reconstruct women's roles to counter the dominant and dominating forms of biblical interpretation presents both the ambiguities and the still fertile possibilities for biblical interpretation and historical reconstruction. This process will be especially compelling not only for the new information it might provide, but also for the way such processes make us as interpreters better attuned to the ethical and political significance for how we argue about women and empire in the past, present, and future. In this fashion struggles with the biblical heritage can be a dangerous, ambiguous, but still relevant component of life in our contemporary contact zones.[84]

Concluding Reflections
and Connections

—————— Reviewing the Present Project ——————

In this work, I have aimed to demonstrate how both Paul's letters and Pauline interpretation are the results of imperially gendered rhetorical activities. To the degree that these claims are apparent and convincing, this study also establishes a number of other assertions. In highlighting the necessity for feminist, postcolonial analysis, it has explicated that a focus on the dynamics of gender, sexuality, ethnicity, and empire is not only appropriate for the study of Paul, but that it might also revitalize biblical scholarship by reformulating our tasks for the twenty-first century. Given the presently persistent and pernicious conditions of injustice, with effects both local and global, and the historical utilization and participation of biblical argumentation in these conditions, such a focus is much needed if our work is to be either interpersonally relevant or ethically accountable.

There are reasons for students of biblical literature and ancient history to be optimistic about such possibilities, because some strands of interpretation have been attending to feminism, postcolonialism, and Roman imperialism. However, it has been rare for scholars to consider how to navigate and evaluate the most relevant intersections of these strands while grappling with the overlaps, gaps, tensions, and conflicts in and between them. Such interactions highlight the clear difficulties and the still manifest possibilities of doing relevantly inter- or multi-disciplinary work. Of course, one should be suspicious of a range of current practices, prevalent in higher education, that prize and promote a generalized trend toward interdisciplinarity, especially as they have modestly emptied interdisciplinarity of any critical import or origin and seldom interrogate to what end this combination or crossing of disciplines operates. Indeed, biblical studies has always involved multiple disciplines and tasks, from philology to history, classical contexts to exegetical details. This has not significantly altered the tendency of too much scholarship to be aligned with the authorities of extraction and oppression, prejudice and profit. Thus, the matter at hand is not whether we should be crossing disciplines, but *how* should we be drawing resources from *which* sets of conversations and toward *what ends*? In the end, our work should rise and fall on its ability to answer the same nagging question I ask of students, colleagues, friends, myself, and all manner of interlocutors: so what? Interdisciplinary work must answer such questions of relevance by addressing not only "what this means," but also "what this does" (or, how it functions).

I attempted to address these kinds of disciplinary questions in the reflections on feminist concepts, postcolonial critics, people's history projects, and pioneers of a politically anti-imperial Paul, among other things in the opening chapters. In doing so, this project made evident the advantages of pursuing a specific kind of trans- or inter-disciplinary trajectory: a feminist, postcolonial analysis of Pauline studies. Drawing upon both the precedent of Elisabeth Schüssler Fiorenza and the contours carved by Musa Dube and Kwok Pui-lan in shaping feminist work that is simultaneously decolonizing, the analysis made manifest the importance of attending to the intersecting structures of domination evident in the first to the twenty-first centuries. It seems unlikely that most of the insights in the analysis that followed would have emerged if the project had not adopted the distinct and explicit foci indicated by the commitments of such scholars.

Attending to the areas of concern outlined by Kwok and answering the guiding questions articulated by Dube led almost ineluctably to a series of key topics for the study of Pauline letters and interpretation, including especially those that are so often overlooked in most malestream scholarship. The evaluative work necessary to chart the relevant histories of interpretation, with these questions in mind, led to a reevaluation of Paul's letter to the Philippians and Pauline interpretation of the letter. In the second chapter, heavenly politics (Phil 3:18-21) and highlighted hymns (Phil 2:6-11) are reconsidered given their interconnections with other troubling rhetorical and historical dynamics. As a result, the presumptions of previous Pauline expositors in pursuit of an anti-imperial or postcolonial Paul are reviewed and challenged for their own gaps and limitations. In addition, we note that those issues raised from early in the work (the circumstances of contact and the practices of mimicry) are demonstrably absent, even in scholarship sensing the significance of empire. Yet, a feminist, postcolonial inquiry into the role of women in conditions of colonizing contact underscores the centrality of travel and interaction for reconstructing historical trajectories for these ancient assemblies. Furthermore, the requisite feminist, postcolonial attention to relations of domination and subordination brings the focus to issues of imitation and authority.

As a result, the analysis was able to concentrate on the richly variegated but also problematic phenomenon of mimicry in both colonial and postcolonial communal contexts. Indeed, mimicry has been a recurrent topic of interest and stress in recent theoretical work in postcolonial studies, most prominently in the case of Homi Bhabha. This theoretical work, however, proves not to be lacking either limits or lessons for various postcolonial and postcolonial feminist scholars, suggesting that those interested in the import of mimicry or of Bhabha's work, in general, for biblical interpretation might want to cast the net a little wider. As we have seen from the numerous insights of Rey Chow, Anne McClintock, and Meyda Yeğenoğlu, there are many reasons and routes for resisting, resituating, and ultimately posing powerful alternatives to Bhabha's theoretical applications of mimicry and hybridity. Thus, with the aid of these insights, the third chapter of this work recognizes and reflects upon how Paul's letters (like Philippians) are attempts to argue through cross-ethnic, cross-gendered claims for imitation within an imperially militarized zone.

Given this view of Pauline letters as particular kinds of rhetorical products, with specific aims, ends, and energies, the task of reconstructing historical dynamics in ancient assemblies like that of Philippi is situated in a different manner. Concepts like contact zone prove fruitful for thinking through the conditions of contact, crossing, and mixing necessary for Paul and others to meet and interact in colonized settings within the Roman Empire. Stressing domains of contact over those of boundary or frontier highlights how empires function through the mutual copresence and involvement of many people, rather than simply as orders of separation. Circumstances are never completely determined by fiat of the imperial authority despite their best efforts. For the ancient historian, this requires attention to more than the "great men" of the past. As both the political context and the specific rhetorics of the letter reveal, to consider the likely range of parties involved in locales like Philippi, we must consider people with a variety of ethnic, cultic, geographic, imperial-political, and gendered origins and positions. To advance further situated knowledges about the *colonia*, the assembly community, or the letter, the elements of travel, contact, and space require more thoughtful consideration.

Such efforts are important, no less, for developing reconstructive historical readings about women in such contact zones as counternarratives to kyriarchal impulses in society and scholarship. Here, the presence of Euodia and Syntyche in the argumentation of the letter and in the community at Philippi seems promising. In attempting to develop non-idealized reconstructions of their potential roles in the assembly at Philippi, the fourth chapter considered a number of relevant dynamics. Described as those who co-struggled with Paul, Euodia and Syntyche could have functioned as missionaries, either traveling to or already based in Philippi. That such struggles could have been against the threats of empire is not an unheard-of role for women mentioned in Paul's letters, given the risks of Prisca or the imprisonment of Junia. The origins of their names indicate a likely Greek origin, and their probable enslaved or emancipated status. Thus, as Greek, potentially long-time residents of Philippi, who were enslaved or manumitted, low status, and possibly poor females in a Roman *colonia*, these two women embodied positions that differ from Paul or most normative subjects for biblical or classical studies.

Nevertheless, the historical roles of Euodia and Syntyche in the community at Philippi are far from straightforward. Does their rhetorical role in the letter signify the existence of alternate models or authorities for the assembly communities? Or, akin to Dube's description of the typescene of land possession, does their appearance indicate Paul's targeted arguments to "possess" the community (and them)? To the degree that the women stand in contradistinction to Paul, their roles could pose as an alternative to the imperial dynamics evident in Paul's argumentation; yet the potential remains that in Euodia and Syntyche, we have simply an imperial-style option different from Rome or Paul. As missionaries or leaders, they could evince another style of collusion, compliance, or collaboration, out of which resistance is still variously possible (as the energies and effects of imperial-colonial powers so often are as well). Such attempts to reconstruct women's roles in colonial contact zones will be especially compelling, not only for the new information it might provide, but also for the way such processes make us as interpreters better attuned to the ethical and political significance for how we argue about women and empire in the past, present, and future.

Regardless of the final details of such inevitably tentative reconstructive efforts, such an analysis historically resituates Pauline authority and challenges Pauline scholars to find ways to not begin and end with Paul's perspective. For historical-critical readings, it highlights a more conflicted copresence of figures and parties in assemblies that are located within, and are themselves even smaller versions of, zones for mixing and interaction. Developing such procedures calls for closer attention to the mixed and interactive communal dynamics at work in those letters and assemblies that we so commonly call Paul's. Considering the variant relations of contact, space, and interaction with empire, in turn, requires that one continue to investigate and formulate the full range of complicated roles women likely played in these communities, beyond simply typical views of Paul's "women-arsenal."

Given where this study has gone, the question raised above remains: so what? What matters about the content and concept of the foregoing analysis? To my mind, there are five clear impulses of this work that I hope its various audiences would take away for further consideration, application, questioning, and critique. Highlighted from the beginning (and evident throughout), the first trajectory stresses the importance of *an increased attention to the interconnections* between various power dynamics and summons biblical studies to an *accompanying shift in methodology*. Too often ignored or isolated, the intersections and mutual influences of gender, sexuality, ethnicity, and empire are crucial for understanding the impact of these seemingly disparate elements for life in either ancient or contemporary kyriarchal contexts. A second trajectory stresses matters of immediate relevance to Pauline studies, but also the study of biblical and ancient literature in general. A change in approach operates as a *corrective to recent work* on the stance of Paul's letters vis-à-vis imperialism, suggesting *closer collaboration and thoughtful interaction with the kinds of cautions, critiques, and concerns raised by feminist, postcolonial, and postcolonial feminist scholars*. In doing so, this study also evokes the clear potential for introducing new elements to postcolonial biblical interpretation. Postcolonial work must proceed with further examination of Pauline materials and could be reasonably reshaped by greater interaction with the wide domain of extra-biblical postcolonial studies, most especially where feminist insights contribute to both.

Following upon and interlaced within these efforts, the third trajectory involves the *consistent tracing of the problematically kyriarchal resonance of the literature covered*, both ancient and academic. Efforts centered on recuperating Paul or redeeming the history of biblical scholarship duck this overwhelming tendency, in both Paul's letters and Pauline interpretation. Rather than residing on the very occasional edges, where cursory acknowledgments of paternalism or peripheral allusions to colonial-era collusions are made, an analysis that focuses upon sexism, racism, ethnocentrism, sexual normativity, and imperial-colonial relations should be at the heart of our pursuits as scholars of some of the most ethically troublesome materials in human history. Nevertheless, the damaging impact of this work as a cultured complicity in kyriarchy should be far from the final word for concerned critics, adherents, and publics. In keeping with a fourth trajectory, some of these alarming aspects can be counteracted by *decentering Paul in the study of these letters*. Alongside feminist historians and people's history advocates, seeking the people besides Paul provides historical resources for the ethical-political struggles of communities marginalized in the past, present, and future. Beyond presenting the possible perspectives of plebeians and peasants, such a shift in reconstructive priority reflects what other promising functions historical processes might still provoke and pursue.

Finally, the fifth trajectory indicates the wider utility of the multiple crossings manifest in this study. As underlined above, this kind of religious studies could be useful for our contemporary contexts. Such work, for example, shows how feminist, postcolonial, and postcolonial feminist studies *needs the contributions of religious studies*. When seeking to analyze the history and rhetoric of gender, sexuality, status, ethnicity, or empire, the specifics of religious institutions, arguments, and practices in the materials studied and the matters critiqued must be treated. To ignore the critical study of religion in these pursuits likely thwarts a more comprehensive understanding and a more effective praxis. Given the historical inclination of powers and peoples to especially cite the precedent and authority of older religious phenomena, concentration on biblical and

Roman-imperial-era materials are particularly crucial if scholars are to be savvy negotiators of such intersections.

—————— Elaborating Further Possibilities ——————

These impulses signify the currently stressed trajectories of the present project, but they are far from comprehensive in describing all the important possibilities for where else such analyses might proceed. From my admittedly limited perspective, at times I can but only hint at some of the more relevant and interconnected trajectories to feminist, postcolonial analysis, but it is nevertheless crucial to indicate further strategies, alliances, and interventions critical to counteracting kyriarchal formations in all their variety and specificity. For example, as occasionally alluded to in the previous chapters and evidenced even by some of Kwok Pui-lan's work, there are many potential interconnections between feminist, postcolonial, and queer approaches.[1] Imperial and colonial authorities often use arguments on erotic grounds to justify particular forms of invasion or intervention. The colonizing (mostly) male authority can claim his superiority, virtue, and civilization by extolling sexual norms (of his own establishment) that the erotically savage or debased colonized people apparently do not embody. Their aberration proves the necessity, even the elevated benefit, of imperial-colonial forces. Feminist, postcolonial analyses, then, should reflect further on such processes of normalization as operations within or overlapping with imperially gendered dynamics.[2] In addition, this set of critical queries should also give considered pause to the normative function, impact, and aspiration of any historiographic effort to find the viewpoint of "typical" people, as scholars focused on history from below or people's history, might be currently inclined. From the homosocial, triangular implications of the "race for Africa" (or any competitive imperial outburst) to the parodic possibilities of mimetic practices, the insights of queer theorists have many contributions to make to the interactions between feminist and postcolonial approaches that should, in turn, help to reformulate critical biblical studies.[3]

This kind of exchange is in no way a one-way street. Rather, in return, the work of transnational feminists like M. Jacqui Alexander foreground neocolonial formations and transnational frameworks to press feminist, queer, and critical race theories to respond to the necessarily multiple crossings of regulatory practice and resistant politics.[4] The immense and still-growing literature of transnational and, especially, transnational feminist scholars is as yet a mostly untapped resource for further critical reflections on the role of biblical interpretation in the project of nationalism.[5] Such work could make Pauline scholars, for example, increasingly attentive to the ways the ethnic reasoning of Paul might be "nationing" his audience(s) as an "imagined political community."[6] In this light, Paul's view of the Philippian heavenly politic is bolstered by the powerful symbolic resonance of a hymnic Christ, the ritual practice of imitating Paul, and the assembly's shared history of struggle.[7]

Increasing attention to the dynamics of such ethnic reasoning, particularly where it crosses boundaries and disciplines, could inspire critics to "provincialize" the study of Paul's assemblies, or the Roman Empire in general.[8] On the historical level, such an effort would involve decentering Paul and Rome in lieu of a focus on the people in the provinces and the peripheries. Feminist historians and critics working on various "histories from below" have begun this project, but attention to how the metropole has constituted subjects both central and peripheral requires further resistance and reformulation. On the disciplinary level, the contributions of "flesh and blood" or "ordinary" readers might demonstrate that interpretation is not the exclusive province of scholars trained in the British, German, or American centers of higher education.[9] As stated in the examinations of the first chapter, this present project does not directly engage in such "reading with" practices, yet it aims to address the concerns of readers "on the ground." It is my genuine hope that the merits and limits of much that has preceded this conclusion will be measured against the critical and creative faculties of such audiences, particularly where they are affected by the dominating dynamics of gender, sexuality, status, race/ethnicity, and empire. These interactions should signal to us how scholarship crosses both nationalized and professionalized borders. Our interpretations and analyses must remain responsible and responsive to multiple contexts, particularly given the way globalization has simultaneously made the world smaller while widening the gulf of traditionally hierarchical differentiations.

Such seemingly contradictory moves in the constantly shifting neocolonial context of the early twenty-first century might explain the continuing influence of hyper-nationalism, even as commerce and information are exchanged in an ostensibly borderless, post-national, digital age. Often this patriotic national fervor is matched with a stiffening sense of a nationally stable ethnic or racial identity. Recent developments in Pauline studies might be responding to the ways a universalist Paul, laboring over and against a legalistic Judaism, was implemented in various nationalist and racializing narratives of the modern era.[10] In many of these reconstructions, scholars have replaced the opponent of Judaism by claiming that Paul's letters represent resistance against the Roman imperial cult or more generally, "paganism." However, this particular strategy for moving away from a supremacist and anti-Semitic conceptualization installs and reinscribes another supremacist and racializing conceptualization evident in many colonial eras and efforts. The non-Christian natives of Africa, Asia, and the Americas were frequently depicted as uncivilized, irrational, and excessively or otherwise aberrantly erotic. The more these "pagan" peoples were thus depicted, the more justified the imperial claims to civilizing and Christianizing appeared. With coinciding religious and sexual rationales for empire, sexuality becomes a key boundary-setter for colonial, national, and religious identity; and reciprocally, religion becomes a key marker of sexual, national, and colonial superiority. Thus, the interpreters' shift from an anti-Jewish to an anti-pagan Paul still involves problematic practices of othering that reinforce historical hierarchies of domination and subordination. Given the distinct roles sexual normativity and racial ideology play in these hierarchies, further concentration on queer, race-critical, and transnational approaches should prove central to continuously critical versions of feminist, postcolonial analysis and of biblical interpretation in general.

Often, as I present various elements of this work that highlight such potentially problematic elements in Pauline argumentation or in contemporary interpretations of Paul, I am met with protestations about the presentation of Paul. The analysis, they interject, seems "too hard on" Paul, deeply unsympathetic to his own specific role or plight in the ancient world. In response, I allow that one would be right to note my starting position of suspicion toward Pauline, even biblical materials. However, one could be even more perceptive in noting that such a position is adopted by myself (and others) because of the historic and contemporary uses to which Paul's arguments have been deployed. For anyone sympathetic to the plight of those oppressed in interlocking structures of domination, then and now, it is hard to ignore the influence and impact of biblical materials in some of the most startlingly dehumanizing practices of humans. Thus, the careful respondent is right to highlight that my sympathies begin more often with these than with Paul or the tradition of interpretation built up around his letters.

To be clear, based on the admittedly limited historical resources that attest to Paul's place in the ancient Mediterranean context ruled by the Romans, Paul of Tarsus was far from being an ancient imperator. It seems likely that there were many more who benefited significantly more from the intersecting privileges of life under Roman imperial and patriarchal authority than this Paul. If one were inclined to monocausal explanations for the fate of people in places like Philippi, Thessalonica, or Corinth, Paul would almost certainly not be the prime mover in determining such fates. Nevertheless, these historical conditions do not preclude the likelihood that the person and the products "Paul" were (or even are) involved in various degrees of complicity and co-optation with kyriarchical orders. Neither do these conditions rule out the further recapitulation and recapitalization of Pauline arguments or Pauline interpreters toward kyriarchical ends, from the first up to and through the beginning of the twenty-first century. Attention to these orders of domination and their intersections in literature and interpretation are seldom at the center of the study of Paul. My efforts herein might mark one attempt to proceed otherwise.

It is possible that the issue is less the details filled in for the person of Paul than the creation and maintenance of a (sub)field designated Pauline studies. Setting aside even the impact of the devotional background and motivation for some (if not most) who study thusly, such a division of labor in biblical studies has perhaps inevitably centered around the figure of Paul, whether one reconstructs an existentialist, rationalist, Hellenist, universalist, apocalypticist, or anti-imperialist Paul. As a result, scholars disciplined as Paulinists almost reflexively have found the need to defend Paul as a means of defending the legitimacy of their own tightly related, individual and corporate enterprises. To do otherwise might require rethinking the entire edifice that is the academic study of Paul. Yet, this is precisely what the work of feminist, postcolonial analysis is calling us to do: to rethink some of the most hallowed methods and cherished assumptions. If one is inclined to care about women, gender, or empire, I suggest that one might try an experiment as a sign of good faith and of solidarity in struggle. Try not to defend the field or its ostensible focus, as a matter of course. Even if one is uncomfortable with reassessing the traditional bounds of this field (Paul's letters), try reading these letters without focusing on the perspective of Paul per se. Some feminist scholars have done as much in recent years, and it appears that practitioners of people's history should be inclined this way as well. Suspending this reflexive defense of Paul could foster new disciplinary habits, where critics take up those challenges raised in the preceding chapters, or mix them with those mentioned in closing here—those still in need of further explication. What new readings might still be possible? What key accountabilities and actions might we still embody in our world today?

In this vein, by way of conclusion, I suggest one further strategy for engaging the imperially gendered argumentation of Paul's letters and Pauline interpretation. In feminist, postcolonial analyses, if one were to find that Paul's letters or interpreters repeat, reuse, or reinforce kyriarchally imperial images or arguments, one would justifiably desire to neither revalorize nor reinscribe such imagery or argument. Nevertheless, one might also identify the still potent possibilities of using Pauline argumentation to different ends. Indeed, for anyone simultaneously invested to any degree in the contemporary authority of biblical materials *and* in efforts against oppression and domination, this possibility seems especially precious. Might there still be creative techniques for recognizing and resisting such dynamics through a reuse? One way to not only decenter but resituate arguments like Paul's is to implement a strategy sprinkled throughout Gayatri Chakravorty Spivak's work, that of *catachresis*.[11] In Spivak's hands, its origin as a term for the "improper use" of a word have been re-appropriated to describe anti-colonial practices that reuse colonizing techniques or institutions against the purposes of colonization (not unlike the resistant form of mimicry considered in chapter 3). If one wishes to be inconsistent with the oppressive practices of biblical argumentation in contemporary reuses, a catachrestic reading could allow for a range of resistant responses.

Such a strategy has very rarely appeared in biblical interpretation, with only recent exceptions like the work of Stephen Moore.[12] Yet, in Moore's application of the concept, the act of catachresis is projected back onto the ancient apocalyptic literature itself. The practices of those loyally adopting Roman imperial language to disloyal ends are highlighted as seditiously

parodying the empire of the first century.[13] There is little to suggest in
such an analysis that *we* might properly use this "improper use" for our
own purposes of loyally disloyal resistance, let alone a faithfully unfaithful
reading of Paul for *the present*. Thus, this specific import of a catachrestic
practice for biblical interpretation is still mostly unexamined. We need not
depend upon an authoritative past to speak with a non-dominating form
of authority about the prospects of resistance and reformulation for the
present and the future. There might still be ways to continue to use these
texts and traditions without continuously perpetuating the problematic
uses. Past models suggest that "proper uses" require fastidiously following
the ostensible intention and argument of the author, the saint, and the
Spirit that creates the text. A present strategy of catachresis suggests that
a spirited use that contradicts where the text clearly keeps company with
kyriarchal impulses is more properly improper when one wishes not to
sanctify domination or oppression.

For Philippians, what other improper uses of heavenly politics, inconsistent with the politics of an imperial Paul, could be formulated? The
examinations above (as in the third chapter) might be indications that the
injunctions to imitate can be used in ways unexpected, or even undesired,
by some first-century community members. Unfaithful readings of the
Christ hymn could create a *chrēsis* of *Christos* that is more faithfully and
consistently consecrated to counter-kyriarchal contestations, despite the
hymn's concluding proclamation of Christ as *kyrios* (2:11), as highlighted
in the second chapter.[14] Paul's gendered argumentation might still engen-
der a gender-based resistance that identifies the potential roles of women
in the community (as in the fourth chapter), but does not treat women's
different experiences under empire identically. Efforts by apostles and
interpreters to limit such roles can be taken not as instructions, but as
signs for how excluded voices must be brought into the center of contemporary interpretive efforts, if not-so-ancient assemblies are to resemble
a more just politic. As suggested by the insights of Chow, McClintock,
and Yeğenoğlu (by the end of the third chapter), cross-gendered, cross-
ethnic arguments to legitimize the travel of imperial authority figures
determined to change and "convert" can be put to cross-purposes, as those
marginalized in these crossed contexts convert colonizers' travel to contest
the territory and "talk back" against the boundaries of exploitation still
manifest in the globally neocolonial exchange.

When being faithful to "Paul" requires either ignoring or reinforcing these kinds of contemporary contextual troubles, one good option involves troubling these dynamics through such faithfully unfaithful interpretations. These avenues for exploration and strategies in struggle suggest that the future of biblical studies might best be glimpsed in the interdisciplinary exchanges encouraged by feminist, postcolonial analysis. It is, in short, time to take the text and interpretation elsewhere. Refusing to be disciplined by disciplinary tradition facilitates the spirit of crossing and mixing necessary to adapt eclectic, strategic, and pragmatic resources for analyses that resist a heritage that oppresses in history and in rhetoric, in image and in action, in the past and in the present, at "home" and "abroad." If they are of any use, proper or improper, the pursuits and processes of the present project of this book should foster recognition, reassessment, reconstruction, and resistance that confront the mixed heritage that is the study of Paul.

List of Abbreviations

AAR	American Academy of Religion
AIC	African Independent Churches
BC (Bell. civ.)	*Civil Wars*
CJ	*Classical Journal*
1–2 Cor	1–2 Corinthians
HTR	*Harvard Theological Review*
IG	*Inscriptiones graecae*
JBL	*Journal of Biblical Literature*
JECS	*Journal of Early Christian Studies*
JFSR	*Journal of Feminist Studies in Religion*
JSNT	*Journal for the Study of the New Testament*
JSTOR	Journal Storage
KJV	*King James Version*
LGBT	Lesbian, Gay, Bisexual, and Transgender/Transsexual
NewDocs	*New Documents Illustrating Early Christianity*
NovT	*Novum Testamentum*
Phil	Philippians
Phlm	Philemon
Rom	Romans
SBL	Society of Biblical Literature
USQR	*Union Seminary Quarterly Review*

Notes

Introduction: Interpretation at the Intersection of Approaches

1. Joseph A. Marchal, *Hierarchy, Unity, and Imitation: A Feminist Rhetorical Analysis of Power Dynamics in Paul's Letter to the Philippians*, Academia Biblica 24 (Atlanta: Society of Biblical Literature; Leiden: Brill, 2006).

2. In fact, some of the first results of this work were included in a volume that viewed itself as presenting feminist and (or?) postcolonial responses. See Marchal, "Military Images in Philippians 1–2: A Feminist Rhetorical Analysis of Scholarship, Philippians, and Current Contexts," in *Her Master's Tools? Feminist and Postcolonial Engagements of Historical-Critical Discourse*, ed. Caroline Vander Stichele and Todd Penner, Global Perspectives on Biblical Scholarship Series (Atlanta: Society of Biblical Literature, 2005), 265–86.

3. For the compelling and exemplary work of two such colleagues of mine from a shared doctoral program, see Uriah Y. Kim, *Decolonizing Josiah: Toward a Postcolonial Reading of the Deuteronomistic History*, The Bible in the Modern World 5 (Sheffield: Sheffield Phoenix, 2006); and Yong-Sung Ahn, *The Reign of God and Rome in Luke's Passion Narrative: An East Asian Global Perspective*, Biblical Interpretation 80 (Leiden: Brill, 2006).

4. For this particular definition, alongside a wide range of approaches that might define feminism differently, see Elisabeth Schüssler Fiorenza, *Wisdom Ways: Introducing Feminist Biblical Interpretation* (Maryknoll: Orbis, 2001), 54–64. Though this definition is in wide circulation in feminist communities, Schüssler Fiorenza is careful to highlight its traditional attribution to Cheris Kramarae and Paula Treichler, though there are no clear sources to verify its origins. See, for example, Schüssler Fiorenza, *The Power of the Word: Scripture and the Rhetoric of Empire* (Minneapolis: Fortress Press, 2007), 12.

5. See Mary Ann Tolbert, "Defining the Problem: The Bible and Feminist Hermeneutics," *Semeia* 28 (1983): 115. For further considerations of how to define a feminist reading in biblical hermeneutics, see Phyllis A. Bird, "What Makes a Feminist Reading Feminist? A Qualified Answer," in *Escaping Eden: New Feminist Perspectives on the Bible*, ed. Harold C. Washington, Susan Lochrie Graham, and Pamela Thimmes (New York: New York University Press, 1999), 124–31; and Thimmes, "What Makes a Feminist Reading Feminist? Another Perspective," in *Escaping Eden*, 132–40.

6. Continuing the narrative of the previous section about reactions to my research, I must admit that I took such links for granted; that is, from such starting points it seemed obvious to me that a feminist also should care about imperial or (neo)colonial

dynamics. Imperialism typically implements gendered expressions and arguments; gender, in turn, is mutually constituted in relation to race, ethnicity, empire, sexuality, and status (all so often shaped in imperial regimes). It is now my view that we must more carefully discuss such relations given the inconsistent historical and theoretical interchanges between postcolonial and feminist work but that feminists must still develop critiques of imperialism and (neo)colonialism. It should be noted, however, that attention to such inter- (or intra-) personal details is not meant to be a celebratory narrative of an enlightened subject operating within but against empires that are patriarchally, or better kyriarchally, structured. There will be numerous occasions to be suspicious of any such claims in the chapters that follow, especially as the author is an imperial pale male.

7. Edward W. Said, *Culture and Imperialism* (New York: Vintage Books, 1993), 9.

8. This focus on both the imperial and the colonial follows the impulse shared by Fernando Segovia in an argument for describing such scholarly activities as "imperial-colonial studies" rather than postcolonial studies, but hesitates to follow the result of renaming the approach for two reasons. The first is simply that postcolonial is the more familiar and widely accepted term in and outside of biblical studies (even as it is much debated). The second is that I do not share Segovia's view of the imperial referring primarily to the center and the colonial to the periphery. For his arguments about these, see Fernando F. Segovia, *Decolonizing Biblical Studies: A View from the Margins* (Maryknoll: Orbis, 2000), 134. Here, Segovia cites Ania Loomba, *Colonialism/Postcolonialism* (New York: Routledge, 1998), 1–19. As will become clear later, my project follows the view that the center and the periphery are in mutually constitutive relations and, thus, Loomba's generalized differentiation is neither particularly helpful nor descriptive.

9. See, for example, the explanations and delineations in Bill Ashcroft, Gareth Griffiths, and Helen Tiffin, *Post-Colonial Studies: The Key Concepts* (London: Routledge, 2000), 186–92; R. S. Sugirtharajah, *Postcolonial Criticism and Biblical Interpretation* (Oxford: Oxford University Press, 2002), 1–4, 11–14, 24–25; and Segovia, "Mapping the Postcolonial Optic in Biblical Criticism: Meaning and Scope," in *Postcolonial Biblical Criticism: Interdisciplinary Intersections*, ed. Stephen D. Moore and Segovia (London: T&T Clark, 2005), 23–78. For another indication of the importance of the material-cultural divide as it runs into postcolonial biblical interpretation, see the manner in which Segovia introduces a commentary volume in Segovia, "Introduction: Configurations, Approaches, Findings, Stances," in *A Postcolonial Commentary on the New Testament Writings*, ed. Segovia and Sugirtharajah (London: T&T Clark, 2007), 1–68.

10. See Sugirtharajah, "A Postcolonial Exploration of Collusion and Construction in Biblical Interpretation," in *The Postcolonial Bible*, ed. Sugirtharajah (Sheffield: Sheffield Academic, 1998), 92.

11. See Musa W. Dube, *Postcolonial Feminist Interpretation of the Bible* (St. Louis: Chalice, 2000), 48. For further reservations about the definition of postcolonial studies in terms of both chronology and gender, see Anne McClintock, "The Angel of Progress: Pitfalls of the Term 'Post-Colonialism,'" *Social Texts* 31/32 (1992): 84–98; and Ella Shohat, "Notes on the 'Post-Colonial,'" *Social Texts* 31/32 (1992): 99–113.

12. For helpful descriptions of the difference between historical and discursive colonization, see Kathleen O'Brien Wicker, "Teaching Feminist Biblical Studies in a

Postcolonial Context," in *Searching the Scriptures: A Feminist Introduction*, ed. Schüssler
Fiorenza (New York: Crossroad, 1993), 1:367–68, 377. See also Laura E. Donaldson,
Decolonizing Feminisms: Race, Gender, and Empire-Building (Chapel Hill: University
of North Carolina Press, 1992).

13. See, for example, Musa W. Dube Shomanah, "Post-Colonial Biblical Interpretations," in *Dictionary of Biblical Interpretation*, gen. ed. John H. Hayes (Nashville:
Abingdon, 1999), 2:299. See also Homi K. Bhabha, *The Location of Culture* (London:
Routledge, 1994), 1–9. The implicitly political resonance of much work in postcolonial
studies is often indicated by the frequency with which the terms decolonizing and anti-
colonial also occur.

14. For an introductory definition to this neologism, see Schüssler Fiorenza, *Wisdom
Ways*, 1, 118–19, 211; and *Rhetoric and Ethic: The Politics of Biblical Studies* (Minneapolis: Fortress Press, 1999), ix. See also Schüssler Fiorenza, *Bread not Stone: The Challenge
of Feminist Biblical Interpretation*, rev. ed. (Boston: Beacon, 1995), 211n6; and *But She
Said: Feminist Practices of Biblical Interpretation* (Boston: Beacon, 1992), 8, 117.

15. Dube, *Postcolonial Feminist Interpretation of the Bible*, 28–36; Kwok Pui-lan,
Postcolonial Imagination and Feminist Theology (Louisville: Westminster John Knox,
2005), 55.

16. Donaldson, *Decolonizing Feminisms*, 5–6.

17. It should be noted that, in the end, Dube argues: "Despite these criticisms, I do
believe that Schüssler Fiorenza's theoretical articulations of *kyriarchy* and *ekklesia* of
women do go a long way toward counteracting imperialism, if followed." Dube, *Postcolonial Feminist Interpretation of the Bible*, 37.

18. Kwok, *Postcolonial Imagination and Feminist Theology*, 55. See also Dube, *Postcolonial Feminist Interpretation of the Bible*, 26.

19. For a few examples of Schüssler Fiorenza's own attempts to represent interlocking, overlapping and/or superimposed kyriarchal relations within wider kyriarchal
arrangements, see some of the diagrams in Schüssler Fiorenza, *Wisdom Ways*, 132–33;
But She Said, 117; and *Discipleship of Equals: A Critical Feminist Ekklesia-logy of Liberation* (New York: Crossroad, 1993), 226.

20. Kwok's comments and my attempt to formulate their place in a larger pyramidal
vision of oppressive structures, for instance, could be seen as continuations of (not con-
tradistinctions from) Schüssler Fiorenza's impulse to create richer, more complex and
dynamically responsive analyses than those facilitated by the category of patriarchy.

21. For more on Schüssler Fiorenza's response to and reflections upon these critiques
and concerns, see Schüssler Fiorenza, *The Power of the Word*, 111–29.

22. See Schüssler Fiorenza, *The Power of the Word*, 10–16, 89–95, 120–21, 125–28.
For a sampling of some of the positions taken in the previous debates, ranging from
"two-system," "anti-systems," and various "one-system" solutions that integrate patriar-
chy into Marxist/materialist analysis or Marxist concepts into anti-patriarchal analysis,
see the following excerpts from the works of: Shulamith Firestone, "The Dialectic of
Sex"; Gayle Rubin, "The Traffic in Women: Notes on the 'Political Economy' of Sex";
Heidi Hartmann, "The Unhappy Marriage of Marxism and Feminism: Towards a More
Progressive Union"; Michele Barrett, "Capitalism and Women's Liberation"; and Linda

Nicholson, "Feminism and Marx: Integrating Kinship with the Economic"; all compiled in Nicholson, ed., *The Second Wave: A Reader in Feminist Theory* (New York: Routledge, 1997), 19–26, 27–62, 97–122, 123–30, and 131–45.

23. Indeed, in stressing an anti-imperial effort in her feminist program, even Schüssler Fiorenza tends to qualify her feminist analysis as a feminist decolonizing approach and her grappling with kyriarchy as a kyriarchal imperialism. See, for example, Schüssler Fiorenza, *The Power of the Word*, 11, 25, 29, and the title of the fourth chapter "Toward a Critical Feminist Decolonizing Interpretation," 111–47.

24. For the establishment of postcolonial theory, many, if not most, refer to the work of Edward W. Said, Gayatri Chakravorty Spivak, and Homi K. Bhabha: Said, *Orientalism*, rev. ed, with new preface and afterword (New York: Vintage, 1994 [1978]); Said, *Culture and Imperialism* (New York: Vintage, 1993); Spivak, *In Other Worlds: Essays in Cultural Politics* (New York: Routledge, 1988); Spivak, *The Post-Colonial Critic: Interviews, Strategies, Dialogues*, ed. Sarah Harasym (New York: Routledge, 1990); Spivak, *A Critique of Postcolonial Reason: Toward a History of the Vanishing Present* (Cambridge: Harvard University Press, 1999); and Bhabha, *The Location of Culture* (London: Routledge, 1994).

25. For such critiques of Said's work, see, for example, Sara Mills, *Discourses of Difference: An Analysis of Women's Travel Writing and Colonialism* (New York: Routledge, 1992), 47–63; and Meyda Yeğenoğlu, *Colonial Fantasies: Towards a Feminist Reading of Orientalism* (Cambridge: Cambridge University Press, 1998), 14–27.

26. Kwok, *Postcolonial Imagination and Feminist Theology*, 80. See also Dube, *Postcolonial Feminist Interpretation of the Bible*, 111-18; Schüssler Fiorenza, *The Power of the Word*, 119–25, as well as the necessity to explicitly address the three interrelated topics, Donaldson and Kwok, ed., *Postcolonialism, Feminism and Religious Discourse* (New York: Routledge, 2002).

27. Here, one could point to places where feminism is admitted as a "cognate discipline" to postcolonial criticism or viewed as a fellow discourse of resistance and emancipation in Sugirtharajah and Segovia's work, respectively. Yet these cognates and commonalities are rarely brought into fruitful or expanded dialogue by a more consistent or persistent engagement of the concerns and critiques of feminist or postcolonial feminist critics. See Sugirtharajah, *Postcolonial Criticism and Biblical Interpretation*, 28–30; and Segovia, *Decolonizing Biblical Studies*, 140–41.

28. For further insights about these two "strands" of biblical interpretation (emphases on postcolonialism and Roman imperialism) in relation to feminist forms and practices, see the opening sections of the following chapter.

29. In many (if not most) cases in this study, I will prefer to use the terms rhetoric or rhetorical over discourse or discursive, though the latter is far more popular in various poststructurally disposed expressions, including as they influence and intersect with feminist and postcolonial theories. The preference for rhetoric is meant to mark a greater emphasis on the perspectival nature of all acts of communication, as well as an increased sense of the force of such acts from, through, and to a particular trajectory. In comparison, discourse strikes this reader as more diffuse in its import, neutral in its force, and general in the current excess of reference. Rhetoric indicates that these acts are efforts to

convince, and highlights that the directionality of such acts expresses, coincides, or reinforces certain power dynamics that require greater attention in feminist, postcolonial analyses. Of course, discourse has been associated with an analysis of power and knowledge, most notably in the work of Michel Foucault. See especially Foucault, *The History of Sexuality: An Introduction*, vol. 1, trans. Robert Hurley (New York: Vintage, 1978 [1976]); and *Power/Knowledge: Selected Interviews and Other Writing 1972–1977*, ed. Colin Gordon, trans. C. Gordon, Leo Marshall, John Mepham, and Kate Soper (New York: Pantheon Books, 1980). For those who associate the discursive with such qualities, one could simply substitute the term in every use of rhetoric to follow. For further reflections on the overlap and difference between discourse and rhetoric (with a different preference), see Elizabeth A. Castelli, *Imitating Paul: A Discourse of Power* (Louisville: Westminster John Knox, 1991), 53–54.

30. A feminist, postcolonial analysis would be derelict in its duties if it failed to note the intensely gendered and imperialized resonances of the high cultural reference to the dual obstacles of Scylla and Charybdis. As depicted in Homeric epic and wider Greek mythology, both creatures are monstrously female obstacles to manly captains of the sea, often preparing for or returning from invasive campaigns for wealth, honor, and glory. Such elements are rarely raised to consciousness when reference to these dangers are made; thus, it might be worth recalling this heightened gender association of the seas (as it likely coincides with imperial aspiration and racialized logics), considering the heightened gender association of land as "virgin territory" in comparable situations.

1. Histories of Interpretation and "People's History" in Pauline Studies

1. On (not explicitly feminist) postcolonial biblical interpretation, see, for example, Fernando F. Segovia, *Decolonizing Biblical Studies: A View from the Margins* (Maryknoll: Orbis, 2000); and R. S. Sugirtharajah, *Asian Biblical Hermeneutics and Postcolonialism: Contesting the Interpretations* (Maryknoll: Orbis, 1998); Sugirtharajah, *The Bible and the Third World: Precolonial, Colonial, and Postcolonial Encounters* (Cambridge: Cambridge University Press, 2001); Sugirtharajah, *Postcolonial Criticism and Biblical Interpretation* (Oxford: Oxford University Press, 2002); Sugirtharajah, *Postcolonial Reconfigurations: An Alternative Way of Reading the Bible and Doing Theology* (St. Louis: Chalice, 2003); and the collections from The Bible and Postcolonialism series: Sugirtharajah, ed., *The Postcolonial Bible* (Sheffield: Sheffield Academic, 1998); Sugirtharajah, ed., *Vernacular Hermeneutics* (Sheffield: Sheffield Academic, 1999); Segovia, ed., *Interpreting beyond Borders* (Sheffield: Sheffield Academic, 2000); Roland Boer, ed., *Last Stop before Antarctica: The Bible and Postcolonialism in Australia* (Sheffield: Sheffield Academic, 2001); Musa W. Dube and Jeffrey L. Staley, eds., *John and Postcolonialism: Travel, Space and Power* (London: Continuum, 2002); and Stephen D. Moore and Segovia, eds., *Postcolonial Biblical Criticism: Interdisciplinary Intersections* (London: T&T Clark International, 2005).

2. Richard A. Horsley, ed., *Paul and Empire: Religion and Power in Roman Imperial Society* (Harrisburg: Trinity Press International, 1997); Horsley, ed., *Paul and Politics: Ekklesia, Israel, Imperium, Interpretation; Essays in Honor of Krister Stendahl* (Harrisburg: Trinity Press International, 2000); Horsley, ed., *Paul and the Roman Imperial Order* (Harrisburg: Trinity Press International, 2004); and Horsley, ed., *Hidden Transcripts and the Arts of Resistance: Applying the Work of James C. Scott to Jesus and Paul* (Atlanta: Society of Biblical Literature, 2004). Some work from this group of scholars may represent the aforementioned overlap; see Horsley, "Submerged Biblical Histories and Imperial Biblical Studies," in *The Postcolonial Bible*, 152–73; Horsley, "Feminist Scholarship and Postcolonial Criticism: Subverting Imperial Discourse and Reclaiming Submerged Histories," in *Walk in the Ways of Wisdom: Essays in Honor of Elisabeth Schüssler Fiorenza*, ed. Shelly Matthews, Cynthia Briggs Kittredge, and Melanie Johnson-Debaufre (Harrisburg: Trinity Press International, 2003); Sze-kar Wan, "Collection for the Saints as Anticolonial Act: Implications of Paul's Ethnic Reconstruction," in *Paul and Politics*, 191–215; Wan, "Does Diaspora Identity Imply Some Sort of Universality? An Asian-American Reading of Galatians," in *Interpreting beyond Borders*, 107–31; Abraham Smith, "'Unmasking the Powers': Toward a Postcolonial Analysis of 1 Thessalonians," in *Paul and the Roman Imperial Order*, 47–66; and Jeremy Punt, "Towards a Postcolonial Reading of Freedom in Paul," in *Reading the Bible in the Global Village: Cape Town* (Atlanta: Society of Biblical Literature, 2002), 125–49, 188–95.

3. For more on these two critical observations, see the following section of the argument (Gaps, Erasures, and Conflicts) and especially the work of Gayatri Chakravorty Spivak, Chandra Talpade Mohanty, and Laura E. Donaldson, cited below.

4. See, for example, Musa W. Dube, *Postcolonial Feminist Interpretation of the Bible* (St. Louis: Chalice, 2000); and Kwok Pui-lan, *Postcolonial Imagination and Feminist Theology* (Louisville: Westminster John Knox, 2005).

5. For reflections and arguments about the meanings of feminist and postcolonial adopted for the purposes of this study, see the opening reflections in the introduction (especially in the section on Starting Points and Parameters).

6. Spivak, "Can the Subaltern Speak?" in *Marxism and the Interpretation of Culture*, ed. Cary Nelson and Lawrence Grossberg (Urbana: University of Illinois Press), 271–313 (296). Whereas here Spivak refers to Western reaction to sati in India, Kwok Pui-lan notes the same imperialist rationale about foot-binding in China in her "Unbinding Our Feet: Saving Brown Women and Feminist Religious Discourse," in *Postcolonialism, Feminism, and Religious Discourse*, ed. Laura E. Donaldson and Kwok (New York: Routledge, 2002), 62–81. For connections to the complex analysis of discourses on the veil in Muslim contexts, see the entries in that volume, as well as the section of six entries on "Harem and the Veil," in *Feminist Postcolonial Theory: A Reader*, ed. Reina Lewis and Sara Mills (New York: Routledge, 2003), 489–609.

7. See Chandra Talpade Mohanty, "Under Western Eyes: Feminist Scholarship and Colonial Discourses," in *Feminism without Borders: Decolonizing Theory, Practicing Solidarity* (Durham: Duke University Press, 2003), 17–42; Kirsten Holst Peterson and Anna Rutherford, eds., *A Double Colonisation: Colonial and Post-Colonial Women's*

Writing (Dangaroo, 1986); Dube, *Postcolonial Feminist Interpretation of the Bible*, 76, 117, 122–23, 174, 184, 201.

8. For these roles, as well as the particular ways women have been figured in nationalist discourses as reproducers, signifiers, and transmitters of ethnic boundaries or difference, see Nira Yuval-Davis and Floya Anthias, eds., *Woman-Nation-State* (Hampshire: MacMillan, 1989), 7–10.

9. Kwok Pui-lan, *Postcolonial Imagination and Feminist Theology*, 66; emphasis added. See also Anne McClintock, "gender dynamics were, from the outset, fundamental to the securing and maintenance of the imperial enterprise." McClintock, *Imperial Leather: Race, Gender and Sexuality in the Colonial Conquest* (New York: Routledge, 1995), 7.

10. McClintock, *Imperial Leather*, 14. Many of the observations made in the introduction to this volume were first presented in McClintock's "The Angel of Progress."

11. See McClintock, "The Lay of the Land: Genealogies of Imperialism," in *Imperial Leather*, 21–74. See also Donaldson, "The Breasts of Columbus: A Political Anatomy of Postcolonialism and Feminist Religious Discourse," in *Postcolonialism, Feminism, and Religious Discourse*, 41–61. For an example of how postcolonial, feminist, and queer theory can be linked profitably in theological discourse, see Kwok, "Postcolonial Feminist Theology: What Is It? How to Do It?" in *Postcolonial Imagination and Feminist Theology*, 125–49.

12. See Kwok, *Postcolonial Imagination and Feminist Theology*, 80–81; Dube, *Postcolonial Feminist Interpretation of the Bible*, 112.

13. See, for example, Patrick Williams and Laura Chrisman, eds., *Colonial Discourse and Post-Colonial Theory: A Reader* (New York: Columbia University Press, 1994), 191–267; Leela Gandhi, *Postcolonial Theory: A Critical Introduction* (New York: Columbia University Press, 1998), 81-101; and John McLeod, *Beginning Postcolonialism* (Manchester: Manchester University Press, 2000), 172–204.

14. Segovia, *Decolonizing Biblical Studies* (2000).

15. Ali A. Mazrui, *Cultural Forces in World Politics* (London: James Curry, 1990), 29; Dube, *Postcolonial Feminist Interpretation of the Bible*, 10–12.

16. Dube, *Postcolonial Feminist Interpretation of the Bible*, 20. See also n. 7 above.

17. Ibid., 118.

18. Ibid.

19. Kwok, *Postcolonial Imagination and Feminist Theology*, 7.

20. Ibid., 7–8; Dube, *Postcolonial Feminist Interpretation of the Bible*, 3–4.

21. Kwok, *Postcolonial Imagination and Feminist Theology*, 8–9.

22. See the four volumes, edited by Horsley, *Paul and Empire* (1997), *Paul and Politics* (2000), *Paul and the Roman Imperial Context* (2004), and particularly the latter half of *Hidden Transcripts* (2004).

23. In a similar manner, colonizers often overtly recognized certain injustices in colonization and included them in their speech-acts but, far from hurting the imperial effort, this recognition and inclusion functions apologetically within their "anti-conquest" claims, facilitating rather than preventing their acts of imperialism. See Dube, *Postcolonial*

Feminist Interpretation of the Bible, 64–67. Here, she is especially referring to David Quint, *Epic and Empire* (Princeton: Princeton University Press, 1993), 99–130.

24. Elisabeth Schüssler Fiorenza, "Paul and the Politics of Interpretation" (40–57), Cynthia Briggs Kittredge, "Corinthian Women Prophets and Paul's Argumentation in 1 Corinthians" (103–9); Sheila Briggs, "Paul on Bondage and Freedom in Imperial Roman Society" (110–23); and Antoinette Clark Wire, "Response: The Politics of the Assembly in Corinth" (124–29), and "Response: Paul and Those outside Power" (224–26). See the rather different concerns about this group of scholars not being as engaged with contemporary postcolonial theory, in Moore, "Postcolonialism," in *Handbook of Postmodern Biblical Interpretation*, ed. A. K. M. Adam (St. Louis: Chalice, 2000), 186–88; and Moore and Segovia, "Postcolonial Biblical Criticisms: Beginnings, Trajectories, Intersection," in *Postcolonial Biblical Criticism*, 7–8. Indeed, this concern could be remedied by a further engagement with feminist practices and postcolonial feminist work.

25. Schüssler Fiorenza, "Paul and the Politics of Interpretation," 50; Briggs, "Paul on Bondage and Freedom," 114–17.

26. Wire, "Response: The Politics of the Assembly in Corinth," 129; Wire, "Response: Paul and Those outside Power," 226. See also Schüssler Fiorenza, "Paul and the Politics of Interpretation," 50, on how the picture changes if "one focuses on the marginal and powerless, such as slaves and/or wo/men."

27. Kittredge, "Corinthian Women Prophets," 103–4.

28. Ibid., 105.

29. Horsley, ed., *Paul and the Roman Imperial Order* (2004); and Horsley, ed., *Hidden Transcripts and the Arts of Resistance: Applying the Work of James C. Scott to Jesus and Paul* (2004), especially the introduction and Part 2, 1–26, 97–171.

30. Jennifer Wright Knust, "Paul and the Politics of Virtue and Vice," in *Paul and the Roman Imperial Order*, 155–74. Could the continued physical placement of women's contributions toward the end of these volumes be a further (subconscious?) indication of precisely how peripheral these methods and concerns are to the project of Paul and politics? See also the *Paul and Empire* and *Hidden Transcripts* volumes.

31. Horsley, "Introduction," in *Paul and the Roman Imperial Order*, 17–18; Efraín Agosto, "Patronage and Commendation, Imperial and Anti-Imperial," in *Paul and the Roman Imperial Order*, 118–22.

32. In the first seven entries in *Paul and the Roman Imperial Order*, for example, only 12 out of 456 footnotes include references to feminist scholarship, two of which are listed only so that the scholar can dismiss them; Neil Elliott, "The Apostle Paul's Self-Presentation as Anti-imperial Performance," 73–74n20; Efraín Agosto, "Patronage and Commendation, Imperial and Anti-Imperial," 119n42. On my reading, the only feminist scholar named in the body of these entries is Gayatri (Chakravorty) Spivak, in Abraham Smith, "'Unmasking the Powers': Toward a Postcolonial Analysis of 1 Thessalonians," 48.

33. Horsley, "Introduction: Jesus, Paul, and the 'Arts of Resistance': Leaves from the Notebook of James C. Scott," in *Hidden Transcripts*, 7, 8.

34. Kittredge makes this exact same point in the beginning of her contribution to this volume, "Reconstructing 'Resistance' or Reading to Resist: James C. Scott and the

Politics of Interpretation," in *Hidden Transcripts*, 145. See, for example, the previous work of Schüssler Fiorenza, Wire, Briggs, and Kittredge, among others.

35. Kittredge, "Reconstructing 'Resistance,'" especially 145–46, 152–55. Like the 2004 volume in this collection, gender plays a central role only in Kittredge's analysis. Of the Works Consulted in this volume, only 13 out of 225 works were written by feminist scholars, eight of which were cited in Kittredge's article.

36. Both Polaski's book and Levine's collection make no reference to postcolonial feminist work, including that of Kwok Pui-lan, Musa W. Dube, or Laura E. Donaldson, or even to any of the above volumes edited by Richard A. Horsley.

37. Polaski, *A Feminist Introduction to Paul* (St. Louis: Chalice, 2005).

38. Luzia Sutter Rehmann, "To Turn the Groaning into Labor: Romans 8:22-23," in *A Feminist Companion to Paul*, ed. Amy-Jill Levine, with Marianne Blickenstaff (Cleveland: Pilgrim, 2004), 74–84, see especially 78–80.

39. Luise Schottroff, "'Law-Free Gentile Christianity'—What About the Women? Feminist Analyses and Alternatives," in *A Feminist Companion to Paul*, 183–94. Though it may be coincidental, it should not go without comment that both of these entries were the sole representatives from outside North America (at least in terms of academic appointment). Could the history of European colonialism and/or the American denial of its empire be at least partially responsible for these differences in topic?

40. Shawn Kelley, *Racializing Jesus: Race, Ideology and the Formation of Modern Biblical Scholarship* (London: Routledge, 2002). On this particular combination, see esp. 7, 148; as well as Said, *Orientalism*, 27–28, 133–48. Further, as Kwok points out, "The persecution of the Other within Europe—the heretics, the witches, and the Jews— was linked with early European expansion and its colonial impulse." Kwok, *Postcolonial Imagination and Feminist Theology*, 16. These intersecting dynamics are not entirely separate from the slave trade or the decimation of Native Americans. For the question of anti-Judaism in (especially feminist) postcolonial interpretation, see the roundtable discussion in *Journal of Feminist Studies in Religion* 20, no. 1 (Spring 2004): 91–132.

41. As Levine explains about her editorial work on the collection: "We were also deliberate in inviting scholars from outside Western Europe, the USA, and Canada; whereas the response rate from this set of invitations was less than ideal . . ." Levine, "Introduction," in *A Feminist Companion to Paul*, 3.

42. Kelley, *Racializing Jesus*, 75–79, 145–50. For Kwok and Dube's concerns with universalism, see Kwok, *Postcolonial Imagination and Feminist Theology*, 36, 48–50, 56, 83, 91; Dube, *Postcolonial Feminist Interpretation of the Bible*, 18, 29, 105, 177, 183.

43. A version of this paper has since been published as "Mutuality Rhetorics and Feminist Interpretation: Examining Philippians and Arguing for Our Lives," *Bible and Critical Theory* 1, no. 3 (August 2005). My thanks to Abraham Smith, who graciously responded to my paper on this occasion and pointed out Shawn Kelley's vital work in this regard.

44. See here especially Donaldson and Kwok, eds., *Postcolonialism, Feminism, and Religious Discourse*.

45. See Spivak, "French Feminism in an International Frame," *In Other Worlds*, 134–53.

46. Kwok, *Postcolonial Imagination and Feminist Theology*, 18, 49. See, for example, Sara Mills, *Discourses of Difference: An Analysis of Women's Travel Writing and Colonialism* (New York: Routledge, 1992); Mary Louise Pratt, *Imperial Eyes: Travel Writing and Transculturation* (New York: Routledge, 1992); Rana Kabbani, *Europe's Myths of Orient: Devise and Rule* (London: Macmillan, 1985); and Jenny Sharpe, *Allegories of Empire: The Figure of Woman in the Colonial Text* (Minneapolis: University of Minnesota Press, 1993).

47. Kwok, *Postcolonial Imagination and Feminist Theology*, 18.

48. For further reflections on the invention of this term and some concerns about its conceptualization, see the discussion in the introductory chapter (especially the section on Starting Points and Parameters).

49. Dube, *Postcolonial Feminist Interpretation of the Bible*, 28–36; Kwok, *Postcolonial Imagination and Feminist Theology*, 55. It should be noted that in the end, Dube argues: "Despite these criticisms, I do believe that Schüssler Fiorenza's theoretical articulations of *kyriarchy* and *ekklesia* of women do go a long way toward counteracting imperialism, if followed." Dube, *Postcolonial Feminist Interpretation of the Bible*, 37.

50. Donaldson, *Decolonizing Feminisms: Race, Gender, and Empire-Building* (Chapel Hill: University of North Carolina Press, 1992), 5–6.

51. For the further problem of identifying with your sources, especially Pauline letters, see Schüssler Fiorenza, "Paul and the Politics of Interpretation," 40–57.

52. Dube, *Postcolonial Feminist Interpretation of the Bible*, 43; Kwok, *Postcolonial Imagination and Feminist Theology*, 66.

53. See the work of Spivak, Donaldson, Mohanty, McClintock, Mills, Pratt, Kabbani, Sharpe (all cited above), and Trinh T. Minh-ha, *Woman, Native, Other: Writing Postcoloniality and Feminism* (Bloomington: Indiana University Press, 1989); Rajeswari Sunder Rajan, *Real and Imagined Women: Gender, Culture, and Postcolonialism* (London: Routledge, 1993); Ann Laura Stoler, *Race and the Education of Desire: Foucault's History of Sexuality and the Colonial Order of Things* (Durham: Duke University Press, 1995); M. Jacqui Alexander and Mohanty, eds., *Feminist Genealogies, Colonial Legacies, Democratic Futures*, Thinking Gender (New York: Routledge, 1997); Chilla Bulbeck, *Re-Orienting Western Feminisms: Women's Diversity in a Postcolonial World* (Cambridge: Cambridge University Press, 1998); Stoler, *Carnal Knowledge and Imperial Power: Race and the Intimate in Colonial Rule* (Berkeley: University of California Press, 2002); Lewis and Mills, eds., *Feminist Postcolonial Theory: A Reader*, among others.

54. Gale A. Yee, *Poor Banished Children of Eve: Woman as Evil in the Hebrew Bible* (Minneapolis: Fortress Press, 2003); Judith E. McKinlay, *Reframing Her: Biblical Women in Postcolonial Focus* (Sheffield: Sheffield Phoenix, 2004); Jean K. Kim, *Woman and Nation: An Intercontextual Reading of the Gospel of John from a Postcolonial Feminist Perspective* (Boston: Brill, 2004); Hisako Kinukawa, "De-colonizing Ourselves as Readers: The Story of the Syro-Phoenician Woman as a Text," in *Distant Voices Drawing Near: Essays in Honor of Antoinette Clark Wire*, ed. Holly E. Hearon (Collegeville: Liturgical, 2004), 131–44; Sharon H. Ringe, "Places at the Table: Feminist and Postcolonial Biblical Interpretation," in *The Postcolonial Bible*, 136–51; Kathleen O'Brien Wicker, "Teaching Feminist Biblical Studies in a Postcolonial Context," in *Searching*

the Scriptures: A Feminist Introduction, ed. Schüssler Fiorenza (New York: Crossroad, 1993), 1:367–80.

55. Kwok, *Discovering the Bible in the Non-Biblical World* (Maryknoll: Orbis, 1995); Kwok, "Jesus/the Native: Biblical Studies from a Postcolonial Perspective," in *Teaching the Bible: The Discourses and Politics of Biblical Pedagogy,* ed. Segovia and Tolbert (Maryknoll: Orbis, 1995), 69–85; Kwok, *Introducing Asian Feminist Theology* (Cleveland: Pilgrim, 2000); Kwok, "Mercy Amba Oduyoye and African Women's Theology," *Journal of Feminist Studies in Religion* 20, no. 1 (2004): 7–22; as well as Donaldson and Kwok, eds., *Postcolonialism, Feminism, and Religious Discourse*; Dube, "Reading for Decolonization (John 4:1-42)," *Semeia* 75 (1996), 37–60; Dube, "Toward a Postcolonial Feminist Interpretation of the Bible," *Semeia* 78 (1997): 11–26; Dube Shomanah, "Scripture, Feminism and Post-Colonial Contexts," in *Women's Sacred Scriptures,* ed. Kwok and Schüssler Fiorenza (London: SCM, 1998), 45–54; Dube Shomanah, "Postcolonial Biblical Interpretations," in *Dictionary of Biblical Interpretation,* ed. John H. Hayes (Nashville: Abingdon, 1999), 2:299–303; Dube, "Consuming the Colonial Cultural Bomb: Translating Badimo into Demons in the Setswana Bible (Matt. 8:28-34; 15:22; 10:8)," *Journal for the Study of the New Testament* 73 (1999): 33–59; as well as O'Brien Wicker, Dube, and Althea Spencer-Miller, eds., *Feminist New Testament Studies: Global and Future Perspectives* (New York: Palgrave MacMillan, 2005).

56. For some of their comments on Paul's letters, including the topics of "the mission to the Gentiles," and Paul's views of women, gender, and sexuality in empire, see Dube, *Postcolonial Feminist Interpretation of the Bible,* 12–14, 181–82; Kwok, *Postcolonial Imagination and Feminist Theology,* 77, 89–93.

57. In particular, see the description in her conclusion; Dube, *Postcolonial Feminist Interpretation of the Bible,* 199–201.

58. Kwok, *Postcolonial Imagination and Feminist Theology,* 81–84.

59. Ibid., 81.

60. For the focus primarily on transnational movements as domain of critique and engagement, see Mohanty, *Feminism without Borders*; Inderpal Grewal and Caren Kaplan, eds., *Scattered Hegemonies: Postmodernity and Transnational Feminist Practices* (Minneapolis: University of Minnesota Press, 1994); Kaplan and Grewal, "Transnational Feminist Cultural Studies: Beyond the Marxism/Poststructuralism/Feminism Divides," *positions* (Fall 1994): 430–45; Grewal, *Home and Harem: Nation, Gender, Empire, and the Cultures of Travel* (Durham: Duke University Press, 1996); Uma Narayan, *Dislocating Cultures: Identities, Traditions, and Third World Feminism* (New York: Routledge, 1997); and M. Jacqui Alexander, *Pedagogies of Crossing: Meditations on Feminism, Sexual Politics, Memory, and the Sacred* (Durham: Duke University Press, 2005).

61. See Horsley and Elliott, among others, as well as the critiques cited above and made by Kittredge, Wire, and Schüssler Fiorenza. On the analytic of domination, see also Schüssler Fiorenza, *Rhetoric and Ethic,* 50; *Wisdom Ways,* 172–75.

62. Kwok, *Postcolonial Imagination and Feminist Theology,* 82.

63. Ibid. For a definition of "contact zone," see, for example, Mary Louise Pratt, *Imperial Eyes*, 4–7. On the hermeneutics of remembrance and reconstruction, see Schüssler Fiorenza, *Rhetoric and Ethic*, 51–52; *Wisdom Ways*, 183–86.

64. Kwok, *Postcolonial Imagination and Feminist Theology*, 83. See, for example, the examination of previous scholarship on mission patterns in Matthew in Dube, *Postcolonial Feminist Interpretation of the Bible*, 157–95. For possible connections to the hermeneutics of suspicion, see Schüssler Fiorenza, *Rhetoric and Ethic*, 50–51; *Wisdom Ways*, 175–77.

65. Historically, empires have identified as imperial, but rationalized their empire by extolling the beneficent, civilizing, and/or paternalistic quality of their rule. Thus, identifying could even be the act of the colonizer. Thus, Pauline scholars must be cautious about how we identify imperial contexts or rhetoric. See n. 51 above and Marchal, "Military Images in Philippians 1–2: A Feminist Rhetorical Analysis of Scholarship, Philippians, and Current Contexts," in *Her Master's Tools? Feminist and Postcolonial Engagements of Historical-Critical Discourse*, ed. Caroline Vander Stichele and Todd Penner (Atlanta: Society of Biblical Literature, 2005), 285–86.

66. Kwok, *Postcolonial Imagination and Feminist Theology*, 83. See, for example, Malika Sibeko and Beverley Haddad, "Reading the Bible 'with' Women in Poor and Marginalized Communities in South Africa," *Semeia* 78 (1997): 83–92; Gerald O. West, *Academy of the Poor: Towards a Dialogical Reading of the Bible* (Sheffield: Sheffield Academic, 1999); and the section "Reading With and From Non-academic Readers," in *Other Ways of Reading: African Women and the Bible*, ed. Dube (Atlanta: Society of Biblical Literature, 2001), 101–42. On the possible connections to a hermeneutics of experience and social location, see Schüssler Fiorenza, *Rhetoric and Ethic*, 49; *Wisdom Ways*, 169–72.

67. For this phrase, see Segovia, *Decolonizing Biblical Studies*, 50.

68. Kwok, *Postcolonial Imagination and Feminist Theology*, 84. Tolbert, "The Politics and Poetics of Location," in *Reading from This Place; Social Location and Biblical Interpretation in the United States*, ed. Segovia and Tolbert (Minneapolis: Fortress Press, 1995), 1:305–17. On potential connections to the hermeneutics of ethical and theological evaluation or transformation, see Schüssler Fiorenza, *Rhetoric and Ethic*, 51, 53–54; *Wisdom Ways*, 177–79, 186–89.

69. Dube, *Postcolonial Feminist Interpretation of the Bible*, 201, cf. 57, 129. The first listing does not include divine representations in the fourth question (57), but they are discussed in the analysis following it and thus added to the later listings (129, 201). The third question also alternately discusses "mutual interdependence" and "condemnation and replacement."

70. Dube's repeated stress on analyzing "this text" in these questions indicates that her approaches are geared primarily toward literary-rhetorical assessment rather than historical reconstructions. Nevertheless, as several feminist rhetorical scholars have demonstrated (Wire, Schüssler Fiorenza, Kittredge), rhetorical analysis of Paul's letters can facilitate an exploration of the various points of view in the potential audience. Thus, in implementing Dube's questions, the following analysis in this study will be

most useful for the initial task, with only a few helpful notes for reconstructing these other perspectives.

71. There are currently plans for seven volumes in a series, edited by Denis R. Janz, on A People's History of Christianity, ranging from Christian Origins and Late Ancient Christianity, through Byzantine, Medieval, and Reformation Christianities, to Modern Christianity to 1900 and Twentieth-Century Global Christianity.

72. Horsley, "Unearthing a People's History," in *Christian Origins* (A People's History of Christianity, Minneapolis: Fortress Press, 2005), 1:1–20.

73. Horsley, "Unearthing," 1–5. See especially p. 5 where Horsley specifically draws upon an overview of historian Peter Burke in developing two tables that highlight the differences between people's history and standard history, or as Burke describes them "new" and "old" history. See Peter Burke, "Overture: The New History; Its Past and Its Future," *New Perspectives on Historical Writing,* ed. Burke, 2nd ed. (University Park, Pa.: Pennsylvania State University Press, 2001), 1–24, especially 3–6. We will have several occasions to return to this overture and the volume as a whole below.

74. Horsley, "Unearthing," 5.

75. Ibid., 2.

76. Ibid., 3–5.

77. Ibid., 11. Here, as he has done before with the edited volume *Hidden Transcripts* (see above), Horsley develops an insight from James C. Scott's work *Domination and the Arts of Resistance* (New Haven: Yale University Press, 1990). As highlighted above, feminist scholars (like Cynthia Briggs Kittredge) have questioned why and how biblical scholars have turned to James C. Scott's work, especially considering that several of the procedures derived from Scott were previously practiced and refined in feminist biblical interpretations. See Kittredge, "Reconstructing 'Resistance' or Reading to Resist: James C. Scott and the Politics of Interpretation," in *Hidden Transcripts*, 145–55.

78. Horsley, "Unearthing," 15–18. Horsley alludes to the contributions of Elisabeth Schüssler Fiorenza and Antoinette Clark Wire in these pages, yet seems to follow their lead rather inconsistently. For example, moments after acknowledging that "we cannot read the history of a Pauline Christianity directly off the pages of Paul's letters" (p. 17), he portrays these texts as providing "windows" (p. 18) to the history. This implied transparency and the oscillating way in which women appear and disappear in these descriptions significantly trouble the potential for feminist, postcolonial analyses under the rubric as Horsley describes it.

79. See especially the brief references to women and feminist approaches in Horsley, "Unearthing," 1, 15.

80. Ibid., 20.

81. Even just a basic search for "history from below" in the JSTOR archive nets articles of widely divergent opinions and arguments about the relative utility of these approaches toward people's or popular history. See, for example, Sabyasachi Bhattacharya, "History from Below," *Social Scientist* 11, no. 4 (Apr. 1983): 3–20; Gerald Strauss, "The Dilemma of Popular History," *Past and Present* 132 (Aug. 1991): 130–49; and William Beik, "The Dilemma of Popular History," *Past and Present* 141 (Nov. 1993): 207–15. The differences within and difficulties of using these approaches should be recognized if Pauline

scholars plan on developing their own form of people's history. The following critical survey covers only those issues most pertinent toward feminist, postcolonial analyses in Pauline studies.

82. As Peter Burke highlights for defining what makes this new kind of history "new," it is often easier to say what it is not. See Burke, "Overture," 2–3. Burke also refers here to the paradigmatic role of nineteenth-century historian Leopold van Ranke in setting the terms for history as a discipline in the West.

83. Ibid., 9.

84. This also resonates with other totalizing, dichotomous forms of homogeneous "opposites" as they continue to operate today, most clearly in the case of the so-called "clash of the civilizations" between the West and now Islam.

85. See, for example, Burke's questions on this matter in Burke, "Overture," 9–10.

86. Jim Sharpe, "History from Below," in *New Perspectives on Historical Writing*, 25–42, 28. See also Burke, "Overture," 10. Here Sharpe is referring especially to the work of Burke, to whom Horsley appealed in his explication of a "people's history" perspective. See Peter Burke, *Popular Culture in Early Modern Europe* (London: Harper & Row, 1978), 23–64; Horsley, "Unearthing," 289, n. 4. Indeed, Horsley refers to these articles by Burke and Sharpe that actually qualify and problematize this perspective on historiography, yet he fails to acknowledge or explicate the impact of these cautions and critiques in his summarizing overview.

87. When attempting to recuperate at least one positive function of history from below for the people, Sharpe's main example is that of the formation of national identity. However, Sharpe does so without inquiring into the fraught dynamics of nationalism. See Sharpe, "History from Below," 37–38.

88. See, for example, their landmark works, Eric J. Hobsbawm, *Primitive Rebels: Studies in Archaic Forms of Social Movement in the 19th and 20th Centuries* (Manchester: Manchester University Press, 1959); and Edward P. Thompson, *The Making of the English Working Class* (New York: Vintage, 1966). For more specific reflections on people's history or history from below, see E. P. Thompson, "History from Below," *Times Literary Supplement* (April 7, 1966), 279–80 (the references to this work in Sharpe, "History from Below," incorrectly list it as running from 269–80); and E. J. Hobsbawm, "History from Below—Some Reflections," in *History from Below: Studies in Popular Protest and Popular Ideology*, ed. Frederick Krantz (Oxford: Basil Blackwell, 1985), 13–27. For further background on the influence and import of British Marxist forms of history, see Harvey J. Kaye, *The British Marxist Historians: An Introductory Analysis* (Cambridge: Polity, 1984); and *The Education of Desire: Marxists and the Writing of History* (New York: Routledge, 1992).

89. For one such set of debates about the relative merits and problems of using Marx's or Marxist insights or strategies for feminist purposes, see the following excerpts from the works of: Shulamith Firestone, "The Dialectic of Sex"; Gayle Rubin, "The Traffic in Women: Notes on the 'Political Economy' of Sex"; Heidi Hartmann, "The Unhappy Marriage of Marxism and Feminism: Towards a More Progressive Union"; Michele Barrett, "Capitalism and Women's Liberation"; and Linda Nicholson, "Feminism and Marx: Integrating Kinship with the Economic," all compiled in Nicholson, ed., *The*

Second Wave: A Reader in Feminist Theory (New York: Routledge, 1997), 19–26, 27–62, 97–122, 123–30, and 131–45.

90. As Sharpe admits about the history from below: "'below' in this context was originally conceived of in terms of a class structure or some other cognate form of social stratification: obviously, writing history from the perspective of women, or indeed, of children, would give different insights into what subordination might entail." Sharpe, "History from Below," 36. Note also the slippage in this quote between women and children as the "other" to the normative subject in/of class. This could be read as either an acknowledgment of the pluriformed hierarchy of who counts in "the below" or an implicit reinforcement of the infantilizing gestures of malestream scholarship towards (not only) women (but also a range of dominated peoples, particularly those colonized by the developed and civilized powers).

91. Thompson, *Making*, 12.

92. See, for example, this kind of recognition in Catherine Hall, "The Tale of Samuel and Jemima: Gender and Working-Class Culture in Nineteenth-Century England," in *E. P. Thompson: Critical Perspectives*, ed. Harvey J. Kaye and Keith McClelland (Philadelphia: Temple University Press, 1990), 78–102 (especially 81); and Joan Wallach Scott, "Women in The Making of the English Working Class," in *Gender and the Politics of History* (New York: Columbia University Press, 1988), 68–90 (especially 69–71). For other, initial elaborations and problematizations of Thompson's form of social history for women's history, see also Sheila Rowbotham, *Hidden from History: Rediscovering Women from the 17th Century to the Present* (New York: Pantheon, 1974); Barbara Taylor, *Eve and the New Jerusalem: Socialism and Feminism in the Nineteenth Century* (New York: Pantheon, 1983).

93. Thompson, *Making*, 9. Both Hall and Scott cite this passage; see Hall, "The Tale," 80; Scott, "Women in *The Making*," 69. It is perhaps ironic that such a conceptualization can refer to the processes of reproduction, yet constantly obscure the differences in positions and relative power according to gendered lines. Thompson again stresses later: "Class is defined by men as they live their own history, and in the end, this is its only definition." See Thompson, *Making*, 11.

94. Hall, "The Tale," 81–82; Scott, "Women in *The Making*," 72–75. The apparently gender-blind but more accurately androcentric viewpoint is also on display in Hobsbawm's work, where the normative position of the historian is repeatedly that of "he." See, for example, Hobsbawm, "History from Below," 24. The norms of perspective lead almost ineluctably to the reinforcement of certain norms in terms of subject matter for historiography.

95. Scott, "Women in *The Making*," 71–72, 76–83.

96. As Scott notes, Thompson argued that his work is akin to a "biography of the English working class from its adolescence until its early manhood." See Thompson, *Making*, 11; also cited in Scott, "Women in *The Making*," 72.

97. Scott, "Women in *The Making*," 76–83. Scott, in particular, points to the manner with which Thompson discusses Joanna Southcott, for example, in *Making*, 382–86.

98. Scott, "Women in *The Making*," 76–79.

99. Ibid., 84.

100. See, for example, the first in the series, edited by Ranajit Guha, *Subaltern Studies I: Writings on South Asian History and Society* (Delhi: Oxford University Press, 1982).

101. A number of the following insights, especially in matters of overview and interconnections between subaltern studies and history from below, are provided by Dipesh Chakrabarty, "Subaltern Studies and Postcolonial Historiography," in *Handbook of Historical Sociology*, ed. Gerard Delanty and Engin F. Isin (London: Sage, 2003), 191–204.

102. See, for example, Antonio Gramsci, *Selections from the Prison Notebooks*, trans. and ed. Quintin Hoare and Geoffrey Nowell-Smith (New York: International Publishers, 1973).

103. See Chakrabarty, "Subaltern Studies," 194–99. For Dirlik's assertion that subaltern studies is merely the application of Thompson's methods, see Arif Dirlik, "The Aura of Postcolonialism: Third World Criticism in the Age of Global Capitalism," in *Contemporary Postcolonial Theory: A Reader*, ed. Padmini Mongia (London: Arnold, 1996), 294–321.

104. Hobsbawm, *Primitive Rebels*, 2.

105. Guha, *Subaltern Studies III: Writing on Indian History and Society* (Delhi: Oxford University Press, 1984), 4–5.

106. Chakrabarty, "Subaltern Studies," 197; Guha, *Elementary Aspects of Peasant Insurgency in Colonial India* (Delhi: Oxford University Press, 1983), 6.

107. Chakrabarty, "Subaltern Studies," 196–97. For further reflections on Hobsbawm's classification of the "pre-political," see Chakrabarty, *Provincializing Europe: Postcolonial Thought and Historical Difference* (Princeton: Princeton University Press, 2000).

108. For these observations and further reflections on the intersections of class, nation, colony, gender, and travels to and from "home," see Inderpal Grewal, *Home and Harem: Nation, Gender, Empire, and the Cultures of Travel* (Durham: Duke University Press, 1996), 12–14, 112–30.

109. Here Chakrabarty would note the influence of a more Foucauldian analysis of power-knowledge on the work of Guha. See Chakrabarty, "Subaltern Studies," 194, 199.

110. Ibid., 198.

111. For further context on the different Edwards Thompson, see Bryan D. Palmer, "Family Tree as 'Liberty Tree'?" in *E.P. Thompson: Objections and Oppositions* (London: Verso, 1994), 11–51. For Edward John Thompson's view, for example, of the "mutiny" of 1857, see his *The Other Side of the Medal* (London: Hogarth, 1925). For one critique of the still-imperialist and Eurocentric mind-set of the elder Thompson's work, see Edward Said, *Culture and Imperialism* (New York: Vintage, 1993), 206–9.

112. See, for example, Spivak's essays, "Subaltern Studies: Deconstructing Historiography," in *In Other Worlds: Essays in Cultural Politics* (New York: Routledge, 1988), 197–221; "Can the Subaltern Speak?" in *Marxism and the Interpretation of Culture*, ed. Cary Nelson and Lawrence Grossberg (Urbana: University of Illinois Press, 1988), 271–313.

113. For some commentary on the intersections of Marxism, postcolonialism, and poststructuralism by biblical scholars (with scattered reflections on Spivak [and even less on feminist approaches] within these), see Stephen D. Moore, "Questions of Biblical Ambivalence and Authority under a Tree outside Delhi, or, the Postcolonial and the Postmodern,"

Roland Boer, "Marx, Postcolonialism, and the Bible," and David Jobling, "'Very Limited Ideological Options': Marxism and Biblical Studies in Postcolonial Scenes," all collected in *Postcolonial Biblical Criticism: Interdisciplinary Intersections*, ed. Moore and Fernando F. Segovia (London: T&T Clark International, 2005), 79–96, 166–83, 184–201.

114. Spivak, "Deconstructing Historiography," 215–19.

115. Ibid., 217–21.

116. Spivak, "Can the Subaltern Speak?" 278.

117. Guha, *Subaltern Studies I*, 8.

118. Spivak, "Can the Subaltern Speak?" 283–85.

119. Ibid., 287.

120. See, for example, Chandra Talpade Mohanty, "Under Western Eyes: Feminist Scholarship and Colonial Discourses," in *Feminism without Borders: Decolonizing Theory, Practicing Solidarity* (Durham: Duke University Press, 2003), 17–41, 255–57; Uma Narayan, "Contesting Cultures: 'Westernization,' Respect for Cultures, and Third-World Feminists," in *Dislocating Cultures: Identities, Traditions, and Third World Feminism* (New York: Routledge, 1997), 1–39.

121. Spivak explains: "Between patriarchy and imperialism, subject-constitution and object-formation, the figure of the woman disappears, not into a pristine nothingness, but into a violent shuttling which is the displaced figuration of the 'third-world woman' caught between tradition and modernization." See Spivak, "Can the Subaltern Speak?" 306.

122. Thompson, *The Poverty of Theory and Other Essays* (London: Merlin, 1979), 210, 222. Spivak's exasperated declaration "The subaltern cannot speak" ("Can the Subaltern Speak?" 308) has caused no end of confusion, debate, and derision among readers of the article. For further explanation and qualification about this conclusion and the ways in which we still are not hearing women's resistance to colonization (now in a more globalized form), see Spivak, "Subaltern Talk: Interview with the Editors," *The Spivak Reader: Selected Works of Gayatri Chakravorty Spivak*, ed. Donna Landry and Gerald MacLean (New York: Routledge, 1996), 287–308; and *A Critique of Postcolonial Reason*, 307–11.

123. Spivak, "Can the Subaltern Speak?" 297–98, 305–7. Spivak refers to Edward (John) Thompson's work *Suttee: A Historical and Philosophical Inquiry into the Hindu Rite of Widow-Burning* (London: George Allen and Unwin, 1928) at several key junctures.

124. Scott, "Women in *The Making*," 84.

125. Indeed, it was the intersection of religious discourse with feminist and postcolonial work that necessitated the specific studies in the volume *Postcolonialism, Feminism, and Religious Discourse*, ed. Donaldson and Kwok (New York: Routledge, 2002).

126. Keith McClelland, "Introduction," in *E. P. Thompson: Critical Perspectives*, 4.

127. Burke, "Overture: The New History," 7.

128. Here, the methodological innovations of Elisabeth Schüssler Fiorenza, Antoinette Clark Wire, and Elizabeth Castelli come most directly to mind.

129. It is appropriate that queer theoretical questions have been introduced in this section of the argument, as this chapter has been reflecting upon whether people's

history might be a suitable partner for feminist, postcolonial analyses in Pauline studies. The mode of this critical reflection, though, should also be checked against the possibly heteronormative, academic tendency to pair "women's topics" with more acceptable or traditional domains or disciplines (its partnered or "husbandly" other?). This signals the even greater importance of adopting a stance of critical assessment and cautious evaluation toward any such potential alliances or collaborations, as well as the necessity of maintaining a distinct focus in pursuing feminist, postcolonial analyses.

2. A Hymn Within and a Heavenly *Politeuma*

1. See Richard A. Horsley, ed., *Paul and Empire: Religion and Power in Roman Imperial Society* (Harrisburg: Trinity Press International, 1997); Horsley, ed., *Paul and Politics: Ekklesia, Israel, Imperium, Interpretation; Essays in Honor of Krister Stendahl* (Harrisburg: Trinity Press International, 2000); Horsley, ed., *Paul and the Roman Imperial Order* (Harrisburg: Trinity Press International, 2004).

2. J. David Hester Amador characterizes the shortcoming of this kind of rhetorical criticism, because it is "a criticism which often avoids judgment or critique concerning the text's rhetorical power or performance. In other words, biblical rhetorical interpretation becomes a criticism that is often arrested before it fulfills its *critical* task." See Amador, *Academic Constraints in Rhetorical Criticism of the New Testament: An Introduction to a Rhetoric of Power* (Sheffield: Sheffield Academic, 1999), 31. For more on this critical task, see Elisabeth Schüssler Fiorenza, *Rhetoric and Ethic: The Politics of Biblical Studies* (Minneapolis: Fortress Press, 1999) 26–30, 58–67, 79–81, 95–102, 123–28; Amador, *Academic Constraints*, 86–94.

3. On the "public health" of and the politics of biblical studies, see Schüssler Fiorenza, "Paul and the Politics of Interpretation," in *Paul and Politics*, 40–57.

4. Horsley, "Introduction" of "Part III: Paul's Counter-Imperial Gospel," in *Paul and Empire*, 140.

5. Horsley, "General Introduction," in *Paul and Empire*, 6; and "Introduction" of "Part III: Paul's Counter-Imperial Gospel," 140.

6. Horsley, "Introduction" of "Part IV: Building an Alternative Society," in *Paul and Empire*, 211.

7. Horsley, "General Introduction," 3–6.

8. Horsley, "Introduction" of "Part III: Paul's Counter-Imperial Gospel," 141.

9. Horsley, "Introduction" of "Part III: Paul's Counter-Imperial Gospel," 142; "Introduction" of "Part IV: Building an Alternative Society," 214.

10. Horsley, "General Introduction," 6.

11. Horsley, "Introduction" of "Part III: Paul's Counter-Imperial Gospel," 143. Here, Horsley cites Neil Elliott, *Liberating Paul: The Justice of God and the Politics of the Apostle* (Maryknoll: Orbis, 1994), 111.

12. Wright, "Paul's Gospel and Caesar's Empire," in *Paul and Politics*, 164.

13. Ibid., 173.

14. Ibid., 178.

15. Ibid., 174–81.

16. Ibid., 179.

17. Richard J. Cassidy, *Paul in Chains: Roman Imprisonment and the Letters of Paul* (New York: Crossroad, 2001), 247–48.

18. Ibid., 17–35, 124–43, 190–210. The tension that Cassidy insists exists between Philippians and Romans 13 only results if the former is unabashedly negative about the empire and the latter unambiguously positive. While the debate about Romans 13:1-7 continues, this study will have a variety of reasons to question such an assessment of Philippians, as does Peter Oakes on another occasion (with very different methods and results). See Oakes, "A State of Tension: Rome in the New Testament," in *The Gospel of Matthew in Its Roman Imperial Context*, ed. John Riches and David C. Sim (London: T&T Clark International, 2005), 75–90.

19. Cassidy, *Paul in Chains*, 192. Cassidy maintains that allusions to the "belly" (*kolia*) in 3:19 must be sexual, since "it is difficult to imagine that the abuse or misuse of food would constitute significant ground for such an explosive rebuke." See Cassidy, *Paul in Chains*, 173. Such a claim seems to ignore other Pauline controversies regarding food (for example, in 1 Corinthians), as well as the connections between food and erotic actions as disciplines of the body in the ancient management of the self. A brief review of the work of Michel Foucault in this regard might prevent such overstatements in the future.

20. Cassidy, *Paul in Chains*, 172–74, 192. A great deal of Cassidy's analysis depends upon uncertain, disputed, or at least unconvincing arguments regarding: a focus on Nero, Paul's imprisonment in Rome, the Roman citizenship of the Philippian audience, as well as Pauline references to persecution in Rome. In developing his thesis, Cassidy primarily adopts a hermeneutics of trust towards Pauline texts, assuming they are transparent in their depiction of historical realities and Paul's own mentalities. The following sections and chapters of analysis in the present work will aim to proceed in a more nuanced manner with regard to the rhetoric of Paul's letters (and, indeed, all discourse).

21. Ibid., 192. Such an argument is another indication of Cassidy's overwhelming faith in the transparency of the text, as is the following reflection from the same page on the same verse: "Whatever its exact nature, this situation is so painful to Paul that it brings tears to his eyes when he ponders it."

22. Ibid., 175–76, 194–95. Not only does Cassidy assume the audience members in the Philippian *ekklesia* are Roman citizens, but he believes they are also veterans and people with higher status. For questions about these factors in the mid-first-century c.e. audience, see Joseph A. Marchal, "Military Images in Philippians 1–2: A Feminist Rhetorical Analysis of Scholarship, Philippians, and Current Contexts," in *Her Master's Tools? Feminist and Postcolonial Engagements of Historical-Critical Discourse*, edited by Caroline Vander Stichele and Todd Penner (Atlanta: Society of Biblical Literature, 2005), 265–86; and Marchal, *Hierarchy, Unity, and Imitation: A Feminist Rhetorical Analysis of Power Dynamics in Paul's Letter to the Philippians,* Academia Biblica 24 (Atlanta: Society of Biblical Literature; Leiden: Brill, 2006), 50–64, 99–112.

23. The different use of the term *hypotassō* ("being subject") here, as opposed to Romans 13:1, 5 (where they are directed toward the governing authorities), is key to

Cassidy's argument that Paul has shifted his point of view due to his imprisonment. See Cassidy, *Paul in Chains*, 176–77, 195–98.

24. Agosto, "Paul vs. Empire: A Postcolonial and Latino Reading of Philippians," *Perspectivas: Occasional Papers* 6 (Fall 2002): 46. It is my understanding that a version of this article will be revised and/or republished as "The Letter to the Philippians," in *A Postcolonial Commentary on the New Testament Writings*, ed. Fernando F. Segovia and R. S. Sugirtharajah (London: T&T Clark International, 2007), 281–93.

25. Agosto, "Paul vs. Empire," 49.

26. Ibid., 45–46.

27. Ibid., 48.

28. Ibid., 49.

29. Ibid.

30. Peter Oakes, "God's Sovereignty over Roman Authorities: A Theme in Philippians," in *Rome in the Bible and the Early Church*, ed. Oakes (Grand Rapids: Paternoster/ Baker Academic, 2002), 126–41. See also Oakes, *Philippians: From People to Letter* (Cambridge: Cambridge University Press, 2001).

31. Oakes, "God's Sovereignty," 139.

32. Ibid., 138.

33. Ibid. Here Oakes is citing with approval Horsley, "Introduction" of "Part III: Paul's Counter-Imperial Gospel," 140.

34. Oakes, "God's Sovereignty," 139. Emphases original.

35. This necessity is demonstrated given the recurrent way in which Horsley's own writing and the collections he has edited are cited as key resources or foundations for most Pauline scholars reconsidering the Roman imperial context.

36. Horsley, "General Introduction," 4.

37. Horsley, "Introduction" of "Part III: Paul's Counter-Imperial Gospel," 141. See also Dieter Georgi, *Theocracy in Paul's Praxis and Theology* (Minneapolis: Fortress Press, 1991), 72–74.

38. Horsley, "Rhetoric and Empire—and 1 Corinthians," in *Paul and Politics*, 72–102.

39. Cassidy, *Paul in Chains*, 181.

40. Ibid., 182.

41. Ibid., 178–82. As was the case with 3:18-21 above, for Cassidy this argument indicates how differently Paul perceives Rome in Philippians than in Romans 13:1-7. See Cassidy, *Paul in Chains*, 179.

42. Ibid., 197. Emphases original.

43. Ibid., 198.

44. Oakes, "God's Sovereignty," 134.

45. Ibid. See also the larger argument in Oakes, *Philippians*, 207–10.

46. Oakes, "God's Sovereignty," 135.

47. Ibid., 136.

48. Ibid., 137. Here Oakes is disputing claims made by Horsley in the "Introduction" of "Part I: The Gospel of Imperial Salvation," 17–22.

49. Oakes, "God's Sovereignty," 137. Here Oakes, like Horsley, is alluding to arguments made by Georgi in his *Theocracy in Paul's Praxis and Theology*, 72–74.

50. Erik M. Heen, "Phil 2:6-11 and Resistance to Local Timocratic Rule: *Isa theō* and the Cult of the Emperor in the East," in *Paul and the Roman Imperial Order*, 125–53.

51. Ibid., 131.

52. Ibid., 141.

53. Ibid., 150–53.

54. Agosto, "Paul vs. Empire," 47.

55. Ibid., 47–48. Agosto's perspective is conditioned by his work on commendation: "Paul's Use of Greco-Roman Conventions of Commendation" (PhD diss., Boston University, 1996); and "Patronage and Commendation, Imperial and Anti-Imperial," in *Paul and Roman Imperial Order*, 103–23. See also his recent study on "servant leadership," *Servant Leadership: Jesus and Paul* (St. Louis: Chalice, 2005).

56. Wright, "Paul's Gospel," 181.

57. Ibid., 174.

58. Ibid., 177.

59. Dube, *Postcolonial Feminist Interpretation of the Bible*, 201, cf. 57, 129. The first listing does not include divine representations in the fourth question (57), but they are discussed in the analysis following it and thus added to the later listings (129, 201). The third question also alternately discusses "mutual interdependence" and "condemnation and replacement."

60. Dube's repeated stress on analyzing "this text" in these questions indicates that her approaches are geared primarily toward literary-rhetorical assessment rather than historical reconstructions. Nevertheless, as several feminist rhetorical scholars have demonstrated (Wire, Schüssler Fiorenza, Kittredge), rhetorical analysis of Paul's letters can facilitate an exploration of the various points of view in the potential audience. Thus, in implementing Dube's questions, the following analysis in this study will be most useful for the initial task, with only a few helpful notes for reconstructing these other perspectives.

61. For some responses to the "aspects of a postcolonial reading" in Agosto, see the response to Agosto by Hjamil A. Martínez-Vázquez, "Postcolonial Criticism in Biblical Interpretation: A Response to Efraín Agosto," *Perspectivas: Occasional Papers* 6 (Fall 2002): 57–63. For other readings of Pauline letters (besides Philippians) using elements of postcolonial theory, see Khoik-Khng Yeo, "The Rhetorical Hermeneutic of 1 Corinthians 8 and Chinese Ancestor Worship," *Biblical Interpretation* 2 (1994): 294–311; Wan, "Collection for the Saints;" Wan, "Does Diaspora Identity Imply Some Sort of Universality?;" Smith, "'Unmasking the Powers;'" Jeremy Punt, "Towards a Postcolonial Reading of Freedom in Paul," in *Reading the Bible in the Global Village: Capetown* (Atlanta: Society of Biblical Literature, 2002), 125–49, 188–95; Vander Stichele and Penner, "Paul and the Rhetoric of Gender," in *Her Master's Tools?* 287–310; Vander Stichele and Penner, "Unveiling Paul: Gendering Ethos in 1 Corinthians 11:2-16," in *Rhetoric, Ethic, and Moral Persuasion in Biblical Discourse*, ed. Thomas H. Olbricht and Anders Eriksson (New York: T&T Clark International, 2005), 214–37; Robert Seesengood, "Hybridity and the Rhetoric of Endurance: Reading Paul's Athletic

Metaphors in a Context of Postcolonial Self-Construction," *Bible and Critical Theory* 1, no. 3 (2005).

62. The following rhetorical analysis depends upon, develops in conversation with, and yet is distinguishable from preceding feminist analyses of Philippians. See especially Carolyn L. Osiek, "Philippians," in *Searching the Scriptures: A Feminist Commentary*, ed. Elisabeth Schüssler Fiorenza (New York: Crossroad, 1994), 2:237–49; Cynthia Briggs Kittredge, *Community and Authority: The Rhetoric of Obedience in the Pauline Tradition* (Harrisburg: Trinity Press International, 1998); Marchal, *Hierarchy, Unity, and Imitation*; "Military Images;" and "'With Friends like These . . .': A Feminist Rhetorical Reconsideration of Scholarship and the Letter to the Philippians," *Journal for the Study of the New Testament* 29, no. 1 (Sept. 2006): 77–106.

63. For a different interpretation of Paul's imprisonment, see Agosto, "Paul vs. Empire," 43–46, 48, 50–51. On Paul's imprisonment, see also Craig S. Wansink, *Chained in Christ: The Experience and Rhetoric of Paul's Imprisonment* (Sheffield: Sheffield Academic, 1996); and Cassidy, *Paul in Chains*. Whether Paul is imprisoned in Ephesus or Rome changes little about the rhetorics and the effects of travel, distance, or the claims of progress.

64. On *parousia*, see Helmut Koester, "Imperial Ideology and Paul's Eschatology in 1 Thessalonians," in *Paul and Empire*, 158–66. The source of the Philippians' joy would also be in their *pistis*, their loyalty or adherence to this message (now imperially cast).

65. For further historical and material considerations of the multiple colonizations of Philippi and the resulting conditions for the possible citizens, veterans, and their descendants, alongside other inhabitants, see Marchal, "Military Images," 271–80; and Marchal, *Hierarchy, Unity, and Imitation*, 50–64, 99–112.

66. See also passages such as 4:15-16 and 21-22 that discuss his travels or situate Paul in another location with greetings to cross some geographical space for the audience.

67. For a helpful, critical, but initial investigation of the power dynamics of Pauline imitation, see Elizabeth A. Castelli, *Imitating Paul: A Discourse of Power* (Louisville: Westminster John Knox, 1991).

68. For Paul as the model, see also 1:3-11, 12-14, 24-26; 2:16-18; 4:2; and perhaps implicitly also 1:30; 2:23-24, 29; 3:7-11; and 4:11-13. Markus Bockmuehl maintains that "the theme of imitation recurs as an integrating focus in every major section of Philippians." See Bockmuehl, *The Epistle to the Philippians* (London: Hendrickson, 1998), 254, as well as the more developed considerations of Pauline imitation given the postcolonial and feminist interest in mimicry (in the third chapter in this study).

69. Tat-siong Benny Liew, "Tyranny, Boundary, and Might: Colonial Mimicry in Mark's Gospel," *Journal for the Study of the New Testament* 73 (1999): 7–31. For the use of mimesis, mimicry, or mimeticism in postcolonial work, see Homi K. Bhabha, *Location of Culture* (London: Routledge, 1994); Rey Chow, *The Protestant Ethnic and the Spirit of Capitalism* (New York: Columbia University Press, 2002); Anne McClintock, *Imperial Leather: Race, Gender and Sexuality in the Colonial Conquest* (New York: Routledge, 1995); and Meyda Yeğenoğlu, "Veiled Fantasies: Cultural and Sexual Difference in the Discourse of Orientalism," in *Feminist Postcolonial Theory*, ed. Reina Lewis and Sara

Mills (New York: Routledge, 2003), 542–66. Reprinted from Yeğenoğlu's monograph, *Colonial Fantasies: Towards a Feminist Reading of Orientalism* (Cambridge: Cambridge University Press, 1998), 39–67. On the concept of mimicry as it relates to Paul's hybridity, see Seesengood, "Hybridity and the Rhetoric of Endurance."

70. On the authoritative, hierarchical dynamics of imitation, see especially Castelli's analysis in *Imitating Paul*. For one conceptualization of the ambivalent agency of the colonized whom are asked to imitate, see Bhabha, *Location of Culture*.

71. See Dube, *Postcolonial Feminist Interpretation of the Bible*, 13–14, 155, 181–83; Kwok, *Postcolonial Imagination and Feminist Theology*, 65. Dube is concerned with a feminist reconstruction of mission and women's roles in "mission texts," because "it proceeds by assuming that the mission to the Gentiles was and is itself liberating, since it does not scrutinize or problematize the strategies of the mission nor the power relations it advocates." See Dube, *Postcolonial Feminist Interpretation of the Bible*, 183. For Dube's analysis, see also Kwesi Dickson's observations about the exclusivist, anti-indigenous tendency of Paul's argumentation, in Dickson, *Uncompleted Mission: Christianity and Exclusivism* (Maryknoll: Orbis, 1991), especially 59–69.

72. For an initial treatment of the problem of difference and boundary in this letter, see "What Difference Does Paul Make? Responding to Rhetorical Constructions of Identity and Community Boundaries in Philippians" (paper presented at the Conference on Rhetorics of Identity: Place, Race, Sex and the Person; Centre for Rhetorics and Hermeneutics at Redlands University and the New Testament Rhetorical Project at Claremont Graduate College, Redlands, Calif., January 2005). Recall also the difference attention to difference makes in the discussions and critical evaluations of "people's history" in the previous chapter.

73. On the apocalyptic aspect of Paul's anti-imperial arguments, see the various entries by Horsley, Koester, and Elliott (among others) in the collections *Paul and Empire*, *Paul and Politics*, and *Paul and the Roman Imperial Order*. Even if one accepts their arguments, the question about whether anti-colonial apocalyptic rhetoric can still be re-deployed as part of a colonizing regime remains to be addressed, especially considering its dualistic argumentation. See Dube, *Postcolonial Feminist Interpretation of the Bible*, 73. Reading Paul as an apocalyptic thinker also requires reconsidering the potentially threatening elements of passages like 3:15 (God's "revelation" for those who think anything different) and 4:3 (inclusion or exclusion in the book of life).

74. For a series of malestream mitigations as to the hierarchical nature of obedience rhetorics, see the overview and critique in Kittredge, *Community and Authority*, 13–36. Victor P. Furnish's claim that Pauline obedience is a kind of loving mutuality is particularly susceptible to this critique. See Furnish, *The Love Command in the New Testament* (Nashville: Abingdon, 1972).

75. For the attribution of sexual perversity to the outsider and colonized people as an imperial rationale, see, in general, Edward W. Said, *Orientalism*, rev. ed. (New York: Vintage, 1994 [1978]); as well as Jennifer Wright Knust, "Paul and the Politics of Virtue and Vice," in *Paul and the Roman Imperial Order*, 155–74; and *Abandoned to Lust: Sexual Slander and Ancient Christianity* (New York: Columbia University Press, 2005).

76. For N. T. Wright's solution to these slurs, as a coded challenge to the empire, see Wright, "Paul's Gospel and Caesar's Empire," 174–81. What eludes Wright here is that Paul's argument likely coincides with and reinforces imperial argumentation. Wright seems initially aware of this possibility (164), but his interpretation does not consider the possibility further.

77. For further critical reflections on this kind of reading of Pauline texts, see Schüssler Fiorenza, "Paul and the Politics of Interpretation," in *Paul and Politics*, 55–56.

78. Dube develops the postcolonial feminist value of interdependence based upon her work with women in African Independent Churches (AICs). See Dube, *Postcolonial Feminist Interpretation of the Bible*, 184–95. In an interrelated way, on the importance of solidarity, as opposed to sisterhood, as a paradigm for decolonizing, transnational feminist organizing, see Mohanty, *Feminism without Borders*, especially 7, 40–45, 110–11.

79. See Dube, *Postcolonial Feminist Interpretation of the Bible*, 184–86.

80. On this phenomenon, Dube comments: "The post-independence experience of many Two-Thirds World countries has also rudely shown that 'independence' from other nations and cultures, even from those that oppressed them, is neither practical nor the best means for survival." Ibid., 185. This raises the question: if Paul *is* anti-imperial, is his position more akin to that of some post-independence authorities than that of an anti-colonial revolutionary?

81. For more on how Paul constructs himself in gendered and imperialist terms in another letter (1 Corinthians), see Vander Stichele and Penner, "Paul and the Rhetoric of Gender"; and "Unveiling Paul."

82. Wright, "Paul's Gospel and Caesar's Empire," 164. On the same page, Wright also suggests: "To say that Paul opposed imperialism is about as politically dangerous as suggesting he was in favor of sunlight, fresh air, and orange juice." Is it not "politically dangerous" because there is a lack of acknowledgment of imperial relations within and extending out from the United States and the United Kingdom (at least by some of its citizenry)? Or is this an indication of how apolitical our analysis of imperialism has been? Nevertheless, as Wright's comments seem to acknowledge (but his analysis fails to develop), Paul is not against imperialism as a dynamic of dominating rule.

83. Kittredge, "Corinthian Women Prophets," in *Paul and Politics*, 107–9.

84. That "commonwealth" is an imperial term that implies commonality, reciprocity, or equality, while masking the exploitative conditions of colonization(s), should give pause to those who want to claim its use here as liberating. On the origins of postcolonial literature as a terminological replacement for "commonwealth literature," see R. S. Sugirtharajah, "A Postcolonial Exploration of Collusion and Construction in Biblical Interpretation," in *The Postcolonial Bible*, ed. Sugirtharajah (Sheffield: Sheffield Academic, 1998), 91–116 (92).

85. For the Roman imperial resonance of these terms, see Dieter Georgi, "God Turned Upside Down," in *Paul and Empire*, 148–57; Elliott, "Romans 13:1-7 in the Context of Imperial Propaganda," in *Paul and Empire*, 184–204; Karl P. Donfried, "The Imperial Cults of Thessalonica and Political Conflict in 1 Thessalonians," in *Paul and Empire*, 215–23 (among others).

86. On military images in Philippians, see, for example, Edgar M. Krentz, "Military Language and Metaphors in Philippians," in *Origins and Method: Towards a New Understanding of Judaism and Christianity; Essays in Honour of John C. Hurd*, ed. Bradley H. McLean (Sheffield: Sheffield Academic, 1993), 105–27; Timothy C. Geoffrion, *The Rhetorical Purpose and the Political and Military Character of Philippians* (Lewiston: Mellen, 1993); and Krentz, "Paul, Games, and the Military," in *Paul in the Greco-Roman World: A Handbook*, ed. J. Paul Sampley (Harrisburg: Trinity Press International, 2003), 344–83. For a summary and assessment of these rhetorics and the scholarly examination of them, see Marchal, "Military Images."

87. For a consideration of patronage and friendship in this letter and the Roman imperial context, see John T. Fitzgerald, "Paul and Friendship," in *Paul in the Greco-Roman World*, 319–43; and Marchal, "With Friends Like These . . ."

88. For interconnections between military and patronage/friendship rhetorics, see Marchal, *Hierarchy, Unity, and Imitation*, 64–70.

89. Kittredge, *Community and Authority*, 37–51; "Corinthian Women Prophets," 105–7. If taken seriously, Kittredge's work on the verb *hypotassethai* ("to be subjected") would nuance some of the positive claims made about Paul by Elliott and Agosto. See Elliott, "The Apostle Paul's Self-Presentation As Anti-Imperial Performance," in *Paul and the Roman Imperial Order*, 73–74; Agosto, "Patronage and Commendation, Imperial and Anti-Imperial," in *Paul and the Roman Imperial Order*, 114.

90. It is here that this study parts ways with the analysis of the hymn offered by Kittredge and other feminist scholars. See Kittredge, *Community and Authority*, 99–100, 110; Luise Schottroff, *Lydia's Impatient Sisters: A Feminist Social History of Early Christianity*, trans. Barbara and Martin Rumscheidt (Louisville: Westminster John Knox, 1995), 43–46. Though the hymn might have offered a pattern of reversal as a hope to those oppressed in various ways by the kyriarchal culture, its imagery and vocabulary are still embedded in this kyriarchal matrix of slave-master (2:7) and subject-ruler (2:9-11). For a similar assertion about the kyriocentric nature of this text, see Briggs, "Can an Enslaved God Liberate? Hermeneutical Reflections on Philippians 2:6-11," *Semeia* 47 (1989): 137–53.

91. Here Kittredge's argument is clear and decisive about the function of the hymn in extolling obedience. See Kittredge, *Community and Authority*, 83–86.

92. On the connection between "fear and trembling" and the obedience of slaves in the Pauline corpus, see Carolyn L. Osiek, *Philippians, Philemon* (Nashville: Abingdon, 2000), 70. Jean K. Kim's interpretation of this hymn from her own Asian contextual position charts this dual danger of the lordship and suffering servant images, most especially in light of Western domination of Asia. Kim, "An Asian Interpretation of Philippians 2.6-11," in *Escaping Eden: New Feminist Perspectives on the Bible*, ed. Harold C. Washington, Susan Lochrie Graham, and Pamela Thimmes (New York: New York University Press, 1999), 104–22 (see especially 104–6). However, her analysis (perhaps problematically) attempts to delineate the difference between the hymn's christological and rhetorical uses instead of viewing them as mutually constructive of each other. On my reading, the preceding arguments of this study (regarding the universalized forms of domination) could fit, though, with Kim's larger theological point about resisting

the exclusivity of the rule of Jesus as world-savior. See Kim, "An Asian Interpretation," 120–22.

93. For a fuller explication of this repeated pattern of "descend in order to ascend" and its connections to the rhetorics of sacrifice, see Marchal, "Mutuality Rhetorics and Feminist Interpretation"; and *Hierarchy, Unity, and Imitation*, 141–143, 171–173.

94. For further arguments that Pauline community language (including the body of Christ and brothers/*adelphoi*) is androcentric, see Jorunn Økland, *Women in Their Place: Paul and the Corinthian Discourse of Gender and Sanctuary Space* (London: T&T Clark International, 2005), 211–17.

95. Both Craig S. de Vos and Peter C. Oakes maintain that the community to which Paul wrote likely was mostly composed of people with lower status. See De Vos, *Church and Community Conflicts: The Relationships of the Thessalonian, Corinthian, and Philippian Churches with Their Wider Civic Communities* (Atlanta: Scholars, 1999), 250–61; Oakes, *Philippians: From People to Letter* (Cambridge: Cambridge University Press, 2001), 57–63. For the impact of relative social standing on the rhetorics of Pauline letters and the communities to which he writes, see Wire, *The Corinthian Women Prophets: A Reconstruction Through Paul's Rhetoric* (Minneapolis: Fortress Press, 1990), 62–71. On Paul's status, with some initial postcolonial analysis, see Seesengood, "Hybridity and the Rhetoric of Endurance."

96. Most scholarship on Philippians has acquiesced to Paul's division of authority in this manner, thus assuming that the call in 4:2 to "think the same thing" portrays a conflict between Euodia and Syntyche, rather than a difference between Paul and the two women. As on previous occasions, Kittredge's argument that Euodia and Syntyche are not in a conflict with each other but with Paul is unique and convincing. See Kittredge, *Community and Authority*, 105–8; and now, Marchal, *Hierarchy, Unity, and Imitation*, 147–52, 189–90; Marchal, "Military Images" and "With Friends . . ."

97. For postcolonial feminist reflections on the roles constructed for women to reinforce colonial and/or communal/nationalist boundaries, see Jean K. Kim, *Woman and Nation: An Intercontextual Reading of the Gospel of John from a Postcolonial Feminist Perspective* (Boston: Brill, 2004).

98. That "the Lord is near" (4:5) might also be a foreboding hint of the end for those who do not accept the letter's specific message of divine peace (4:7, 9). Peace is the province of the Romans since Augustus's reign established a "Pax Romana."

99. See Mary Rose D'Angelo, "Abba and 'Father': Imperial Theology and the Traditions about Jesus," *Journal of Biblical Literature* 111 (1992): 611–30; and "Early Christian Sexual Politics and Roman Imperial Family Values: Rereading Christ and Culture," in *The Papers of the Henry Luce III Fellows in Theology*, ed. Christopher I. Wilkins (Pittsburgh: Association of Theological Schools, 2003), 6:23–48.

100. Kittredge, "Corinthian Women Prophets," 105.

101. Even if this chapter still proves unconvincing that this argumentation repeats, reinscribes, or coincides with imperialism, there is still no assurance that Paul's letters function to decolonize. See, for example, Dube's three questions about rhetorical methods of decolonizing in *Postcolonial Feminist Interpretation of the Bible*, 97.

102. Kwok, *Postcolonial Imagination and Feminist Theology*, 10.

103. On "erotic triangles," the homosocial/homoerotic contest for authority, and the maintenance of power, see Eve Kosofsky Sedgwick, *Between Men: English Literature and Male Homosocial Desire*, Gender and Culture (New York: Columbia University Press, 1985), especially 21–27. For the interweaving of this kind of analysis with postcolonial feminist concerns, see Donaldson, "A Passage to 'India': Colonialism and Filmic Representation," in *Decolonizing Feminisms*, 88–101. For the specific roles constructed for Korean women and similar gestures in the Gospel of John, see Kim, *Woman and Nation*, 5–18, 90–141.

104. For this pattern in ancient visual culture, see, for example, Davina C. Lopez, "Reading Galatians in Light of Images of Roman Imperial Gender Constructs" (paper delivered at the annual meeting of the Society of Biblical Literature, San Antonio, Tex., November 2004); and her study, *Apostle to the Conquered: Reimaging Paul's Mission* (Minneapolis: Fortress Press, 2008); Rene Rodgers, "Female Representation in Roman Art: Feminizing the Provincial Other," in *Roman Imperialism and Provincial Art*, ed. Sarah Scott and Jane Webster (New York: Cambridge University Press, 2004), 69–93; and in general on imperialism, see McClintock, *Imperial Leather*, among others.

105. On the importance of manliness in the empire see, for example, D'Angelo, "Abba and 'Father'"; and "Early Christian Sexual Politics"; Craig A. Williams, *Roman Homosexuality: Ideologies of Masculinity in Classical Antiquity* (New York: Oxford University Press, 1999); Vander Stichele and Penner, "Paul and the Rhetoric of Gender"; and Virginia Burrus, *"Begotten, Not Made": Conceiving Manhood in Late Antiquity* (Stanford: Stanford University Press, 2000).

106. Because such an assessment would require a lengthier and more complicated analysis than can be offered at this initial stage, refer to the attempt to engage postcolonial and postcolonial feminist work on mimesis, mimicry, and mimeticism, in the following chapter.

107. For a feminist engagement with the perils of nationalism and globalization, see the roundtable discussion in *Journal of Feminist Studies in Religion* 21, no. 1 (Spring 2005): 111–54.

108. Dube, *Postcolonial Feminist Interpretation of the Bible*, 52. See also Uma Narayan's analysis of nationalist and/or nativist formations in response to localized forms of feminist activism, in "Contesting Cultures: 'Westernization,' Respect for Cultures, and Third-World Feminists," in *Dislocating Cultures: Identities, Traditions, and Third World Feminism* (New York: Routledge, 1997), 2–39.

109. For the phrases, "almost the same, but not quite," and "almost the same, but not white," see Bhabha, *The Location of Culture*, 86 and 89, respectively.

110. Kwok, *Postcolonial Imagination and Feminist Theology*, 82.

111. For a similar assessment in terms of another Pauline letter, see Kittredge, "Corinthian Women Prophets," 103–9; Antoinette Clark Wire, "Response: The Politics of the Assembly in Corinth," in *Paul and Politics*, 124–29.

112. See, for example, Schüssler Fiorenza, "Paul and the Politics of Interpretation," 50; Kittredge, "Corinthian Women Prophets," 105.

3. The Rhetorics of Imitation and Postcolonial Theories of Mimicry

1. For a more expansive, detailed analysis of the modeling rhetorics in the letter to the Philippians (on which some of this analysis is based), see Joseph A. Marchal, *Hierarchy, Unity, and Imitation: A Feminist Rhetorical Analysis of Power Dynamics in Paul's Letter to the Philippians*, Academia Biblica 24 (Atlanta: Society of Biblical Literature, 2006), 180–90. For a rhetorical analysis of the whole of the letter, as the arguments develop, see *Hierarchy, Unity, and Imitation*, 115–56. This analysis depends upon, develops in conversation with, and yet is distinguishable from preceding feminist analyses of Philippians. See especially Carolyn L. Osiek, "Philippians," in *Searching the Scriptures: A Feminist Commentary*, ed. Elisabeth Schüssler Fiorenza (New York: Crossroad, 1994), 2:237–49; and Cynthia Briggs Kittredge, *Community and Authority: The Rhetoric of Obedience in the Pauline Tradition* (Harrisburg: Trinity Press International, 1998).

2. Kittredge's argument is clear and decisive about the function of the hymn in extolling obedience. See Kittredge, *Community and Authority*, 83–86.

3. Thus, the *functional* role of this argument is supporting, even if the mind-set of Paul or membership in the community involved a more significant *theological* role for Christ. References to Christ are used to bolster the preeminence of Paul's model in the argumentation. At one point in the letter, Paul's self-description seems comparable to the arc of this hymn (loss to gain in 3:7-11), while Paul maintains an aim of "becoming like him" (3:10). (The more associated Paul becomes with respected figures in the community, the more his model status is elevated.)

4. As already mentioned above, the use of further arguments by model can reinforce others, especially when they are compatible with each other. As Lucie Olbrechts-Tyteca and Chaïm Perelman maintain: "Close adherence to a recognized model guarantees the value of the behavior. The person following the model enjoys an enhanced value, and can thus, in turn, serve as model." See Olbrechts-Tyteca and Perelman, *The New Rhetoric: A Treatise on Argumentation*, trans. John Wilkinson and Purcell Weaver (Notre Dame: University of Notre Dame Press, 1969) [originally published as *La Nouvelle Rhétorique: Traité de l'Argumentation* (Paris: Universitaires de France, 1958)], 364.

5. It should be noted, of course, that the "me" Paul presented in the letter likely does not correspond accurately to "the historical Paul," as his self-depiction involved the selection of certain information and modes of presentation for his specific rhetorical purposes on this occasion. See, for example, the arguments of Todd Penner and Caroline Vander Stichele, "Unveiling Paul: Gendering *Ethos* in 1 Corinthians 11:2-16," in *Rhetoric, Ethic, and Moral Persuasion in Biblical Discourse*, ed. Thomas H. Olbricht and Anders Eriksson (New York: T&T Clark International, 2005), 214–37.

6. Elizabeth A. Castelli, *Imitating Paul: A Discourse of Power* (Louisville: Westminster John Knox, 1991), 23–33. Here, Castelli highlights the multiple meanings of "skirt"—to avoid because of danger or fear of controversy or to move along an edge or border—to describe Pauline scholarship and the issue of power (see especially p. 23).

7. For Castelli's description of Michel Foucault's conception of power, see Castelli, *Imitating Paul*, 35–58. For one convenient collection of some of Foucault's reflections on this topic, see Foucault, *Power/Knowledge: Selected Interviews and Other Writing*

1972–1977, ed. Colin Gordon; trans. C. Gordon, Leo Marshall, John Mepham, and Kate Soper (New York: Pantheon, 1980).

8. See Castelli, *Imitating Paul*, 23.

9. Ibid., 13.

10. Unlike most past scholarship, Castelli clearly states the hierarchical aspect of imitation. See Castelli, *Imitating Paul*, 16, 21–22, 86–87. On the role of imitation in the master-apprentice model of pedagogy, see Elisabeth Schüssler Fiorenza, *Wisdom Ways: Introducing Feminist Biblical Interpretation* (Maryknoll: Orbis, 2001), 30.

11. For brief summaries of the main aspects of ancient Greco-Roman discourses of imitation or mimesis, see Castelli, *Imitating Paul*, 16, 86–87.

12. Ibid., 89–117.

13. Ibid., 95–97.

14. See Markus Bockmuehl, *The Epistle to the Philippians* (London: Hendrickson, 1998). On imitation in Paul, see also Benjamin Fiore, "Paul, Exemplification, and Imitation," in *Paul in the Greco-Roman World: A Handbook*, ed. J. Paul Sampley (Harrisburg: Trinity Press International, 2003), 228–57; and Brian J. Dodd, *Paul's Paradigmatic "I": Personal Example as Literary Strategy* (Sheffield: Sheffield Academic, 1999).

15. See Bockmuehl, *Epistle*, 254.

16. Ibid., 1. On the same page, Bockmuehl also notes: "St Paul's letter to Philippi sparkles with joy—the sort of life-giving, heart-refreshing joy that is tangibly transforming in its effect on the mundane realities of everyday existence."

17. Ibid., 229.

18. Ibid., 228.

19. For a similarly defensive view of Paul's modeling, see Frederick W. Weidmann, "An (Un)Accomplished Model: Paul and the Rhetorical Strategy of Philippians 3:3-17," in *Putting Body and Soul Together: Essays in Honor of Robin Scroggs*, ed. Virginia Wiles, Alexandra Brown, and Graydon F. Snyder (Valley Forge: Trinity Press International, 1997), 245–57; and Andrew D. Clarke, "'Be Imitators of Me': Paul's Model of Leadership," *Tyndale Bulletin* 49 (1998): 329–60. Weidmann's article is, in part, in response to Robert T. Fortna, "Philippians: Paul's Most Egocentric Letter," in *The Conversation Continues: Festschrift for J. Louis Martyn*, ed. Fortna and Beverly R. Gaventa (Nashville: Abingdon, 1990), 220–34.

20. On the tendency of scholars to lump "following Jesus" traditions with Paul's calls for imitation, see Castelli, *Imitating Paul*, 24–26.

21. See Schüssler Fiorenza, "Paul and the Politics of Interpretation," in *Paul and Politics: Ekklesia, Israel, Imperium, Interpretation; Essays in Honor of Krister Stendahl*, ed. Richard A. Horsley (Harrisburg: Trinity Press International, 2000), 40–57, 44.

22. For a similar point, see Marchal, "Military Images in Philippians 1–2: A Feminist Rhetorical Analysis of Scholarship, Philippians, and Current Contexts," in *Her Master's Tools? Feminist and Postcolonial Engagements of Historical-Critical Discourse*, ed. Caroline Vander Stichele and Todd Penner (Atlanta: Society of Biblical Literature, 2005), 285–86.

23. See Bockmuehl, *Epistle*, 229. Here Bockmuehl refers to the third and fourth chapters of Castelli's book (59–117), which ironically comprise the most "typically"

academic portions of the work: a philological/social-historical survey of classical sources and an exegetical close reading of a series of biblical texts. Bockmuehl seems also to mis-recognize Castelli's methodology. Overall, one might say the study engages in ideology critique or discursive diagnosis, as it adapts a Foucauldian analytic rather than a Der-ridean deconstruction. Oddly enough, Derrida and deconstruction are mentioned only briefly among a range of other topics in the conclusion (119–36), to which Bockmuehl was apparently not referring. Thus, similar to his treatment of Philippians, Bockmuehl generalizes, misidentifies, and erases certain dynamics in Castelli's and his own texts.

24. See, for example, Musa W. Dube, *Postcolonial Feminist Interpretation of the Bible* (St. Louis: Chalice, 2000), 60–67.

25. This is a point that Castelli insists upon throughout the study. See, for example, Castelli, *Imitating Paul*, 13, 16, 18, 21–33.

26. Ibid., 17, 116–17.

27. See, for example, Foucault's reflections on prohibitions and the repressive hypoth-esis in psychology in Foucault, *The History of Sexuality: An Introduction*, trans. Robert Hurley (New York: Vintage, 1990), 1:3–49.

28. See Castelli, *Imitating Paul*, 43–44, 48.

29. Ibid., 32–33.

30. Paul's argumentation likely was shaped by the dynamics of the rhetorical situ-ation. Paul may not have been the sole founder of the discourse on display in the let-ter, especially if one conceives of the letter as a response and one part of an ongoing exchange between parties. Thus, arguments about imitation likely were shaped by others in the community/ies to which Paul wrote. See, for example, Antoinette Clark Wire, *The Corinthian Women Prophets: A Reconstruction through Paul's Rhetoric* (Minneapolis: Fortress Press, 1990); Cynthia Briggs Kittredge, "Rethinking Authorship in the Let-ters of Paul: Elisabeth Schüssler Fiorenza's Model of Pauline Theology," in *Walk in the Ways of Wisdom: Essays in Honor of Elisabeth Schüssler Fiorenza*, ed. Shelly Matthews, Kittredge, and Melanie Johnson-Debaufre (Harrisburg: Trinity Press International, 2003), 318–33; and Kittredge, "Feminist Rethinking of Paul" (paper presented at the annual meeting of the Society of Biblical Literature, Philadelphia, November 2005).

31. See Castelli, *Imitating Paul*, 136.

32. On the tension between the call to imitate and the inability to ever actually achieve such sameness, see, for example, Castelli, *Imitating Paul*, 68, 71, 75, 86–87.

33. The wide variety of critical theorists that reflect upon imitation, mimesis, simi-larity, or simulation cannot possibly be represented in an inquiry focused in the way this one is. Nevertheless, the connections between feminist and feminist/queer theorists of mimicry, like Luce Irigaray and Judith Butler, and the postcolonial work of Bhabha have been under-recognized and under-theorized as mutually influential or possibly constitu-tive for Bhabha's observations. This should raise some initial suspicions about Bhabha's own inclinations or biases in terms of gender. For further analysis, see the observations below.

34. For more on this kind of colony, see Craig S. de Vos, *Church and Community Conflicts: The Relationship of the Thessalonian, Corinthian, and Philippian Churches with Their Wider Civic Communities* (Atlanta: Scholars, 1999), 112–15, 246–47; Barbara

Levick, ed., *The Government of the Roman Empire: A Sourcebook* (London: Croom Helm, 1988), 73–74, 316; and Adrian N. Sherwin-White, *The Roman Citizenship*, 2d ed. (Oxford: Clarendon, 1973), 316–19. In fact, by this point in the history of Philippi, the locale had been colonized multiple times. For an overview of the Thasian, Macedonian, and Roman colonizations of Philippi, see Paul Collart, *Villes de Macédoine: depuis ses origins jusqu'à la fin de l'époque romaine* (École Française d'Athènes: Paris, 1937); Lilian Portefaix, *Sisters Rejoice: Paul's Letter to the Philippians and Luke-Acts as Received by First-Century Philippian Women* (Stockholm: Almqvist & Wiksell, 1988), 59–60; Lukas Bormann, *Philippi: Stadt und Christengemeinde zur Zeit des Paulus* (Leiden: Brill, 1995); Peter Pilhofer, *Philippi I: Die erste christliche Gemeinde Europas* (Tübingen: J. C. B. Mohr, 1995); De Vos, *Church and Community Conflicts*, 233–50, 275–87; and Peter Oakes, *Philippians: From People to Letter* (Cambridge: Cambridge University Press, 2001), 1–54.

35. See Kwok Pui-lan, *Postcolonial Imagination and Feminist Theology* (Louisville: Westminster John Knox, 2005), 8–9.

36. See, for example, Fernando F. Segovia's focus on both ancient texts and modern readings in his elucidation of a "postcolonial optic" in Segovia, *Decolonizing Biblical Studies: A View from the Margins* (Maryknoll: Orbis, 2000), 125–29. See also Dube, *Postcolonial Feminist Interpretation*, 3–4; and Kwok, *Postcolonial Imagination*, 7–8.

37. See, at least initially, the entry on mimicry in Bill Ashcroft, Gareth Griffiths, and Helen Tiffin, *Post-Colonial Studies: The Key Concepts* (London: Routledge, 2000), 139–42. For the case of India, see V. S. Naipaul, *The Mimic Men* (London: Deutsch, 1967).

38. See Thomas Babington Macaulay, "Minute on Education," in *Sources of Indian Tradition*, ed. William Theodore de Bary (New York: Columbia University Press, 1958), 2:49; as cited in Homi Bhabha, "Of Mimicry and Man: The Ambivalence of Colonial Discourse," in *The Location of Culture* (London: Routledge, 1994), 85–92, 87.

39. On the efforts to work against this trend in colonialist forms of classical archaeology, history, and art, see the contributions in *Roman Imperialism: Post-Colonial Perspectives*, ed. Jane Webster and Nicholas J. Cooper (Leicester: School of Archaeological Studies, 1996); *Dialogues in Roman Imperialism: Power, Discourse, and Discrepant Experience in the Roman Empire*, ed. David J. Mattingly (Portsmouth: Journal of Roman Archaeology, British Academy, 1997); and *Roman Imperialism and Provincial Art*, ed. Sarah Scott and Jane Webster (Cambridge: Cambridge University Press, 2003).

40. For the influence of and reaction to Roman imperial institutions and social forms in Paul's letters, see the various entries in Richard A. Horsley, ed., *Paul and Empire: Religion and Power in Roman Imperial Society* (Harrisburg: Trinity Press International, 1997); Horsley, ed., *Paul and Politics: Ekklesia, Israel, Imperium, Interpretation; Essays in Honor of Krister Stendahl* (Harrisburg: Trinity Press International, 2000); Horsley, ed., *Paul and the Roman Imperial Order* (Harrisburg: Trinity Press International, 2004); and Horsley, ed., *Hidden Transcripts and the Arts of Resistance: Applying the Work of James C. Scott to Jesus and Paul* (Atlanta: Society of Biblical Literature, 2004). Many of these entries, in fact, point out that Paul mimics or repeats imperial terminology in order to use it in another fashion. On various Greek forms of imitation in the politicized

context of the empire, see Tim Whitmarsh, *Greek Literature and the Roman Empire: The Politics of Imitation* (Oxford: Oxford University Press, 2001).

41. For the use of Bhabha in biblical interpretation, see Tat-siong Benny Liew, "Tyranny, Boundary, and Might: Colonial Mimicry in Mark's Gospel," *JSNT* 73 (1999): 7–31; Erin Runions, *Changing Subjects: Gender, Nation and Future in Micah* (Sheffield: Sheffield Academic, 2002); Stephen D. Moore, "Questions of Biblical Ambivalence and Authority under a Tree outside Delhi; or, the Postcolonial and the Postmodern," in *Postcolonial Biblical Criticism: Interdisciplinary Intersections*, ed. Moore and Fernando F. Segovia (London: T&T Clark International, 2005), 79–96; and Robert Seesengood "Hybridity and the Rhetoric of Endurance: Reading Paul's Athletic Metaphors in a Context of Postcolonial Self-Construction," *Bible and Critical Theory* 1, no. 3 (2005). For the purposes of this study, Liew's article ("Tyranny, Boundary, and Might") is especially useful in light of the present, specific topic and his similarly suspicious approach to any prematurely celebratory reaction to colonial mimicry.

42. See Bhabha, "Of Mimicry and Man," 85–92, 85.

43. See Bhabha, "Sly Civility," in *The Location of Culture*, 100.

44. Here, Bhabha's difficulties (or generalized lack of will for) grappling with the gendered aspects of the colonial scene would be especially improved by an engagement with Judith Butler's work on gendered performativity and parodic forms of resistance (in fact, Butler's first work on these concepts predates a significant amount of Bhabha's reflections on mimicry). See Butler, *Gender Trouble: Feminism and the Subversion of Identity* (New York: Routledge, 1990); *Bodies That Matter: On the Discursive Limits of "Sex"* (New York: Routledge, 1993); and *Undoing Gender* (New York: Routledge, 2004).

45. See, for example, Bhabha's "Sly Civility," 93–101.

46. On this, Bhabha writes: "The *menace* of mimicry is its *double* vision which in disclosing the ambivalence of colonial discourse also disrupts its authority." See Bhabha, "Of Mimicry and Man," 88. On the move from mimicry to menace or mockery, see also Bhabha, "Of Mimicry and Man," 91; "Articulating the Archaic: Cultural Difference and Colonial Nonsense," in *The Location of Culture*, 123–38, 137.

47. See Bhabha, "Of Mimicry and Man," 86, 89. For the conjoined phrase "not quite/ not white," see ibid., 92.

48. See Bhabha, "The Commitment to Theory," in *The Location of Culture*, 19–39, 28.

49. See Seesengood, "Hybridity and the Rhetoric of Endurance."

50. See Daniel Boyarin, *A Radical Jew: Paul and the Politics of Identity* (Berkeley: University of California Press, 1994), 79. Interestingly, though Boyarin does not directly refer to Bhabha in this work, Bhabha did provide approving comments on the back jacket (at least in the 1997 paperback edition).

51. For the use of Boyarin and this specific question, see Seesengood, "Hybridity and the Rhetoric of Endurance," 16–3.

52. Castelli also considered the ambiguous power dynamics of imitation, in terms of both its emulative and authoritative aspects. On this ambiguity, see Castelli, *Imitating Paul*, 16, 21–22, 30–31, 68–71, 140–41. However, Castelli also repeatedly stresses the authoritative aspect over and above the possible import of this ambiguity.

53. See Bockmuehl, *Epistle*, 254.

54. To grasp the efforts to which Paul goes to drive home this point, one need only note the amount of times he also draws upon a divine authority to shore up his arguments: 1:8, 20, 28; 2:5-13, 27; 3:9, 15: 4:7, 9, 13, 19. For an analysis of the argument from divine authority, see Marchal, *Hierarchy, Unity, and Imitation*, 176–78.

55. See Wire, *The Corinthian Women Prophets*, 10.

56. For one such instance of the reuse of the Bible in the colonial contact zone, see Bhabha, "Signs Taken for Wonders: Questions of Ambivalence and Authority under a Tree outside Delhi, May 1817," in *The Location of Culture*, 102–22. Indeed, Bhabha's (at least) cursory interest in the colonial resignification of the authoritative uses of the Bible might explain some of the interest biblical scholars have shown in his work. See, for example, Moore's reflections on this particular anecdote in Moore, "Questions of Biblical Ambivalence," 85–93.

57. See Rey Chow, "Where Have All the Natives Gone?" in *Feminist Postcolonial Theory: A Reader*, ed. Reina Lewis and Sara Mills (London: Routledge, 2003), 324–49, 330. Reprinted from *Displacements: Cultural Identities in Question*, ed. Angelika Bammer (Bloomington: Indiana University Press, 1994), 125–51. Here, Chow is engaging Benita Parry who implements Bhabha to critique Gayatri Chakravorty Spivak's essay, "Can the Subaltern Speak?" in *Marxism and the Interpretation of Culture*, ed. Cary Nelson and Lawrence Grossberg (Urbana: University of Illinois Press, 1988), 271–313. See Parry, "Problems in Current Theories of Colonial Discourse," *Oxford Literary Review* 9:1–2 (1987): 27–58.

58. To continue Chow's incisive argument, "What Bhabha's word 'hybridity' revives, in the masquerade of deconstruction, anti-imperialism and 'difficult' theory, is an old functionalist notion of what a dominant culture permits in the interest of maintaining its own equilibrium." See Chow, "Where Have All the Natives Gone?" 330. In a similar manner, Liew contrasts his use of "colonial mimicry" to Bhabha's definition: "I am using 'mimicry' to refer to a reinscription or a duplication of colonial ideology by the colonized." See Liew, "Tyranny," 13, n. 9. Liew's article also refers to and elaborates upon Chow's earlier work on diaspora. See Chow, *Writing Diaspora: Tactics of Intervention in Contemporary Cultural Studies* (Bloomington: Indiana University Press, 1993).

59. See, particularly, Chow, "Keeping Them in Their Place: Coercive Mimeticism and Cross-Ethnic Representation," in *The Protestant Ethnic*, 95–127.

60. See Chow, "Keeping Them in Their Place," 106. By raising the questions of "What is the genuine import of such openings?" and "Whom do they benefit?" (on the same page), Chow highlights those questions that Judith Butler seems to be repeatedly examining and re-examining in terms of her theories of performativity and parodic resistance. See, for example, Butler, *Gender Trouble*, 142–49; *Bodies That Matter*, 1–16, 121–40, 233–42; *Undoing Gender*, 40–101. This is precisely where a closer engagement with sex/gender/sexuality and the body would help Bhabha and sharpen the work of other postcolonial critics. Earlier in the volume, Chow is also critical of Fredric Jameson's similar failure to ask who gets to create and use stereotypes. See Chow, "Brushes with the-Other-as-Face: Stereotyping and Cross-Ethnic Representation," in *The Protestant Ethnic*, 54–59, and 207n12.

61. See Chow, "Keeping Them in Their Place," 105–6. For reflections on how stereo-type intersects with dynamics of duplication and imitation, see also Chow, "Brushes with the-Other-as-Face," 50–94.

62. See Chow, "Keeping Them in Their Place," 103.

63. Ibid., 103–8.

64. Ibid., 104.

65. See Trinh T. Minh-ha, *Woman, Native, Other: Writing Postcoloniality and Feminism* (Bloomington: Indiana University Press, 1989), 52. Trinh is considerably less sanguine than Bhabha about the possibilities for resistant imitation. The full quote reads: "'Be like *us*.' The goal pursued is the spread of a hegemonic dis-ease. Don't be us, this self-explanatory motto warns. Just be 'like' and bear the chameleon's fate, never infecting *us* but only yourself, spending your days muting, putting on/taking off glasses, trying to please all and always at odds with myself who is no self at all." It is interesting to note that neither Bhabha nor Chow refer to Trinh in either of the works examined here, but Castelli does in her conclusion. See Castelli, *Imitating Paul*, 133–35.

66. See Chow, "Keeping Them in Their Place," 104–6.

67. See ibid., 106–7. Chow explains that Bhabha's form of mimicry "is still, by and large, governed by the white man as the original, with the supposedly important difference that the unsuccessful imitation of the colonized subject is now deemed equally worthy of critical attention." See ibid., 106.

68. Ibid., 107–8. For her development of this concept as it refigures interpellation, see the remainder of the chapter, ibid., 108–27.

69. Ibid., 107.

70. See Frantz Fanon, *Black Skin, White Masks*, trans. Charles Lam Markmann (New York: Grove, 1967 [1952]), 10, 228.

71. This concept could be echoing Butler's comments that "the notion of gender parody defended here does not assume that there is an original which such parodic identities imitate. Indeed, the parody is *of* the very notion of an original . . . so gender parody reveals that the original identity after which gender fashions itself is an imitation without an origin." See Butler, *Gender Trouble*, 138.

72. See Chow, "Keeping Them in Their Place," 107.

73. Ibid., 104.

74. For Chow's reflections on the term "woman" as it is configured relative to "ethnicity," see Chow, "When Whiteness Feminizes . . . : Some Consequences of a Supplementary Logic," in *The Protestant Ethnic*, 153–82.

75. See Buell and Johnson Hodge, "The Politics of Interpretation: The Rhetoric of Race and Ethnicity in Paul," *JBL* 123, no. 2 (2004): 235–51. Buell coined the term "ethnic reasoning" "to refer to the set of discursive strategies whereby ancient authors construe collective identity in terms of peoplehood." See Buell, "Rethinking the Relevance of Race for Early Christian Self-Definition," *HTR* 94 (2001): 451; "Race and Universalism in Early Christianity," *JECS* 10 (2002): 432–41.

76. See Buell and Johnson Hodge, "The Politics of Interpretation," 236–38. For Chow's elucidation of the simultaneous understanding of ethnicity as universal

(something everyone has/is) and particular/local (something only others or foreigners have/are), see Chow, "The Protestant Ethnic and the Spirit of Capitalism," in *The Protestant Ethnic*, 19–49.

77. See Buell and Johnson Hodge, "The Politics of Interpretation," 244. On this particular strategy, they also refer to Jonathan M. Hall, *Ethnic Identity in Greek Antiquity* (Cambridge: Cambridge University Press, 1997), 47. In a similar manner, Liew points out that Mark's own colonial mimicry maintains absolutized structures of exclusive authority for Jesus and of binary insider-outsider characterizations. See Liew, "Tyranny," 13–23.

78. If Paul is developing an argument for "an imagined political community" in Philippi (and elsewhere), his efforts fit with Benedict Anderson's analysis of how nations are created. See Benedict Anderson, *Imagined Communities: Reflections on the Origins and Spread of Nationalism* (London: Verso, 1983), 6. See also Terry Eagleton, Jameson, and Edward W. Said, *Nationalism, Colonialism, and Literature* (Minneapolis: University of Minnesota Press, 1990). For reflections on the gendered aspects of nationalist readings of scriptures, see Jean K. Kim, *Woman and Nation: An Intercontextual Reading of the Gospel of John from a Postcolonial Feminist Perspective* (Boston: Brill, 2004).

79. See Chow, "Keeping Them in Their Place," 103.

80. On the combination of hierarchy with unity rhetorics, see below and also Marchal, *Hierarchy, Unity, and Imitation*; Buell and Johnson Hodge, "The Politics of Interpretation," 250.

81. See Buell and Johnson Hodge, "The Politics of Interpretation," 249. For a different conception of Paul's efforts at "ethnic reconstruction," see Sze-Kar Wan, "Collection for the Saints as Anticolonial Act: Implications of Paul's Ethnic Reconstruction," in *Paul and Politics*, 191–215.

82. Dube's work has analyzed how collaboration leads colonized peoples to fight against each other. Whereas this study focuses on such possibilities within communities that know Paul (or between Paul and them), Dube refers to the internal divisions of various competing interest groups in Roman Palestine. See Dube, *Postcolonial Feminist Interpretation*, 51–52. Furthermore, Dube argues that Matthew is an example of "a collaborative postcolonial narrative that arises from among the colonized but that deflects the focus from the root cause of oppression, the imperialists, and focuses instead on other victims." See Dube, *Postcolonial Feminist Interpretation*, 135.

83. On the phenomenon, see especially Shawn Kelley, *Racializing Jesus: Race, Ideology and the Formation of Modern Biblical Scholarship* (London: Routledge, 2002).

84. To their credit, Buell and Johnson Hodge note (though only briefly) the "highly gendered" tenor of Paul's ethnic reasoning. See Buell and Johnson Hodge, "The Politics of Interpretation," 246, n. 39.

85. McClintock writes: "The ironically generic 'Man' in Bhabha's title ("Of Mimicry and Man") both conceals and reveals that Bhabha is really only talking about men. By eliding gender difference, however, Bhabha implicitly ratifies gender power, so that masculinity becomes the invisible norm of postcolonial discourse." See Anne McClintock, *Imperial Leather: Race, Gender and Sexuality in the Colonial Conquest* (New York: Routledge, 1995), 64–65.

86. See Kwok, *Postcolonial Imagination*, 80–81; Dube, *Postcolonial Feminist Interpretation*, 112.

87. See Meyda Yeğenoğlu, "Veiled Fantasies: Cultural and Sexual Difference in the Discourse of Orientalism," in *Feminist Postcolonial Theory*, 542–66. Reprinted from Yeğenoğlu's monograph, *Colonial Fantasies: Towards a Feminist Reading of Orientalism* (Cambridge: Cambridge University Press, 1998), 39–67.

88. See Fanon, *A Dying Colonialism*, trans. Haakon Chevalier (New York: Grove, 1965), 37–38; as quoted in Yeğenoğlu, "Veiled Fantasies," 543.

89. See Yeğenoğlu, "Veiled Fantasies," 545. For the variance and valence of Muslim readings of veiling practices, see for example, Leila Ahmed, *Women and Gender in Islam: Historical Roots of a Modern Debate* (New Haven: Yale University Press, 1992), 144–68; Asma Barlas, *"Believing Women" in Islam: Unreading Patriarchal Interpretations of the Qur'an* (Austin: University of Texas Press, 2002), 26–27, 31, 53–58, 124, 158–66. See also Yeğenoğlu, "Sartorial Fabric-ations: Enlightenment and Western Feminism," *Postcolonialism, Feminism, and Religious Discourse*, ed. Laura E. Donaldson and Kwok Pui-lan (New York: Routledge, 2002), 82–99. Portions reprinted from Yeğenoğlu, *Colonial Fantasies*.

90. See Yeğenoğlu, "Veiled Fantasies," 548–52. Yeğenoğlu builds upon Joan Riviere's critique of Western (more specifically Nietzschean) views of women as masquerade. See Riviere, "Womanliness as Masquerade," *Formations of Fantasy*, ed. Victor Burgin, James Donald, and Cora Kaplan (London: Methuen, 1986), 35–44.

91. See Yeğenoğlu, "Veiled Fantasies," 556.

92. See ibid., 554.

93. See ibid., 557–58; Fanon, *A Dying Colonialism*, 44; and Malek Alloula, *The Colonial Harem*, trans. Myrna and Wlad Godzich (Minneapolis: University of Minnesota Press, 1986), 7.

94. See Yeğenoğlu, "Veiled Fantasies," 557.

95. See Luce Irigaray, *Speculum of the Other Woman*, trans. Gillian C. Gill (Ithaca: Cornell University Press, 1985); *This Sex Which Is Not One*, trans. Catherine Porter (Ithaca: Cornell University Press, 1985).

96. See, for example, Irigaray, *This Sex*, 76. Once more, the question must be asked how different Bhabha's analysis might have been if he had chosen to significantly engage with either Irigaray's or Butler's work on mimicry, performativity, subversion, or parody. Whereas there is one slight reference to Butler toward the end of *The Location of Culture* (219), there are none to Irigaray, whose work was available in French in the 1970s and in English by the early 1980s. Indeed, Irigaray's work was so controversial and debated that a key volume about the utility of her work was published in the same year as Bhabha's collection. See *Engaging with Irigaray: Feminist Philosophy and Modern European Thought*, ed. Carolyn Burke, Naomi Schor, and Margaret Whitford (New York: Columbia University Press, 1994).

97. See Yeğenoğlu, "Veiled Fantasies," 559.

98. See ibid.

99. See ibid., 559–60. Yeğenoğlu argues that "what the colonial gaze saw in the Algerian women's disturbing mimicry was a displacement of its own representation of the

veil." See Yeğenoğlu, "Veiling Fantasies," 559. In response to Bhabha, Reina Lewis and Sara Mills also observe that only certain conditions facilitate a counterinsurgent practice of mimicry. See Lewis and Mills, "Introduction," in *Feminist Postcolonial Theory*, 3. For further concerns about Bhabha's (and others') emphasis on psychoanalytic concepts to the detriment of materialist analysis, see Sara Mills, "Gender and Colonial Space," in *Feminist Rhetorical Theory*, 692–719, 693–97. Reprinted from *Gender, Space and Culture* 3, no. 2 (1996): 125–47. On the need for critical reflection in feminist examinations of experience and ethical evaluation, see Elisabeth Schüssler Fiorenza, *Rhetoric and Ethic: The Politics of Biblical Studies* (Minneapolis: Fortress, 1999), 49–51; *Wisdom Ways: Introducing Feminist Biblical Interpretation* (Maryknoll: Orbis, 2001), 169–72, 177–79.

100. See Yeğenoğlu, "Veiled Fantasies," 560.

101. See McClintock, *Imperial Leather*, 15.

102. McClintock comments, at length: "But if mimicry always displays a slippage between identity and difference, doesn't one need to elaborate how colonial mimicry differs from anti-colonial mimicry; if colonial and anti-colonial mimicry are formally identical in their founding ambivalence, why did colonial mimicry succeed for so long?" Continuing on the opposite page, McClintock questions, "Above all, how does one explain how dominant powers become dominant in the first place?" See McClintock, *Imperial Leather*, 64–65.

103. See McClintock, *Imperial Leather*, 5.

104. See ibid., 64.

105. See, for example, McClintock's introduction, subtitled "Postcolonialism and the Angel of Progress," or other sections of the work, such as those labeled "Panoptical Time," "Anachronistic Space," "Degeneration: A Triangulated Discourse," or "Degeneration and the Family Tree," in *Imperial Leather*, 1–17, 36–42, 46–51.

106. See McClintock, *Imperial Leather*, 66.

107. See ibid., 67–68.

108. See ibid., 65.

109. See ibid., 64.

110. See ibid., 62.

111. See ibid., 7. See also Kwok, *Postcolonial Imagination*, 66.

112. On these "porno-tropics," see McClintock, "The Lay of the Land: Genealogies of Imperialism," in *Imperial Leather*, 21–24; and Laura E. Donaldson, "The Breasts of Columbus: A Political Anatomy of Postcolonialism and Feminist Religious Discourse," in *Postcolonialism, Feminism, and Religious Discourse*, 41–61.

113. See Kipling, *Kim* (London; Penguin, 1987); and McClintock's analysis in *Imperial Leather*, 66–71.

114. See McClintock, *Imperial Leather*, 70.

115. See ibid.

116. See Spivak, *A Critique of Postcolonial Reason: Toward a History of the Vanishing Present* (Cambridge: Harvard University Press, 1999), xii (though it is a concern throughout this work, see especially 157, 187, 353–58, 397–400).

117. See McClintock, *Imperial Leather*, 42–51.

118. See ibid., 45.

119. See ibid., 41–42, 353–57. For the particular ways women have been figured in nationalist discourses as reproducers, signifiers, and transmitters of ethnic boundaries or difference, see Nira Yuval-Davis and Floya Anthias, eds., *Woman-Nation-State* (Hampshire: MacMillan, 1989), 7–10. The politics and practices of mimicry are not limited to these, or to biblical scholars', concerns. In a related argument, Uma Narayan charts how third world subjects (often third-world feminists) are asked to mime very specific, constricted roles as emissary, mirror, or insider for Western academic contexts. See Narayan, "Through the Looking-Glass Darkly: Emissaries, Mirrors, and Authentic Insiders as Preoccupations," in *Dislocating Cultures: Identities, Traditions, and Third World Feminism* (New York: Routledge, 1997), 119–57.

120. See McClintock, *Imperial Leather*, 365–68; Fanon, *A Dying Colonialism*, 48–58.

121. See Fanon, *A Dying Colonialism*, 58; McClintock, *Imperial Leather*, 366.

122. See McClintock, *Imperial Leather*, 45, 357.

123. In a similar fashion, see also McClintock's critique of Marjorie Garber's universalization of all transvestism as representing crisis and disruption, in *Imperial Leather*, 67–69, 174–76, 200–202. Garber's work is *Vested Interests: Cross-Dressing and Cultural Authority* (New York: Routledge, 1992).

124. See McClintock, *Imperial Leather*, 175.

125. Kwok highlights the limitations of any liberal paradigm of cultural diversity that prizes the idea of including many voices and perspectives, when it does not confront the dominant white culture. The question of how these multiple people or possibilities are included raises issues of who "sets the table." See Kwok, *Postcolonial Imagination*, 42.

126. Schüssler Fiorenza's neologism "kyriarchy," for example, highlights how multiple and mutually influential structures of domination and subordination function together, evident not only in sexism, but also in racism, classism, ethnocentrism, heterosexism, colonialism, nationalism, and militarism. For an introductory explanation of this definition and discussion of its use for a feminist, postcolonial analysis, see the introductory chapter (especially the section on Starting Points and Parameters).

127. On the basis of the description of Euodia and Syntyche as "co-workers" and "those who struggled with me in the gospel" in 4:3, many scholars argue for their prominence and possible leadership roles in the community. For further considerations of their roles, see Lillian Portefaix, *Sisters Rejoice: Paul's Letter to the Philippians and Luke-Acts as Received by First-Century Philippian Women* (Stockholm: Almqvist & Wiksell, 1988), 135–54; Mary Rose D'Angelo, "Women Partners in the New Testament," *JFSR* 6 (1990): 65–86; Wendy Cotter, "Women's Authority Roles in Paul's Churches: Countercultural or Conventional?" *NovT* 36 (1994): 350–72; Nils A. Dahl, "Euodia and Syntyche and Paul's Letter to the Philippians," in *The Social World of the First Christians: Essays in Honor of Wayne A. Meeks*, ed. L. Michael White and O. Larry Yarbrough (Minneapolis: Fortress Press, 1995), 3–15; Kittredge, *Community*, 90–94, 105–10.

128. See Schüssler Fiorenza, *Wisdom Ways*, 185. See also Schüssler Fiorenza, *Rhetoric and Ethic*, 51–52. Dube, in fact, suggests that feminist analyses should also begin to focus more often on texts that do not feature women, because "gender constructions pervade

all social spheres of life." See Dube, "Rahab Says Hello to Judith: A Decolonizing Feminist Reading," in *Toward a New Heaven and a New Earth: Essays in Honor of Elisabeth Schüssler Fiorenza*, ed. Fernando F. Segovia (Maryknoll: Orbis, 2003), 54–72, 60.

129. See, for example, Edgar M. Krentz, "Military Language and Metaphors in Philippians," in *Origins and Method: Towards a New Understanding of Judaism and Christianity; Essays in Honour of John C. Hurd*, ed. Bradley H. McLean (Sheffield: Sheffield Academic, 1993), 105–27; Timothy C. Geoffrion, *The Rhetorical Purpose and the Political and Military Character of Philippians* (Lewiston: Mellen, 1993); Krentz, "Paul, Games, and the Military," in *Paul in the Greco-Roman World: A Handbook*, ed. J. Paul Sampley (Harrisburg: Trinity Press International, 2003), 344–83; and Jennifer Bird, "Paul Wants You! A Re-Interpretation of the Letter to the Philippians" (presentation at the international meeting of the Society of Biblical Literature, Edinburgh, Scotland, July 2006). For a summary and assessment of these rhetorics and the scholarly examination of them, see Marchal "Military Images"; and *Hierarchy, Unity, and Imitation*, 29–34, 50–72.

130. On the theme of absence and presence in military situations, see Krentz, "Military Language," 119; "Paul," 355.

131. On the military resonance of this Greek term (*synēthlēsan*), see Portefaix, *Sisters*, 141; Geoffrion, *Rhetorical Purpose*, 209–10; Krentz, "Paul," 362.

132. The argument is asking not for unity between Euodia and Syntyche (as most scholars still assume), but for the two women's conformity with and imitation of Paul. Most scholars reinscribe Paul's authoritative status and thus assume that Euodia and Syntyche could not have been in conflict with Paul. See, among the most recent examples, Bockmuehl, *Epistles*, 238–42; Gordon D. Fee, *Philippians* (Downers Grove: Intervarsity, 1999), 167–71; Paul A. Holloway, *Consolation in Philippians: Philosophical Sources and Rhetorical Strategy* (Cambridge: Cambridge University Press, 2001), 146–48; Peter S. Oakes, *Philippians: From People to Letter* (Cambridge: Cambridge University Press, 2001), 114, 123–24; Carolyn L. Osiek, *Philippians, Philemon* (Nashville: Abingdon, 2000), 110–13; and Davorin Peterlin, *Paul's Letter to the Philippians in the Light of Disunity in the Church* (Leiden: Brill, 1995), 101–32. As on previous occasions, Kittredge's argument that Euodia and Syntyche are not in a conflict with each other but with Paul is unique and convincing. See Kittredge, *Community and Authority*, 105–8; and, now, Marchal, *Hierarchy, Unity and Imitation*, 147–52; "Military Images"; and "With Friends like These."

133. For further arguments that Pauline community language (including the body of Christ and brothers/*adelphoi*) is androcentric, see Jorunn Økland, *Women In Their Place: Paul and the Corinthian Discourse of Gender and Sanctuary Space* (London: T&T Clark International, 2005), 211–17.

134. Given the shared intimacy of both familial and patronal expressions, scholars would do well to reconsider patronage in light of these pluriform, imperial dynamics. On patronage and friendship in this letter and the Roman imperial context, see John T. Fitzgerald, "Paul and Friendship," in *Paul in the Greco-Roman World*, 319–43; and Marchal, "With Friends like These."

135. For further reflections, akin to McClintock's and Yeğenoğlu's, on the attribution of sexual perversity to the outsider and colonized people as an imperial rationale, see

Said, *Orientalism*, rev. ed. (New York: Vintage, 1994 [1978]), as well as Jennifer Wright Knust, "Paul and the Politics of Virtue and Vice," in *Paul and the Roman Imperial Order*, 155–74; and *Abandoned to Lust: Sexual Slander and Ancient Christianity* (New York: Columbia University Press, 2005). See also the reflections of Jean K. Kim on the placement of responsibilities for (re)production on maternal figures in *Woman and Nation*, 61–89, 169–94.

136. See Mary Rose D'Angelo, "Abba and 'Father': Imperial Theology and the Traditions about Jesus," *JBL* 111 (1992): 611–30; D'Angelo, "Early Christian Sexual Politics and Roman Imperial Family Values: Rereading Christ and Culture," in *The Papers of the Henry Luce III Fellows in Theology*, ed. Christopher I. Wilkins (Pittsburgh: Association of Theological Schools, 2003), 6:23–48.

137. See McClintock, *Imperial Leather*, 70.

138. See Fanon, *A Dying Colonialism*, trans. Haakon Chevalier (New York: Grove, 1965), 37–38; as quoted in Yeğenoğlu, "Veiled Fantasies," 543.

139. See, for example, Dube, *Postcolonial Feminist Interpretation*, 23–43; Kwok, *Postcolonial Imagination*, 18, 49.

140. For the advocates of an anti-imperial Paul, see most of the entries in the volumes edited by Horsley. For a range of feminist responses to these, see the following entries in the *Paul and Politics* volume: Schüssler Fiorenza, "Paul and the Politics of Interpretation" (40–57), Kittredge, "Corinthian Women Prophets and Paul's Argumentation in 1 Corinthians" (103–9), Sheila Briggs, "Paul on Bondage and Freedom in Imperial Roman Society" (110–23), and Wire, "Response: The Politics of the Assembly in Corinth" (124–29), and "Response: Paul and Those outside Power" (224–26). For further analysis of both, see the two preceding chapters.

141. See, for example, Dube, "Rahab Says Hello," 68.

142. See Fanon, *A Dying Colonialism*, 58; McClintock, *Imperial Leather*, 366.

143. This raises the possibility that the distance between the communities (in Corinth, or Philippi, or others) and Paul could have functioned similarly to the dynamics of veiling described by Yeğenoğlu. Paul writes to try to make the audience members' actions transparent to his gaze; however, upon reception of the letter, the audience "sees" what Paul has to say, but Paul cannot easily "see" what their responses are. Like the veiled Algerian women, the audience members can see without being seen.

4. Women in the Contact Zone

1. Kwok Pui-lan, *Postcolonial Imagination and Feminist Theology* (Louisville: Westminster John Knox, 2005), 82.

2. These concerns run throughout Musa Dube's various works, but most notably in Dube, *Postcolonial Feminist Interpretation of the Bible* (St. Louis: Chalice, 2000), particularly 57–58, 65–70, 92, 105, 115. For further reflections on borders, space, placement, and travel, see the volumes *Interpreting beyond Borders*, ed. Fernando F. Segovia (Sheffield: Sheffield Academic, 2000); and *John and Postcolonialism: Travel, Space and Power*, ed. Dube and Jeffrey L. Staley (New York: Sheffield Academic, 2002).

3. For a repetitive focus on the interrelated manner in which colonial-era arguments mutually construct these categories, see Inderpal Grewal, *Home and Harem: Nation, Gender, Empire, and the Cultures of Travel* (Durham: Duke University Press, 1996). For critical transnational feminist reflections on concepts of "home," see Chandra Talpade Mohanty, with Biddy Martin, "What's Home Got to Do with It?" in *Feminism without Borders: Decolonizing Theory, Practicing Solidarity* (Durham: Duke University Press, 2003), 85–105, 260–61.

4. Mary Louise Pratt, *Imperial Eyes: Travel Writing and Transculturation* (London: Routledge, 1992), 4.

5. Ibid., 6.

6. Ibid.

7. Ibid., 7.

8. On the possibilities for finding hints of others' views of space within the colonizer's texts, see Sara Mills, *Gender and Colonial Space* (Manchester: Manchester University Press, 2005), 136–57.

9. Grewal, *Home and Harem*, 1–20.

10. For this point, see especially Grewal, *Home and Harem*, 4.

11. Ibid. For the continuing relevance of Pratt's concept of the contact zone in postcolonial feminist work, see, for example, Mills, *Gender and Colonial Space*, 34–38.

12. For the use of such a strategy in biblical studies and historical approaches, in general, see the overview of issues for the history of interpretation (in chapter 1) and the references to the work of Elisabeth Schüssler Fiorenza and Joan W. Scott. For its use within postcolonial feminist studies (or analyses of women in colonial discourse), see Jenny Sharpe, *Allegories of Empire: The Figure of Woman in the Colonial Text* (Minneapolis: University of Minnesota Press, 1993), 17; and Mills, *Gender and Colonial Space*, 143.

13. Gayatri Chakravorty Spivak, "Can the Subaltern Speak?" in *Marxism and the Interpretation of Culture*, ed. Cary Nelson and Lawrence Grossberg (Urbana: University of Illinois Press, 1988), 271–313, esp. 292. See also its citation in Mills, *Gender and Colonial Space*, 146. Mills elaborates on this issue further: "White theorists working within post-colonial theory need to be very aware of their motivations for analysing colonial texts, perhaps to the point of analysing the extent to which they are trying to construct their academic selves as beyond reproach or criticism of racism." See Mills, *Gender and Colonial Space*, 157.

14. For extensive reflections on the significance of social location in the fields of biblical interpretation, see Fernando F. Segovia and Mary Ann Tolbert, eds., *Reading from This Place*, 2 vols. (Minneapolis: Fortress Press, 1995).

15. Pratt, *Imperial Eyes*, 213.

16. Laura E. Donaldson, "Gospel Hauntings: The Postcolonial Demons of New Testament Criticism," in *Postcolonial Biblical Criticism: Interdisciplinary Intersections*, ed. Stephen D. Moore and Fernando F. Segovia (London: T&T Clark International, 2005), 97–113. On this point (especially on page 102), Spivak is again being summarized and/or redeployed. See Spivak, *A Critique of Postcolonial Reason: Toward a History of the Vanishing Present* (Cambridge: Harvard University Press, 1999), 191.

17. On the ethical-political grounds of feminist rhetorical and historical studies of the Bible, see Schüssler Fiorenza, *Rhetoric and Ethic: The Politics of Biblical Studies* (Minneapolis: Fortress Press, 1999), especially 17–81.

18. Ibid., 52.

19. Mills, *Gender and Colonial Space*, 19.

20. Pratt borrows and re-situates this ethnographic concept that is meant "to describe how subordinated or marginal groups select and invent from materials transmitted to them by a dominant or metropolitan culture." See Pratt, *Imperial Eyes*, 6. According to Pratt, transculturation was coined by Fernando Ortiz as early as the 1940s. See Ortiz, *Contrapunto Cubano* (Caracas: Biblioteca Ayacucho, 1978).

21. Pratt, *Imperial Eyes*, 4–7. See also the point Grewal makes in *Home and Harem*, 9, as well as the structure of the work as a whole (Part I: English Imperial Culture; Part II: Euroimperial Travel and Indian Women), focusing on those who move in, to, and from both England and India.

22. See, for example, Spivak, *A Critique of Postcolonial Reason*, as well as Grewal's particular concerns with celebratory conceptions of the colonial hybrid or mime, in *Home and Harem*, 3, 16–17, 179–229. See also the qualification in the previous chapter of Bhabha's work by Rey Chow, Meyda Yeğenoğlu, and Anne McClintock.

23. For feminist and anticolonial or postcolonial studies on the life and work of Mary Kingsley, see Sara Mills, *Discourses of Difference: An Analysis of Women's Travel Writing and Colonialism* (London: Routledge, 1991), especially 153–74; Pratt, *Imperial Eyes*, 201–27; and Alison Blunt, *Travel, Gender, and Imperialism: Mary Kingsley and West Africa* (New York: Guilford, 1994).

24. The main sources of information provided by Kingsley to the imperial audience were her *Travels in West Africa: Congo Français, Corisco and Cameroons* (London: Macmillan, 1987; London: Virago, 1986); *West African Studies* (London: Macmillan, 1899); and *The Story of West Africa* (London: Horace Marshall, 1900).

25. On the Thasian and Macedonian colonizations of Philippi, see Herodotus, 7.112; Appian, *BC* 4.105; Diodorus Siculus 11.70.5; 12.68.1-3; 16.3.7; 16.8.6-7; Paul Collart, *Philippes: Villes de Macédoine: depuis ses origins jusqu'à la fin de l'époque romaine* (École Française d'Athènes: Paris, 1937), 54, 68–85, 133–60, 258; Holland L. Hendrix, "Philippi," in *Anchor Bible Dictionary*, ed. David N. Freedman (New York, 1992), 5:314; Lilian Portefaix, *Sisters Rejoice: Paul's Letter to the Philippians and Luke-Acts as Received by First-Century Philippian Women* (Stockholm: Almqvist & Wiksell, 1988), 59–60; Craig S. de Vos, *Church and Community Conflicts: The Relationships of the Thessalonian, Corinthian, and Philippian Churches with Their Wider Civic Communities* (Atlanta: Scholars, 1999), 234–35; Chaido Koukouli-Chrysantaki, "Colonia Iulia Augusta Philippensis," in *Philippi at the Time of Paul and after His Death*, ed. Charalambos Bakirtzis and Helmut Koester (Harrisburg: Trinity Press International, 1998), 5–7; Peter S. Oakes, *Philippians: From People to Letter* (Cambridge: Cambridge University Press, 2001), 12. On the battle of Philippi and the initial Roman settlement, see Strabo 7.331 (frag. 41); Pliny 4.42; Collart, *Philippes*, 227; Portefaix, *Sisters Rejoice*, 60; Koukouli-Chrysantaki, "Colonia," 5–35, 8; Craig S. de Vos, *Church and Community Conflicts*, 234; Oakes, *Philippians*, 13. For further reflections on this history, see Joseph

A. Marchal, "Military Images in Philippians 1–2: A Feminist Rhetorical Analysis of Scholarship, Philippians, and Current Contexts," in *Her Master's Tools? Feminist and Postcolonial Engagements of Historical-Critical Discourse,* ed. Caroline Vander Stichele and Todd Penner (Atlanta: Society of Biblical Literature, 2005), 265–86; and *Hierarchy, Unity, and Imitation: A Feminist Rhetorical Analysis of Power Dynamics in Paul's Letter to the Philippians,* Academia Biblica 24 (Atlanta: Society of Biblical Literature; Leiden: Brill, 2006).

26. Tat-siong Benny Liew and Vincent L. Wimbush, "Contact Zones and Zoning Contexts: From the Los Angeles 'Riot' to a New York Symposium," *USQR* 56 (2003): 21–40.

27. See Oakes, *Philippians*; Marchal, "Military Images" and *Hierarchy, Unity, and Imitation,* 99–112. The potential irony of this scholarly trend of seeing progress or benefit and its (potentially complicit) analogues in recent military-imperial beliefs that invasion and occupation should be greeted as "liberation" are striking.

28. In Oakes's terms, there was a "double land-loss," "first by Greek and then by many of the poorer Roman colonists." See Oakes, *Philippians,* 49.

29. Oakes, *Philippians,* 73–74. On the Thracians, see Hendrix, "Philippi," 313–17, 314; De Vos, *Church and Community Conflicts,* 240, 243; Oakes, *Philippians,* 30, 73. Oakes argues that as the years pass, the Thasian and Macedonian colonizers became indistinguishable from each other, which is why he uses the more general term "Greeks" for them. Eventually in his study, Oakes adopts "Greeks" as a term for all residents in the colony that are clearly not Roman, including Thracians and later Greek-speaking arrivals. See Oakes, *Philippians,* 12, 18, 73–74.

30. On the inscriptions, see for example, Collart, *Philippes,* 315; Peter Pilhofer, *Philippi I: Die erste christliche Gemeinde Europas* (Tübingen: J. C. B. Mohr, 1995), 92. For claims about the "Roman-ness" of the population, see Lukas Bormann, *Philippi: Stadt und Christengemeinde zur Zeit des Paulus* (Leiden: Brill, 1995), 52. Nevertheless, these do not demonstrate that Romans were in the majority in Philippi, or that the majority somehow benefited from Roman colonization. See De Vos, *Church and Community Conflicts,* 242–47; Oakes, *Philippians,* 35; Marchal, *Hierarchy, Unity, and Imitation,* 99–112.

31. As de Vos points out for Philippi, "Like other Roman *coloniae,* the average citizen would have had limited political power given the strongly hierarchical and oligarchic system." De Vos, *Church and Community Conflicts,* 247. For the social-political relations in Roman colonies and Philippi specifically, see de Vos, *Church and Community Conflicts,* 110–15, 245–47.

32. For some of the recent debates on how to measure and delineate poverty in Pauline studies, see the exchange between Steven J. Friesen, "Poverty in Pauline Studies: Beyond the So-Called New Consensus," John Barclay, "Poverty in Pauline Studies: A Response to Steven Friesen," and Peter Oakes, "Constructing Poverty Scales for Graeco-Roman Society: A Response to Steven Friesen's 'Poverty in Pauline Studies,'" all in the *Journal for the Study of the New Testament* 26, no. 3 (March 2004): 323–61, 363–66, 367–71.

33. Oakes estimates that around 20 percent of Philippi's first century population was enslaved. Oakes also chooses to differentiate between the impoverished majority

(subsistence) and the "poor" as those who are regularly and unhealthily below subsistence level, which he also estimates at 20 percent. See *Philippians*, 17, 49–50. Although de Vos takes issue with many of Oakes's precisely enumerated figures for the make-up of Philippi (and the community to which the letter was written), most of his observations about the population of the colony do not significantly contradict the general trajectory of Oakes's evaluations. See de Vos, *Church and Community Conflicts*, 240–44. For the dynamics of slavery in the Roman world, the Pauline letters, and biblical interpretation in general, see the special issue of *Semeia* 83/84 (1998), edited by Allen Dwight Callahan, Richard A. Horsley, and Abraham Smith, *Slavery in Text and Interpretation*.

34. On women's doubled or tripled colonization, see Dube, *Postcolonial Feminist Interpretation of the Bible*, 113–23, 174, 184, 201.

35. For brief reflections upon the problematics of Paul's "mission to the Gentiles," see Dube, Kwok, and previous chapters. Paul's claims to be the apostle to the Gentiles have significant connections to colonizers' claims to a protective mission, as with Daisy Bates's title of "Protector of the Aborigines." See Mills, *Gender and Colonial Space*, 143; and Kay Schaffer, *Women and the Bush: Forces of Desire in the Australian Cultural Tradition* (Cambridge: Cambridge University Press, 1988).

36. For further, yet rather different reflections on Paul's imprisonment, see Efraín Agosto, "Paul vs. Empire: A Postcolonial and Latino Reading of Philippians," *Perspectivas: Occasional Papers* 6 (Fall 2002): 43–46, 48, 50–51; Craig S. Wansink, *Chained in Christ: The Experience and Rhetoric of Paul's Imprisonment* (Sheffield: Sheffield Academic, 1996); and Richard J. Cassidy, *Paul in Chains: Roman Imprisonment and the Letters of Paul* (New York: Crossroad, 2001).

37. Paul's exemplary character is also stressed by his ability to move forward in space and time towards the appropriate goal (in 3:13–14). These kinds of moves, alongside the recurrent references to Paul's *parousia*, were considered in greater depth in chapter 2 above.

38. For further reflections on this pattern in Paul's argumentation in both 1 Corinthians and Philippians, see Wire, *The Corinthian Women Prophets: A Reconstruction through Paul's Rhetoric* (Minneapolis: Fortress Press, 1990), 58–71; Marchal, *Hierarchy, Unity, and Imitation*, 142–43, 171–73, 185–86, 199–200.

39. See especially Pratt, *Imperial Eyes*, 38–85; Sara Mills, *Discourses of Difference*, 125–94.

40. See, for example, Edgar M. Krentz, "Military Language and Metaphors in Philippians," in *Origins and Method: Towards a New Understanding of Judaism and Christianity; Essays in Honour of John C. Hurd*, ed. Bradley H. McLean (Sheffield: Sheffield Academic, 1993), 105–27; Timothy C. Geoffrion, *The Rhetorical Purpose and the Political and Military Character of Philippians* (Lewiston: Mellen, 1993); Krentz, "Paul, Games, and the Military," in *Paul in the Greco-Roman World: A Handbook*, ed. J. Paul Sampley (Harrisburg: Trinity Press International, 2003): 344–83; and Jennifer Bird, "Paul Wants You! A Re-Interpretation of the Letter to the Philippians" (presentation at the international meeting of the Society of Biblical Literature, Edinburgh, Scotland, July 2006). For a summary and assessment of these rhetorics and the scholarly examination of them, see Marchal "Military Images;" and *Hierarchy, Unity, and Imitation*, 29–34, 50–72.

41. Here Paul seems to take on another role exercised in colonial-imperial rule, that of the social engineer (even if the claims are that it is "for the good" of the subjects, as often claimed by "social progress" or reformist apologists for empire). See, for example, Pratt, *Imperial Eyes*, 155–71.

42. In the context of British imperial presence in India, for example, the colonial presence was bolstered by an ideology of separation that developed along the "fears" of sexualized intermingling and the supposed need to protect white women's purity. At the same time, the desire for separation by indigenous populations (seen roundly as oppressive from the perspective of Western imperial eyes) is likely better explained in terms of the legitimate fears of violence against women enacted by militarized groups of colonizers. See the striking analysis of accounts of sexual assault in Sharpe, *Allegories of Empire*, 1–24.

43. See here, especially, Mills, "Gender and Colonial Space," in *Feminist Postcolonial Theory: A Reader*, ed. Reina Lewis and Mills (New York: Routledge, 2003), 692–719 (707); reprinted from *Gender, Space and Culture* 3, no. 2 (1996): 125–47.

44. Jorunn Økland, *Women In Their Place: Paul and the Corinthian Discourse of Gender and Sanctuary Space* (London: T&T Clark International, 2005), 39–77. In the analysis of this dynamic, Økland builds upon the observations of historian Yvonne Hirdman. See especially Økland, *Women in Their Place*, 59; and Hirdman, *Genussystemet—teoretiska funderingar kring kvinnors sociala underordning* (Uppsala: Maktutredningen, 1988).

45. Økland, *Women in Their Place*, 67–71; Mills, *Gender and Colonial Space*, 31–34, 102–35. See also Partha Chatterjee, *The Nation and Its Fragments: Colonial and Postcolonial Histories* (Princeton: Princeton University Press, 1993), 135–58.

46. Mills, *Gender and Colonial Space*, 132.

47. See, for example, the analysis of Caren Kaplan, *Questions of Travel* (Durham: Duke University Press, 1996).

48. See the arguments in the preceding chapter for this allusion to Frantz Fanon's view of anti-colonial women. See Fanon, *A Dying Colonialism*, trans. Haakon Chevalier (New York: Grove, 1965), 58; Anne McClintock, *Imperial Leather: Race, Gender and Sexuality in the Colonial Conquest* (New York: Routledge, 1995), 366. Furthermore, in projecting such roles onto the other figures named in Paul's letters, while remaining obsessively focused upon the (historical, social, political, rhetorical, or theological) primacy of Paul, many Pauline scholars repeat similar gaps in the construction of colonizing subjects (as travelers) and the colonized as objects (passive and static, staying in place). Grewal's study is dedicated to exposing the acts of erasure this involves by charting Indian women's travels, which are also conditioned by colonial dynamics. See Grewal, *Home and Harem*, 179–229.

49. D'Angelo, "Euodia," in *Women in Scripture: A Dictionary of Named and Unnamed Women in the Hebrew Bible, the Apocryphal/Deuterocanonical Books, and the New Testament*, ed. Carol Meyers, Toni Craven, and Ross S. Kraemer (Grand Rapids: Eerdmans, 2000), 79. See also D'Angelo, "Syntyche," in *Women in Scripture*, 159; and "Women Partners in the New Testament," *JFSR* 6 (1990): 65–86.

50. See, for example, Sara Mills, *Discourses of Difference: An Analysis of Women's Travel Writing and Colonialism* (London: Routledge, 1991); Alison Blunt and Gillian Rose, eds., *Writing Women and Space: Colonial and Postcolonial Geographies* (New York: Guilford, 1994); and Blunt, *Travel, Gender, and Imperialism*. For more on European women's roles in colonialist activities and Orientalist constructions (not only travel writers), see Helen Callaway, *Gender, Culture, and Empire* (Urbana: University of Illinois Press, 1987); Dea Birkett, *Spinsters Abroad* (London: Basil Blackwell, 1989); Margaret Strobel, *European Women and the Second British Empire* (Bloomington: Indiana University Press, 1991); Reina Lewis, *Gendering Orientalism: Race, Femininity and Representation* (London: Routledge, 1996).

51. See, for example, a number of the contributions to *Western Women and Imperialism: Complicity and Resistance*, ed. Nupur Chaudhuri and Margaret Strobel (Bloomington: Indiana University Press, 1992); and *Gender and Imperialism*, ed. Clare Midgley (Manchester: Manchester University Press, 1998). See especially Jane Haggis, "White Women and Colonialism: Towards a Non-Recuperative History," in *Gender and Imperialism*, 45–75. Recall also the point Kwok Pui-lan made (cited above in chapter 1): "Judging from the magnitude of women's participation in mission and the amount of money raised to support such activities, the women's missionary movement must be regarded as the largest women's movement in the nineteenth and early twentieth centuries." See Kwok, *Postcolonial Imagination and Feminist Theology*, 18. For women missionaries, see Barbara N. Ramusack, "Cultural Missionaries, Maternal Imperialists, Feminist Allies: British Women Activists in India, 1865–1945," Leslie A. Flemming, "A New Humanity: American Missionaries' Ideals for Women in North India, 1870–1930," and Sylvia M. Jacobs, "Give a Thought to Africa: Black Women Missionaries in Southern Africa," in *Western Women and Imperialism*, 119–36, 191–206, 207–28.

52. See, for example, Cynthia Briggs Kittredge, *Community and Authority: The Rhetoric of Obedience in the Pauline Tradition* (Harrisburg: Trinity Press International, 1998), 108.

53. On the basis of the description of Euodia and Syntyche as "co-workers" and "those who struggled with me in the gospel" in 4:3, many scholars argue for their prominence and possible leadership roles in the community. For further considerations of their roles, see Portefaix, *Sisters Rejoice*, 135–54; D'Angelo, "Women Partners in the New Testament;" Wendy Cotter, "Women's Authority Roles in Paul's Churches: Countercultural or Conventional?" *NovT* 36 (1994): 350–72; Nils A. Dahl, "Euodia and Syntyche and Paul's Letter to the Philippians" in *The Social World of the First Christians: Essays in Honor of Wayne A. Meeks*, ed. L. Michael White and O. Larry Yarbrough (Minneapolis: Fortress Press, 1995), 3–15; Kittredge, *Community and Authority*, 90–94, 105–10. D'Angelo and Kittredge were among the first to develop this argument in the face of most malestream biblical interpretation of the passage. See Kittredge, *Community and Authority*, 105–8; D'Angelo, "Women Partners"; and, now, Marchal, *Hierarchy, Unity and Imitation*, 147–52; "Military Images"; and "'With Friends like These . . .': A Feminist Rhetorical Reconsideration of Scholarship and the Letter to the Philippians," *Journal for the Study of the New Testament* 29, no. 1 (Sept. 2006): 77–106, as well as the two preceding chapters.

54. For rather more optimistic views of Paul's anti-imperial stance, see the overview and analysis of a number of Pauline interpreters in chapter 2.

55. The exact location of Paul's imprisonment on this occasion is still debated. Yet, no matter how one theorizes this historical point, the dynamics at work in the letter remain similar, if not the same.

56. On the remarkable history of the gender remarking of Junia in biblical interpretation, see Bernadette J. Brooten, "'Junia . . . Outstanding among the Apostles' (Romans 16:7)," in *Women Priests: A Catholic Commentary on the Vatican Declaration*, ed. Leonard and Arlene Swidler (New York: Paulist, 1977), 141–44.

57. As interpreters of this Roman imperial era literature, Pauline scholars should consider not just how such terminology is influenced by this setting, but also how formative colonizing dynamics seem to have been to the development of the entire edifice resulting from this/these movement(s). To the extent one can meaningfully ascribe these traditions as part of the origins of Christianity/ies, scholars must recognize that early Christian movements may not have become (or descended or degraded into) "imperial Christianity," but that the very conditions of its origins make it colonizing from its "start." This would significantly complicate conversations about "the origins" of Christianity (or Judaism(s), for that matter).

58. See Liddell and Scott, *Greek-English Lexicon*, 7th ed. (Oxford: Clarenden, 1996). Though these names could give much-needed clues into the potential roles or backgrounds of these women, scholars of biblical antiquity (Dale B. Martin) and of more contemporary colonial scenes (Spivak) have cautioned about drawing too strong a correlation between etymology and meaning. See Spivak, "Can the Subaltern Speak?" 305–6; and Martin, *"Arsenokoitēs* and *Malakos*: Meanings and Consequences," in *Biblical Ethics & Homosexuality: Listening to Scriptures*, ed. Robert L. Brawley (Louisville: Westminster John Knox, 1996), 117–36.

59. The patronym I bear is likely from the French word *maréchal*, potentially indicating at least my patrilineal descent from either a militarily elevated family or possibly a family of smiths (as in *maréchal-ferrant*, "blacksmith"). As a twenty-first-century American of French and Irish descent, I benefit from the intertwined histories of settler colonization in North America and of extended European colonial efforts in a range of locales. I also remain complicit in a militarized and increasingly decentralized (or globalized) neocolonialism, despite my efforts to oppose such forces. For the once subordinate (as "Celtic Calibans") but now racially elevated status of Irish people (particularly in the United States) and the dependence of such status upon differential relations to various colonial and neocolonial powers, see Anne McClintock, *Imperial Leather*, 52–56; as well as Noel Ignatiev, *How the Irish Became White* (New York: Routledge, 1996); Matthew Frye Jacobson, *Whiteness of a Different Color: European Immigrants and the Alchemy of Race* (Cambridge: Harvard University Press, 1999). For one treatment of the current, globalized form of empire, see Michael Hardt and Antonio Negri, *Empire* (Cambridge: Harvard University Press, 2000).

60. De Vos, *Church and Community Conflicts*, 252–56. The Euodia references are in *New Docs.* 4.178–179; *IG* 5.2.277; and *CJ* 1.391. The third reference describes a Euodia

married to a man of Judean descent, who would have likely been of lower status as well. See de Vos, *Church and Community Conflicts*, 256.

61. Oakes, *Philippians*, 64.

62. Contrary to some of the previous scholarship on Roman-era slavery and the practice of manumission as "more humanitarian," manumitted slaves remained in an obligatory relationship with their "former" masters. Manumission did not undermine slavery, but reinforced it and the social control both institutions sought. For reflections on manumission and its relevance for the interpretation of Paul's letters, see Sheila Briggs, "Paul on Bondage and Freedom in Imperial Roman Society," in *Paul and Politics: Ekklesia, Israel, Imperium, Interpretation; Essays in Honor of Krister Stendahl*, ed. Richard A. Horsley (Harrisburg: Trinity Press International, 2000), 110–23.

63. Community members with such status would also have difficulties (or at least differences) in identifying with a pattern of surrendering status to gain a position (the descend-to-ascend trend repeated in the letter to the Philippians).

64. Markus Bockmuehl reminds us that the KJV rendered Euodia as Euodias. See Bockmuehl, *The Epistle to the Philippians* (London: Hendrickson, 1998), 238. Further back in history, D'Angelo explains that Theodore of Mopsuestia altered Syntyche's name to Syntyches in the late fourth or early fifth century C.E. See D'Angelo, "Syntyche," 159; as well as Brooten, "Junia." It is difficult to discern if these name changes occurred because it was hard to imagine or stomach Paul having so many women co-workers or two women being co-workers together. In either case, both display the tendency for interconnected gender and sexual norms to impinge on biblical interpretation. For further reflections about the nature of Euodia's and Syntyche's partnership, see D'Angelo, "Women Partners."

65. Kittredge, *Community and Authority*, 107.

66. See, for example, Davorin Peterlin, *Paul's Letter to the Philippians in the Light of Disunity in the Church* (Leiden: Brill, 1995), 159–60.

67. De Vos, *Church and Community Conflicts*, 255, 258.

68. For more on the potential tensions between the Roman elites and their subjects, especially as they are tied to resettlement, confiscation, and veterans' concerns in Rome's transformation from republic to empire, see Marchal, *Hierarchy, Unity, and Imitation*, 53–62.

69. Despite her attention to gender in analyzing imperial travel writing, it is indeed striking that Pratt does not include gendered dynamics in her delineation of the "contact zone" concept. This is one of the benefits in considering Grewal's further theorization and contextualization of the term. See the introductory section above.

70. Unlike recent seemingly biologically based gendered differentiations, ancients seemed to have conceived of masculinity as a status that could be exclusively attained only by those enacting the correct practices of gender, sexuality, ethnicity, age, ability, status, and imperial-colonial placement (among others). For more on the ancient rhetorics of masculinity, see Thomas Laqueur, *Making Sex: Body and Gender from the Greeks to Freud* (Cambridge: Harvard University Press, 1990); Maud Gleason, *Making Men: Sophists and Self-Presentation in Ancient Rome* (Princeton: Princeton University Press, 1995); Jonathan Walters, "Invading the Roman Body: Manliness and Impenetrability

in Roman Thought," in *Roman Sexualities*, ed. Judith P. Hallett and Marilyn B. Skinner (Princeton: Princeton University Press, 1997), 29–43; Craig A. Williams, *Roman Homosexuality: Ideologies of Masculinity in Classical Antiquity* (New York: Oxford University Press, 1999); Erik Gunderson, *Staging Masculinity: The Rhetoric of Performance in the Roman World* (Ann Arbor: University of Michigan Press, 2000); and Virginia Burrus, *"Begotten, not Made": Conceiving Manhood in Late Antiquity* (Stanford: Stanford University Press, 2000).

71. See, especially, Dube, *Postcolonial Feminist Interpretation of the Bible*, 118–19.

72. Dube, *Postcolonial Feminist Interpretation of the Bible*, 119. On the Pocahontas perplex as described in postcolonial feminist work, see the work of Rayna Green, "The Pocahontas Perplex: The Image of Indian Women in American Culture," *Massachusetts Review* (Autumn 1975): 698–714; as cited and developed in reflecting on the story of Ruth by Laura E. Donaldson, "The Sign of Orpah: Reading Ruth through Native Eyes," in *Vernacular Hermeneutics*, ed. R. S. Sugirtharajah (Sheffield: Sheffield Academic, 1999), 20–36. For similar dynamics in terms of the characterization of women in the Gospel of John, see also Jean K. Kim, *Woman and Nation: An Intercontextual Reading of the Gospel of John from a Postcolonial Feminist Perspective* (Boston: Brill, 2004). For women as the grounds of contestation in colonial contexts, see also Lata Mani, "Contentious Traditions: The Debate on Sati in Colonial India," in *Recasting Women*, ed. Kum-Kum Sangari and Sudesh Vaid (Delhi: Kali for Women, 1989), 88–126.

73. Økland, *Women In Their Place*; Donaldson, "The Breasts of Columbus: A Political Anatomy of Postcolonialism and Feminist Religious Discourse," in *Postcolonialism, Feminism, and Religious Discourse*, ed. Donaldson and Kwok Pui-lan (New York: Routledge, 2002), 41–61; and Anne McClintock, *Imperial Leather*, especially 21–24.

74. For one compelling instance of imperial claims to uninhabited land or empty space (*terra nullius*) in the Australian context, see Mills, *Gender and Colonial Space*, 140.

75. See also Grewal, *Home and Harem*, 9.

76. Pauline scholarship frequently casts a "Paul in their own image." Hence, this phenomenon might also be damaging opportunities for more properly reconceiving the potential historical roles of the figure they claim to prize so dearly.

77. Kittredge, "Rethinking Authorship in the Letters of Paul: Elisabeth Schüssler Fiorenza's Model of Pauline Theology," in *Walk in the Ways of Wisdom: Essays in Honor of Elisabeth Schüssler Fiorenza*, ed. Shelly Matthews, Kittredge, and Melanie Johnson-Debaufre (Harrisburg: Trinity Press International, 2003), 318–33.

78. For Kittredge's argument that the hymn reflects the authorial work of Euodia and Syntyche, among others in the community, see Kittredge, "Rethinking Authorship," 324–26.

79. For reflections on the potential sexual violence involved with most wars, military encampments, or occupations, see Marchal, "Military Images," 277–80.

80. For such qualifications, see the various entries in the two volumes *Western Women and Imperialism* and *Gender and Imperialism*, but perhaps especially contributions like Padma Anagol, "Indian Christian Women and Indigenous Feminism, c.1850–c.1920," in *Gender and Imperialism*, 79–103. See also Ian Tyrell, *Woman's*

World/Woman's Empire: The Women's Christian Temperance Union in International Perspective, 1880–1930 (Chapel Hill: University of North Carolina Press, 1991).

81. Scholars of imperial and colonial formations have increasingly come to recognize that imperial powers do not operate in exclusively monolithic fashion, but are much more diffuse, heterogeneous, improvisatory, and even contradictory in their exercise of power and their justifications (the latter frequently coming as legitimizing afterthoughts than as items on a colonial structural agenda). For example, the rationales for the British imperial presence in India altered not in direct response to historical conditions or political decisions "from the top," but primarily as the necessary means to justify their continued hold on to power. See, for example, Sharpe, *Allegories of Empire*, 6–11; McClintock, *Imperial Leather*, 9–17; Pratt, *Imperial Eyes*, 1–11; and Mills, *Gender and Colonial Space*, 14–16.

82. See the arguments in chapter 2, for example, but most especially Kittredge's note that Paul works to "both subvert and reinscribe the imperial system." See Kittredge, "Corinthian Women Prophets and Paul's Argumentation in 1 Corinthians," in *Paul and Politics*, 105.

83. See N. T. Wright, "Paul's Gospel and Caesar's Empire," in *Paul and Politics*, 164.

84. Such concluding observations, though, should also be engaged with suspicion about any easy identification of ancient figures with contemporary processes, especially as practiced by a hyphenated pale male who might be prone to position the people and/or the process in a manner similar to his own positionality: that is, mixing or vacillating between complicity and resistance.

5. Concluding Reflections and Connections

1. See, for example, the "requeering sexuality" section of her "Postcolonial Feminist Theology: What is It? How to Do It?" in *Postcolonial Imagination and Feminist Theology* (Louisville: Westminster John Knox, 2005), 125–49; and "A Postcolonial Reading: Sexual Morality and National Politics: Reading Biblical 'Loose Women,'" in *Engaging the Bible: Critical Readings from Contemporary Women*, ed. Choi Hee An and Katheryn Pfisterer Darr (Minneapolis: Fortress Press, 2006), 21–46. It is striking that even in recent volumes on the "interdisciplinary intersections" of postcolonial theory with other theories or critical topics, there are no entries on the intersections of postcolonial and queer theories. See, for example, *Postcolonial Biblical Criticism: Interdisciplinary Intersections*, ed. Stephen D. Moore and Fernando F. Segovia (London: T&T Clark International, 2005). This absence is all the more remarkable given at least two of the contributors' previous work in queer approaches (Moore and Roland Boer) and based on the introductory comments (5), the entry that most engages sexuality (Tat-siong Benny Liew's) had to be commissioned only after the initial session neglected race/ethnicity. This particular gap might also be an indication of what a minor role gender plays in much postcolonial biblical scholarship. Clearly, then, there is plenty of room for further

focused reflections on the interconnections within and between feminist, postcolonial, and queer approaches in biblical studies.

2. Just as resistant forms of solidarity were/are not always apparent between feminist and anticolonial activists, one should remain aware that struggles against homophobia and heterosexism have not always been continuous with anti-imperial or decolonizing efforts. See, for example, Robert F. Aldrich, *Colonialism and Homosexuality* (London: Routledge, 2003); and Joseph A. Boone, "Vacation Cruises; or, The Homoerotics of Orientalism," in *Feminist Postcolonial Theory: A Reader*, ed. Reina Lewis and Sara Mills (New York: Routledge, 2003), 460–86.

3. As indicated at several points in the analysis of mimicry in the third chapter, Judith Butler's work on parody and performativity might critically resituate any application of Homi Bhabha's theoretical apparatus. Attention to the role of desire and the similarity of rivals in contests (colonial or otherwise) are key foci for the work of Eve Kosofsky Sedgwick.

4. See, for a more recent example, Alexander, *Pedagogies of Crossing: Meditations on Feminism, Sexual Politics, Memory, and the Sacred* (Durham: Duke University Press, 2005). Alexander's work might also be notable for students of religion given the way she weaves an analysis of the sacred and the secular into expansively multiple and heterogeneous examinations. For her own reflections on white gay corporate tourism and state heterosexualization, see the chapters on "Imperial Desire/Sexual Utopias: White Gay Capital and Transnational Tourism," and "Transnationalism, Sexuality, and the State: Modernity's Traditions at the Height of Empire," in *Pedagogies of Crossing*, 66–88, 181–254.

5. For a feminist engagement with the perils of nationalism and globalization in religious studies, see the roundtable discussion in *Journal of Feminist Studies in Religion* 21, no. 1 (Spring 2005): 111–54. A prominent sampling of transnational feminist work (outside of biblical studies) would likely include works like Chandra Talpade Mohanty, *Feminism without Borders: Decolonizing Theory, Practicing Solidarity* (Durham: Duke University Press, 2003); Inderpal Grewal and Caren Kaplan, eds., *Scattered Hegemonies: Postmodernity and Transnational Feminist Practices* (Minneapolis: University of Minnesota Press, 1994); Grewal, *Home and Harem: Nation, Gender, Empire, and the Cultures of Travel* (Durham: Duke University Press, 1996); Uma Narayan, *Dislocating Cultures: Identities, Traditions, and Third World Feminism* (New York: Routledge, 1997); Alexander and Mohanty, eds., *Feminist Genealogies, Colonial Legacies, Democratic Futures* (New York: Routledge, 1997); and Kaplan, Norma Alarcon, and Minoo Moallem, eds., *Between Woman and Nation: Nationalisms, Transnational Feminisms, and the State* (Durham: Duke University Press, 1999).

6. The key study for the invention of common histories, symbols, rituals, beliefs, and origins as integral to the development of nations as imagined political communities is Benedict Anderson, *Imagined Communities: Reflections on the Origins and Spread of Nationalism* (London: Verso, 1983). See also the later reflections in Terry Eagleton, Fredric Jameson, and Edward W. Said, *Nationalism, Colonialism and Literature* (Minneapolis: University of Minnesota Press, 1990).

7. For the possibility of Paul using his ethnicity/nationality as one among the con-quered nations to create solidarity across and among these peoples, see Davina C. Lopez, *Apostle to the Conquered: Reimagining Paul's Mission,* Paul in Critical Contexts (Min-neapolis: Fortress Press, 2008). Here, Paul might be similar in strategy to that expressed by postcolonial poet Aimé Césaire: "As there are hyena-men and panther-men, I shall be a Jew-man / a kaffir-man / a Hindu-from-Calcutta-man / a man from-Harlem-who-does-not-vote." Césaire, *Notebook of a Return to My Native Land,* trans. Mireille Rosello with Annie Pritchard (Newcastle upon Tyne: Bloodaxe, 1995), 85. The analogy between the two, however, might also extend to their similarly androcentric perspective.

8. For a recent transnationally postcolonial effort to reconceive the influence and circulation of metropolitan perspectives for the study of ostensible centers and peripher-ies, see Dipesh Chakrabarty, *Provincializing Europe: Postcolonial Thought and Historical Difference* (Princeton: Princeton University Press, 2000). For one potential example of such a trend in the study of the Roman imperial era, see Susan E. Alcock, *Graecia Capta: Landscapes of Roman Greece* (Cambridge: Cambridge University Press, 1993).

9. See, for example, the section on reading with and from non-academic readers in Musa W. Dube, ed., *Other Ways of Reading: African Women and the Bible* (Atlanta: Society of Biblical Literature, 2001), 101–42; as well as Gerald O. West, ed., *Reading Other-Wise: Socially Engaged Scholars Reading with Their Local Communities* (Atlanta: Society of Biblical Literature, 2007); West, *The Academy of the Poor: Towards a Dialogi-cal Reading of the Bible* (Sheffield: Sheffield Academic, 1999).

10. However, despite this "new consensus" on Paul in biblical studies, there has been a marked rise in this idea of an "apostle of universalism" against legalism in (mostly) secular, Eurocentric philosophy. See, most recently, Alain Badiou, *Saint Paul: The Foun-dation of Universalism,* trans. Ray Brassier (Stanford: Stanford University Press, 2003); Slavoj Zizek, *The Puppet and the Dwarf: The Perverse Core of Christianity* (Cambridge: MIT Press, 2003); and Giorgio Agamben, *The Time That Remains: A Commentary on the Letter to the Romans,* trans. Patricia Dailey (Stanford: Stanford University Press, 2005).

11. Although there is no definitive location for discerning the particular way(s) Spi-vak deploys this critical strategy, some of the places where it figures in her own argumen-tation include: "Can the Subaltern Speak?" *Marxism and the Interpretation of Culture,* ed. Cary Nelson and Lawrence Grossberg (Urbana: University of Illinois, 1988), 271–313, especially 297, 303; Spivak, with Ellen Rooney, "'In a Word': *Interview,"* in *Outside in the Teaching Machine* (New York: Routledge, 1993), 1–23, especially 12–14; "More on Power/Knowledge," in *Outside in the Teaching Machine,* 25–51, especially 26–29, 37–39; "Marginality in the Teaching Machine," in *Outside in the Teaching Machine,* 53–76, especially 64–70 and the chapter's note 30 on 298; "Limits and Openings of Marx in Derrida," in *Outside in the Teaching Machine,* 97–119, especially 118–19; and *A Critique of Postcolonial Reason: Toward a History of the Vanishing Present* (Cambridge: Harvard University Press, 1999), 14, 140–42, 179–80, 250–54, 285, 321–23. See also the entry on catachresis in Bill Ashcroft, Gareth Griffiths, and Helen Tiffin, *Post-Colonial Studies: The Key Concepts* (London: Routledge, 2000), 34 (which, incidentally, Stephen Moore also cites [see below]).

12. See, for example, Stephen D. Moore, *Empire and Apocalypse: Postcolonialism and the New Testament* (Sheffield: Sheffield Phoenix, 2006), especially 37–38, 105–6.

13. In these instances, Moore highlights the use of *basileia* (and in a secondary way, an imperial-style cult) in Mark and Revelation as catachrestic. In this way, much of Moore's argument parallels those scholars (examined in chapter 2) who view Paul's reuse of imperial imagery as inherently seditious or resistant to empire. As this study has shown, though, such claims about an anti-imperial/postcolonial Paul obscure the imperial ends to which the arguments reuse such images and arguments, especially as they are consistent with certain gendered, erotic, and ethnic elements to imperialism. Thus, in shifting the catachrestic reading to the twenty-first-century interpreter (as this concluding reflection suggests), we should remain vigilant as to how even catachrestic strategies can reinforce kyriarchy, particularly when it is not balanced against the other aims of feminist, postcolonial analysis. The test of its utility will revolve around these dynamics of complicity and co-optation within resistance.

14. The biblical and classical use of *chrēsis* for the use made of various "vessels" for erotic activity, including women, slaves, foreigners, and conquered peoples is deserving of greater reflection in biblical interpretation, especially given the way this Greek term reappears in Pauline argumentation reflecting intersecting gendered, erotic, economic, ethnic, imperial, and slave status dynamics in letters like Romans and Philemon. See, for example, the use of *chrēsis*, *achrēstos*, and *euchrēstos* in Rom 1:26-27 and Phlm 10–11. For some reflection on the former text and the utility of the catachrestic strategy, see Joseph A. Marchal, "Inconsistent Consistencies and Improper Uses: Recent Approaches to Gender, Romans 1, and the Need for a Feminist, Postcolonially Queer Analysis" (paper presented at the annual meeting of the Society of Biblical Literature, San Diego, November 2007).

Bibliography

Agamben, Giorgio. *The Time That Remains: A Commentary on the Letter to the Romans*. Translated by Patricia Dailey. Meridian: Crossing Aesthetics. Stanford: Stanford University Press, 2005.

Agosto, Efraín. "Patronage and Commendation, Imperial and Anti-Imperial." In *Paul and the Roman Imperial Order*, edited by Richard A. Horsley, 103–23. Harrisburg: Trinity Press International, 2004.

———. "Paul vs. Empire: A Postcolonial and Latino Reading of Philippians." *Perspectivas: Occasional Papers* 6 (Fall 2002): 37–56.

———. "Paul's Use of Greco-Roman Conventions of Commendation." Ph.D. diss., Boston University, 1996.

———. *Servant Leadership: Jesus and Paul*. St. Louis: Chalice, 2005.

Ahmed, Leila. *Women and Gender in Islam: Historical Roots of a Modern Debate*. New Haven: Yale University Press, 1992.

Ahn, Yong-Sung. *The Reign of God and Rome in Luke's Passion Narrative: An East Asian Global Perspective*. Biblical Interpretation 80. Leiden: Brill, 2006.

Alcock, Susan E. *Graecia Capta: Landscapes of Roman Greece*. Cambridge: Cambridge University Press, 1993.

Aldrich, Robert F. *Colonialism and Homosexuality*. London: Routledge, 2003.

Alexander, M. Jacqui. *Pedagogies of Crossing: Meditations on Feminism, Sexual Politics, Memory, and the Sacred*. Durham: Duke University Press, 2005.

Alexander, M. Jacqui, and Chandra Talpade Mohanty, eds. *Feminist Genealogies, Colonial Legacies, Democratic Futures*. Thinking Gender. New York: Routledge, 1997.

Alloula, Malek. *The Colonial Harem*. Translated by Myrna and Wlad Godzich. Minneapolis: University of Minnesota Press, 1986.

Anagol, Padma. "Indian Christian Women and Indigenous Feminism, c.1850–c.1920." In *Gender and Imperialism*, edited by Clare Midgley, 79–103. Studies in Imperialism. Manchester: Manchester University Press, 1998.

Anderson, Benedict. *Imagined Communities: Reflections on the Origins and Spread of Nationalism*. London: Verso, 1983.

181

Ashcroft, Bill, Gareth Griffiths, and Helen Tiffin. *Post-Colonial Studies: The Key Concepts*. London: Routledge, 2000.

Badiou, Alain. *Saint Paul: The Foundation of Universalism*. Translated by Ray Brassier. Cultural Memory in the Present. Stanford: Stanford University Press, 2003.

Bakirtzis, Charalambos, and Helmut Koester, eds. *Philippi at the Time of Paul and after His Death*. Harrisburg: Trinity Press International, 1998.

Barlas, Asma. *"Believing Women" in Islam: Unreading Patriarchal Interpretations of the Qur'an*. Austin: University of Texas Press, 2002.

Beik, William. "The Dilemma of Popular History." *Past and Present* 141 (Nov. 1993): 207–15.

Bhabha, Homi K. "Articulating the Archaic: Cultural Difference and Colonial Nonsense." In *The Location of Culture*, 123–38. London: Routledge, 1994.

———. "The Commitment to Theory." In *The Location of Culture*, 19–39. London: Routledge, 1994.

———. *The Location of Culture*. London: Routledge, 1994.

———. "Of Mimicry and Man: The Ambivalence of Colonial Discourse." In *The Location of Culture*, 85–92. London: Routledge, 1994.

———. "Signs Taken for Wonders: Questions of Ambivalence and Authority under a Tree outside Delhi, May 1817." In *The Location of Culture*, 102–22. London: Routledge, 1994.

———. "Sly Civility." In *The Location of Culture*, 93–101. London: Routledge, 1994.

Bhattacharya, Sabyasachi. "History from Below." *Social Scientist* 11, no. 4 (Apr. 1983): 3–20.

Bird, Phyllis A. "What Makes a Feminist Reading Feminist? A Qualified Answer." In *Escaping Eden: New Feminist Perspectives on the Bible*, edited by Harold C. Washington, Susan Lochrie Graham, and Pamela Thimmes, 124–31. New York: New York University Press, 1999.

Birkett, Dea. *Spinsters Abroad*. London: Basil Blackwell, 1989.

Blunt, Alison. *Travel, Gender, and Imperialism: Mary Kingsley and West Africa*. Mappings: Society/Theory/Space. New York: Guilford, 1994.

Blunt, Allison, and Gillian Rose, eds. *Writing Women and Space: Colonial and Postcolonial Geographies*. Mappings: Society/Theory/Space. New York: Guilford, 1994.

Bockmuehl, Markus. *The Epistle to the Philippians*. Black's New Testament Commentary. London: Hendrickson, 1998.

Boer, Roland, ed. *Last Stop before Antarctica: The Bible and Postcolonialism in Australia*. The Bible and Postcolonialism. Sheffield: Sheffield Academic, 2001.

Boone, Joseph A. "Vacation Cruises; or, The Homoerotics of Orientalism." In *Feminist Postcolonial Theory: A Reader*, edited by Reina Lewis and Sara Mills, 460–86. New York: Routledge, 2003.

Bormann, Lukas. *Philippi: Stadt und Christengemeinde zur Zeit des Paulus*. Novum Testamentum Supplement Series 78. Leiden: Brill, 1995.

Boyarin, Daniel. *A Radical Jew: Paul and the Politics of Identity*. Berkeley: University of California Press, 1994.

Briggs, Sheila. "Can an Enslaved God Liberate? Hermeneutical Reflections on Philippians 2:6–11." *Semeia* 47 (1989): 137–53.

———. "Paul on Bondage and Freedom in Imperial Roman Society." In *Paul and Politics: Ekklesia, Israel, Imperium, Interpretation; Essays in Honor of Krister Stendahl*, edited by Richard A. Horsley, 110–23. Harrisburg: Trinity Press International, 2000.

Brooten, Bernadette J. "'Junia . . . Outstanding among the Apostles' (Romans 16:7)." In *Women Priests: A Catholic Commentary on the Vatican Declaration*, edited by Leonard and Arlene Swidler, 141–44. New York: Paulist Press, 1977.

Buell, Denise Kimber. "Race and Universalism in Early Christianity." *Journal of Early Christian Studies* 10 (2002): 432–41.

———. "Rethinking the Relevance of Race for Early Christian Self-Definition." *Harvard Theological Review* 94 (2001): 449–76.

———. *Why This New Race: Ethnic Reasoning in Early Christianity*. New York: Columbia University Press, 2005.

Buell, Denise Kimber, and Caroline Johnson Hodge. "The Politics of Interpretation: The Rhetoric of Race and Ethnicity in Paul." *Journal of Biblical Literature* 123, no. 2 (2004): 235–51.

Bulbeck, Chilla. *Re-Orienting Western Feminisms: Women's Diversity in a Postcolonial World*. Cambridge: Cambridge University Press, 1998.

Burke, Carolyn, Naomi Schor, and Margaret Whitford, eds. *Engaging with Irigaray: Feminist Philosophy and Modern European Thought*. New York: Columbia University Press, 1994.

Burke, Peter, ed. *New Perspectives on Historical Writing*. 2d ed. University Park: Pennsylvania State University Press, 2001.

———. "Overture: The New History; Its Past and Its Future." In *New Perspectives on Historical Writing*, edited by Burke, 1–24. 2d ed. University Park: Pennsylvania State University Press, 2001.

———. *Popular Culture in Early Modern Europe*. London: Harper & Row, 1978.

Burrus, Virginia. *"Begotten, not Made:" Conceiving Manhood in Late Antiquity*. Figurae. Stanford: Stanford University Press, 2000.

Butler, Judith. *Bodies That Matter: On the Discursive Limits of "Sex."* New York: Routledge, 1993.

———. *Gender Trouble: Feminism and the Subversion of Identity.* Thinking Gender. New York: Routledge, 1990.

———. *Undoing Gender.* New York: Routledge, 2004.

Callahan, Allen Dwight, Richard A. Horsley, and Abraham Smith, eds. *Slavery in Text and Interpretation.* Semeia 83/84. Atlanta: Society of Biblical Literature, 1998.

Callaway, Helen. *Gender, Culture, and Empire.* Urbana: University of Illinois Press, 1987.

Cassidy, Richard J. *Paul in Chains: Roman Imprisonment and the Letters of Paul.* New York: Crossroad, 2001.

Castelli, Elizabeth A. *Imitating Paul: A Discourse of Power.* Literary Currents in Biblical Interpretation. Louisville: Westminster John Knox, 1991.

Césaire, Aimé. *Notebook of a Return to My Native Land.* Translated by Mireille Rosello with Annie Pritchard. Newcastle upon Tyne: Bloodaxe, 1995.

Chakrabarty, Dipesh. "Subaltern Studies and Postcolonial Historiography." In *Handbook of Historical Sociology*, edited by Gerard Delanty and Engin F. Isin, 191–204. London: Sage, 2003.

———. *Provincializing Europe: Postcolonial Thought and Historical Difference.* Princeton: Princeton University Press, 2000.

Chatterjee, Partha. *The Nation and Its Fragments: Colonial and Postcolonial Histories.* Princeton: Princeton University Press, 1993.

Chaudhuri, Nupur, and Margaret Strobel, eds. *Western Women and Imperialism: Complicity and Resistance.* Bloomington: Indiana University Press, 1992.

Choi Hee An and Katheryn Pfisterer Darr, eds. *Engaging the Bible: Critical Readings from Contemporary Women.* Minneapolis: Fortress Press, 2006.

Chow, Rey. "Brushes with the-Other-as-Face: Stereotyping and Cross-Ethnic Representation." In *The Protestant Ethnic and the Spirit of Capitalism*, 50–94. New York: Columbia University Press, 2002.

———. "Keeping Them in Their Place: Coercive Mimeticism and Cross-Ethnic Representation." In *The Protestant Ethnic and the Spirit of Capitalism*, 95–127. New York: Columbia University Press, 2002.

———. "The Protestant Ethnic and the Spirit of Capitalism." In *The Protestant Ethnic and the Spirit of Capitalism*, 19–49. New York: Columbia University Press, 2002.

———. *The Protestant Ethnic and the Spirit of Capitalism.* New York: Columbia University Press, 2002.

————. "When Whiteness Feminizes . . . : Some Consequences of a Supplementary Logic." In *The Protestant Ethnic and the Spirit of Capitalism*, 153–82. New York: Columbia University Press, 2002.

————. "Where Have All the Natives Gone?" In *Feminist Postcolonial Theory: A Reader*, edited by Reina Lewis and Sara Mills, 324–49. London: Routledge, 2003.

————. *Writing Diaspora: Tactics of Intervention in Contemporary Cultural Studies*. Bloomington: Indiana University Press, 1993.

Clarke, Andrew D. "'Be Imitators of Me': Paul's Model of Leadership." *Tyndale Bulletin* 49 (1998): 329–60.

Collart, Paul. *Philippes: Villes de Macédoine: depuis ses origins jusqu'à la fin de l'époque romaine*. École Française d'Athènes: Paris, 1937.

Cotter, Wendy. "Women's Authority Roles in Paul's Churches: Countercultural or Conventional?" *Novum Testamentum* 36 (1994): 350–72.

Dahl, Nils A. "Euodia and Syntyche and Paul's Letter to the Philippians." In *The Social World of the First Christians: Essays in Honor of Wayne A. Meeks*, edited by L. Michael White and O. Larry Yarbrough, 3–15. Minneapolis: Fortress Press, 1995.

D'Angelo, Mary Rose. "Abba and 'Father': Imperial Theology and the Traditions about Jesus." *Journal of Biblical Literature* 111 (1992): 611–30.

————. "Early Christian Sexual Politics and Roman Imperial Family Values: Rereading Christ and Culture." In *The Papers of the Henry Luce III Fellows in Theology*, edited by Christopher I. Wilkins, 6:23–48. Pittsburgh: Association of Theological Schools, 2003.

————. "Euodia." In *Women in Scripture: A Dictionary of Named and Unnamed Women in the Hebrew Bible, the Apocryphal/Deuterocanonical Books, and the New Testament*, edited by Carol Meyers, Toni Craven, and Ross S. Kraemer, 79. Grand Rapids: Eerdmans, 2000.

————. "Syntyche." In *Women in Scripture: A Dictionary of Named and Unnamed Women in the Hebrew Bible, The Apocryphal/Deuterocanonical Books, and the New Testament*, edited by Carol Meyers, Toni Craven, and Ross S. Kraemer, 159. Grand Rapids: Eerdmans, 2000.

————. "Women Partners in the New Testament." *Journal of Feminist Studies in Religion* 6 (1990): 65–86.

De Vos, Craig S. *Church and Community Conflicts: The Relationships of the Thessalonian, Corinthian, and Philippian Churches with Their Wider Civic Communities*. Society of Biblical Literature Dissertation Series 168. Atlanta: Scholars, 1999.

Dickson, Kwesi. *Uncompleted Mission: Christianity and Exclusivism*. Maryknoll: Orbis, 1991.

Dirlik, Arif. "The Aura of Postcolonialism: Third World Criticism in the Age of Global Capitalism." In *Contemporary Postcolonial Theory: A Reader*, edited by Padmini Mongia, 294–321. London: Arnold, 1996.

Dodd, Brian J. *Paul's Paradigmatic "I": Personal Example as Literary Strategy.* Journal for the Study of the New Testament Supplement Series 177. Sheffield: Sheffield Academic, 1999.

Donaldson, Laura E. "The Breasts of Columbus: A Political Anatomy of Postcolonialism and Feminist Religious Discourse." In *Postcolonialism, Feminism, and Religious Discourse*, edited by Donaldson and Kwok Pui-lan, 41–61. New York: Routledge, 2002.

———. *Decolonizing Feminisms: Race, Gender, and Empire-Building.* Chapel Hill: University of North Carolina Press, 1992.

———. "Gospel Hauntings: The Postcolonial Demons of New Testament Criticism." In *Postcolonial Biblical Criticism: Interdisciplinary Intersections*, edited by Stephen D. Moore and Fernando F. Segovia, 97–113. The Bible and Postcolonialism. London: T&T Clark International, 2005.

———. "The Sign of Orpah: Reading Ruth through Native Eyes." In *Vernacular Hermeneutics*, edited by R. S. Sugirtharajah, 20–36. The Bible and Postcolonialism. Sheffield: Sheffield Academic, 1999.

Donaldson, Laura E., and Kwok Pui-lan, eds. *Postcolonialism, Feminism and Religious Discourse.* New York: Routledge, 2002.

Donfried, Karl P. "The Imperial Cults of Thessalonica and Political Conflict in 1 Thessalonians." In *Paul and Empire: Religion and Power in Roman Imperial Society*, edited by Richard A. Horsley, 215–23. Harrisburg: Trinity Press International, 1997.

Dube, Musa W. "Consuming the Colonial Cultural Bomb: Translating Badimo into Demons in the Setswana Bible (Matt. 8:28-34; 15:22; 10:8)." *Journal for the Study of the New Testament* 73 (1999): 33–59.

———, ed. *Other Ways of Reading: African Women and the Bible.* Global Perspectives on the Bible Series. Atlanta: Society of Biblical Literature, 2001.

———. *Postcolonial Feminist Interpretation of the Bible.* St. Louis: Chalice, 2000.

———. "Rahab Says Hello to Judith: A Decolonizing Feminist Reading." In *Toward a New Heaven and a New Earth: Essays in Honor of Elisabeth Schüssler Fiorenza*, edited by Fernando F. Segovia, 54–72. Maryknoll: Orbis, 2003.

———. "Toward a Postcolonial Feminist Interpretation of the Bible." *Semeia* 78 (1997): 11–26.

Dube, Musa W., and Jeffrey L. Staley, eds. *John and Postcolonialism: Travel, Space and Power.* Bible and Postcolonialism. London: Continuum, 2002.

Dube Shomanah, Musa W. "Postcolonial Biblical Interpretations." In *Dictionary of Biblical Interpretation*, edited by John H. Hayes, 2:299–303. Nashville: Abingdon, 1999.

———. "Scripture, Feminism and Post-Colonial Contexts." In *Women's Sacred Scriptures*, edited by Kwok Pui-lan and Elisabeth Schüssler Fiorenza, 45–54. London: SCM, 1998.

Eagleton, Terry, Frederic Jameson, and Edward W. Said. *Nationalism, Colonialism, and Literature*. Minneapolis: University of Minnesota Press, 1990.

Elliott, Neil. "The Apostle Paul's Self-Presentation as Anti-Imperial Performance." In *Paul and the Roman Imperial Order*, edited by Richard A. Horsley, 67–88. Harrisburg: Trinity Press International, 2004.

———. *Liberating Paul: The Justice of God and the Politics of the Apostle*. Maryknoll: Orbis, 1994.

———. "Romans 13:1-7 in the Context of Imperial Propaganda." In *Paul and Empire: Religion and Power in Roman Imperial Society*, edited by Richard A. Horsley, 184–204. Harrisburg: Trinity Press International, 1997.

Fanon, Frantz. *Black Skin, White Masks*. Translated by Charles Lam Markmann. New York: Grove, 1967 [1952].

———. *A Dying Colonialism*. Translated by Haakon Chevalier. New York: Grove, 1965.

Fee, Gordon D. *Philippians*. Intervarsity Press New Testament Commentary Series 11. Downers Grove, Ill.: Intervarsity, 1999.

Fiore, Benjamin. "Paul, Exemplification, and Imitation." In *Paul in the Greco-Roman World: A Handbook*, edited by J. Paul Sampley, 228–57. Harrisburg: Trinity Press International, 2003.

Fitzgerald, John T. "Paul and Friendship." In *Paul in the Greco-Roman World: A Handbook*, edited by J. Paul Sampley, 319–43. Harrisburg: Trinity Press International, 2003.

Fortna, Robert T. "Philippians: Paul's Most Egocentric Letter." In *The Conversation Continues: Festschrift for J. Louis Martyn*, edited by Fortna and Beverly R. Gaventa, 220–34. Nashville: Abingdon, 1990.

Foucault, Michel. *The History of Sexuality: An Introduction*. Vol. 1. Translated by Robert Hurley. New York: Vintage, 1978 [1976].

———. *Power/Knowledge: Selected Interviews and Other Writing 1972–1977*. Edited by Colin Gordon and translated by C. Gordon, Leo Marshall, John Mepham, and Kate Soper. New York: Pantheon, 1980.

Friesen, Steven J. "Poverty in Pauline Studies: Beyond the So-Called New Consensus." *Journal for the Study of the New Testament* 26, no. 3 (Mar. 2004): 323–61.

Furnish, Victor P. *The Love Command in the New Testament.* Nashville: Abingdon, 1972.

Gandhi, Leela. *Postcolonial Theory: A Critical Introduction.* New York: Columbia University Press, 1998.

Garber, Marjorie. *Vested Interests: Cross-Dressing and Cultural Authority.* New York: Routledge, 1992.

Geoffrion, Timothy C. *The Rhetorical Purpose and the Political and Military Character of Philippians.* Lewiston: Mellen, 1993.

Georgi, Dieter. "God Turned Upside Down." In *Paul and Empire: Religion and Power in Roman Imperial Society,* edited by Richard A. Horsley, 148–57. Harrisburg: Trinity Press International, 1997.

———. *Theocracy in Paul's Praxis and Theology.* Minneapolis: Fortress Press, 1991.

Gleason, Maud. *Making Men: Sophists and Self-Presentation in Ancient Rome.* Princeton: Princeton University Press, 1995.

Gramsci, Antonio. *Selections from the Prison Notebooks.* Translated and edited by Quintin Hoare and Geoffrey Nowell-Smith. New York: International Publishers, 1973.

Grewal, Inderpal. *Home and Harem: Nation, Gender, Empire, and the Cultures of Travel.* Post-Contemporary Interventions. Durham: Duke University Press, 1996.

Grewal, Inderpal, and Caren Kaplan, eds. *Scattered Hegemonies: Postmodernity and Transnational Feminist Practices.* Minneapolis: University of Minnesota Press, 1994.

Guha, Ranajit. *Elementary Aspects of Peasant Insurgency in Colonial India.* Delhi: Oxford University Press, 1983.

———, ed. *Subaltern Studies I: Writings on South Asian History and Society.* Delhi: Oxford University Press, 1982.

———, ed. *Subaltern Studies III: Writing on Indian History and Society.* Delhi: Oxford University Press, 1984.

Guha, Ranajit, and Gayatri Chakravorty Spivak, eds. *Selected Subaltern Studies.* New York: Oxford University Press, 1988.

Gunderson, Erik. *Staging Masculinity: The Rhetoric of Performance in the Roman World.* Ann Arbor: University of Michigan Press, 2000.

Haggis, Jane. "White Women and Colonialism: Towards a Non-Recuperative History." In *Gender and Imperialism,* edited by Clare Midgley, 45–75. Studies in Imperialism. Manchester: Manchester University Press, 1998.

Hall, Catherine. "The Tale of Samuel and Jemima: Gender and Working-Class Culture in Nineteenth-Century England." In *E. P. Thompson: Critical*

Perspectives, edited by Harvey J. Kaye and Keith McClelland, 78–102. Philadelphia: Temple University Press, 1990.

Hall, Jonathan M. *Ethnic Identity in Greek Antiquity.* Cambridge: Cambridge University Press, 1997.

Hallett, Judith P., and Marilyn B. Skinner, eds. *Roman Sexualities.* Princeton: Princeton University Press, 1997.

Hardt, Michael, and Antonio Negri. *Empire.* Cambridge: Harvard University Press, 2000.

Hearon, Holly E., ed. *Distant Voices Drawing Near: Essays in Honor of Antoinette Clark Wire.* Collegeville: Liturgical, 2004.

Heen, Erik M. "Phil 2:6-11 and Resistance to Local Timocratic Rule: *Isa theō* and the Cult of the Emperor in the East." In *Paul and the Roman Imperial Order*, edited by Richard A. Horsley, 125–53. Harrisburg: Trinity Press International, 2004.

Hendrix, Holland L. "Philippi." In *Anchor Bible Dictionary.* Vol. 5, edited by David N. Freedman, 313–17. New York: Doubleday, 1992.

Hester Amador, J. David. *Academic Constraints in Rhetorical Criticism of the New Testament: An Introduction to a Rhetoric of Power.* Journal for the Study of the New Testament Supplement Series 174. Sheffield: Sheffield Academic, 1999.

Hobsbawm, Eric J. "History from Below—Some Reflections." In *History from Below: Studies in Popular Protest and Popular Ideology*, edited by Frederick Krantz, 13–27. Oxford: Basil Blackwell, 1985.

———. *Primitive Rebels: Studies in Archaic Forms of Social Movement in the 19th and 20th Centuries.* Manchester: Manchester University Press, 1959.

Holloway, Paul A. *Consolation in Philippians: Philosophical Sources and Rhetorical Strategy.* Society for New Testament Studies Monograph Series 112. Cambridge: Cambridge University Press, 2001.

Horsley, Richard A., ed. *Christian Origins.* Vol. 1, *A People's History of Christianity.* Minneapolis: Fortress Press, 2005.

———. "Feminist Scholarship and Postcolonial Criticism: Subverting Imperial Discourse and Reclaiming Submerged Histories." In *Walk in the Ways of Wisdom: Essays in Honor of Elisabeth Schüssler Fiorenza*, edited by Shelly Matthews, Cynthia Briggs Kittredge, and Melanie Johnson-Debaufre, 297–317. Harrisburg: Trinity Press International, 2003.

———. "General Introduction." In *Paul and Empire: Religion and Power in Roman Imperial Society*, edited by Horsley, 1–8. Harrisburg: Trinity Press International, 1997.

————, ed. *Hidden Transcripts and the Arts of Resistance: Applying the Work of James C. Scott to Jesus and Paul.* Semeia Studies 48. Atlanta: Society of Biblical Literature, 2004.

————. "Introduction: Jesus, Paul, and the 'Arts of Resistance': Leaves from the Notebook of James C. Scott." In *Hidden Transcripts and the Arts of Resistance: Applying the Work of James C. Scott to Jesus and Paul,* edited by Horsley, 1–26. Semeia Studies. Atlanta: Society of Biblical Literature, 2004.

————. "Introduction" of "Part I: The Gospel of Imperial Salvation." In *Paul and Empire: Religion and Power in Roman Imperial Society,* edited by Horsley, 10–24. Harrisburg: Trinity Press International, 1997.

————. "Introduction" of "Part III: Paul's Counter-Imperial Gospel." In *Paul and Empire: Religion and Power in Roman Imperial Society,* edited by Horsley, 140–47. Harrisburg: Trinity Press International, 1997.

————. "Introduction" of "Part IV: Building an Alternative Society." In *Paul and Empire: Religion and Power in Roman Imperial Society,* edited by Horsley, 206–14. Harrisburg: Trinity Press International, 1997.

————. "Introduction." In *Paul and the Roman Imperial Order,* edited by Horsley, 1–23. Harrisburg: Trinity Press International, 2004.

————, ed. *Paul and Empire: Religion and Power in Roman Imperial Society.* Harrisburg: Trinity Press International, 1997.

————, ed. *Paul and Politics: Ekklesia, Israel, Imperium, Interpretation; Essays in Honor of Krister Stendahl.* Harrisburg: Trinity Press International, 2000.

————, ed. *Paul and the Roman Imperial Order.* Harrisburg: Trinity Press International, 2004.

————. "Rhetoric and Empire—and 1 Corinthians." In *Paul and Politics: Ekklesia, Israel, Imperium, Interpretation; Essays in Honor of Krister Stendahl,* edited by Horsley, 72–102. Harrisburg: Trinity Press International, 2000.

————. "Submerged Biblical Histories and Imperial Biblical Studies." In *The Postcolonial Bible,* edited by R. S. Sugirtharajah, 152–73. Bible and Postcolonialism. Sheffield: Sheffield Academic, 1998.

————. "Unearthing a People's History." In *Christian Origins. A People's History of Christianity,* edited by Horsley, 1:1–20. Minneapolis: Fortress Press, 2005.

Ignatiev, Noel. *How the Irish Became White.* New York: Routledge, 1996.

Irigaray, Luce. *Speculum of the Other Woman.* Translated by Gillian C. Gill. Ithaca: Cornell University Press, 1985.

————. *This Sex Which Is Not One.* Translated by Catherine Porter. Ithaca: Cornell University Press, 1985.

Jacobson, Matthew Frye. *Whiteness of a Different Color: European Immigrants and the Alchemy of Race.* Cambridge: Harvard University Press, 1999.

Kabbani, Rana. *Europe's Myths of Orient: Devise and Rule.* London: Macmillan, 1985.

Kaplan, Caren. *Questions of Travel.* Durham: Duke University Press, 1996.

Kaplan, Caren, and Inderpal Grewal. "Transnational Feminist Cultural Studies: Beyond the Marxism/Poststructuralism/Feminism Divides." *positions* (Fall 1994): 430–45.

Kaplan, Caren, Norma Alarcon, and Minoo Moallem, eds. *Between Woman and Nation: Nationalisms, Transnational Feminisms, and the State.* Durham: Duke University Press, 1999.

Kaye, Harvey J. *The British Marxist Historians: An Introductory Analysis.* Cambridge: Polity, 1984.

————. *The Education of Desire: Marxists and the Writing of History.* New York: Routledge, 1992.

Kaye, Harvey J., and Keith McClelland, eds. *E. P. Thompson: Critical Perspectives.* Philadelphia: Temple University Press, 1990.

Kelley, Shawn. *Racializing Jesus: Race, Ideology and the Formation of Modern Biblical Scholarship.* Biblical Limits. London: Routledge, 2002.

Kim, Jean K. "An Asian Interpretation of Philippians 2.6-11." In *Escaping Eden: New Feminist Perspectives on the Bible,* edited by Harold C. Washington, Susan Lochrie Graham, and Pamela Thimmes, 104–22. New York: New York University Press, 1999.

————. *Woman and Nation: An Intercontextual Reading of the Gospel of John from a Postcolonial Feminist Perspective.* Biblical Interpretation 69. Boston: Brill, 2004.

Kim, Uriah Y. *Decolonizing Josiah: Toward a Postcolonial Reading of the Deuteronomistic History.* The Bible in the Modern World 5. Sheffield: Sheffield Phoenix, 2006.

Kingsley, Mary H. *The Story of West Africa.* London: Horace Marshall, 1900.

————. *Travels in West Africa: Congo Français, Corisco and Cameroons.* London: Macmillan, 1987; London: Virago, 1986.

————. *West African Studies.* London: Macmillan, 1899.

Kinukawa, Hisako. "De-colonizing Ourselves as Readers: The Story of the Syro-Phoenician Woman as a Text." In *Distant Voices Drawing Near: Essays in Honor of Antoinette Clark Wire,* edited by Holly E. Hearon, 131–44. Collegeville: Liturgical, 2004.

Kipling, Rudyard. *Kim.* London: Penguin, 1987.

Kittredge, Cynthia Briggs. *Community and Authority: The Rhetoric of Obedience in the Pauline Tradition.* Harvard Theological Studies 45. Harrisburg: Trinity Press International, 1998.

————. "Corinthian Women Prophets and Paul's Argumentation in 1 Corinthians." In *Paul and Politics: Ekklesia, Israel, Imperium, Interpretation; Essays in Honor of Krister Stendahl,* edited by Richard A. Horsley, 103–9. Harrisburg: Trinity Press International, 2000.

————. "Feminist Rethinking of Paul." Paper presented at the annual meeting of the Society of Biblical Literature. Philadelphia, November 2005.

————. "Reconstructing 'Resistance' or Reading to Resist: James C. Scott and the Politics of Interpretation." In *Hidden Transcripts and the Arts of Resistance: Applying the Work of James C. Scott to Jesus and Paul,* edited by Richard A. Horsley, 145–55. Semeia Studies. Atlanta: Society of Biblical Literature, 2004.

————. "Rethinking Authorship in the Letters of Paul: Elisabeth Schüssler Fiorenza's Model of Pauline Theology." In *Walk in the Ways of Wisdom: Essays in Honor of Elisabeth Schüssler Fiorenza,* edited by Shelly Matthews, Kittredge, and Melanie Johnson-Debaufre, 318–33. Harrisburg: Trinity Press International, 2003.

Knust, Jennifer Wright. *Abandoned to Lust: Sexual Slander and Ancient Christianity.* Gender, Theory, and Religion. New York: Columbia University Press, 2005.

————. "Paul and the Politics of Virtue and Vice." In *Paul and the Roman Imperial Order,* edited by Richard A. Horsley, 155–74. Harrisburg: Trinity Press International, 2004.

Koester, Helmut. "Imperial Ideology and Paul's Eschatology in 1 Thessalonians." In *Paul and Empire: Religion and Power in Roman Imperial Society,* edited by Richard A. Horsley, 158–66. Harrisburg: Trinity Press International, 1997.

Koukouli-Chrysantaki, Chaido. "Colonia Iulia Augusta Philippensis." In *Philippi at the Time of Paul and after His Death,* edited by Charalambos Bakirtzis and Helmut Koester, 5–35. Harrisburg: Trinity Press International, 1998.

Krentz, Edgar M. "Military Language and Metaphors in Philippians." In *Origins and Method: Towards a New Understanding of Judaism and Christianity; Essays in Honour of John C. Hurd,* edited by Bradley H. McLean, 105–27. Journal for the Study of the New Testament Supplement Series 86. Sheffield: Sheffield Academic, 1993.

————. "Paul, Games, and the Military." In *Paul in the Greco-Roman World: A Handbook*, edited by J. Paul Sampley, 344–83. Harrisburg: Trinity Press International, 2003.

Kwok, Pui-lan. *Discovering the Bible in the Non-Biblical World*. The Bible & Liberation. Maryknoll: Orbis, 1995.

————. *Introducing Asian Feminist Theology*. Introductions in Feminist Theology. Cleveland: Pilgrim, 2000.

————. "Jesus/the Native: Biblical Studies from a Postcolonial Perspective." In *Teaching the Bible: The Discourses and Politics of Biblical Pedagogy*, edited by Fernando F. Segovia and Mary Ann Tolbert, 69–85. Maryknoll: Orbis, 1995.

————. "Mercy Amba Oduyoye and African Women's Theology." *Journal of Feminist Studies in Religion* 20, no. 1 (2004): 7–22.

————. *Postcolonial Imagination and Feminist Theology*. Louisville: Westminster John Knox, 2005.

————. "A Postcolonial Reading: Sexual Morality and National Politics; Reading Biblical 'Loose Women.'" In *Engaging the Bible: Critical Readings from Contemporary Women*, edited by Choi Hee An and Katheryn Pfisterer Darr, 21–46. Minneapolis: Fortress Press, 2006.

————. "Unbinding Our Feet: Saving Brown Women and Feminist Religious Discourse." In *Postcolonialism, Feminism, and Religious Discourse*, edited by Laura E. Donaldson and Kwok, 62–81. New York: Routledge, 2002.

Kwok, Pui-lan, and Elisabeth Schüssler Fiorenza, eds. *Women's Sacred Scriptures*. Concilium. London: SCM, 1998.

Laqueur, Thomas. *Making Sex: Body and Gender from the Greeks to Freud*. Cambridge: Harvard University Press, 1990.

Levick, Barbara, ed. *The Government of the Roman Empire: A Sourcebook*. London: Croom Helm, 1988.

Levine, Amy-Jill. "Introduction." in *A Feminist Companion to Paul*, edited by Levine with Marianne Blickenstaff, 1–12. Cleveland: Pilgrim, 2004.

Levine, Amy-Jill, with Marianne Blickenstaff, eds. *A Feminist Companion to Paul*. Cleveland: Pilgrim, 2004.

Lewis, Reina. *Gendering Orientalism: Race, Femininity and Representation*. Gender, Racism, Ethnicity. London: Routledge, 1996.

Lewis, Reina, and Sara Mills. "Introduction." In *Feminist Postcolonial Theory: A Reader*, edited by Lewis and Mills, 1–21. New York: Routledge, 2003.

————, eds. *Feminist Postcolonial Theory: A Reader*. New York: Routledge, 2003.

Liew, Tat-siong Benny. "Tyranny, Boundary, and Might: Colonial Mimicry in Mark's Gospel." *Journal for the Study of the New Testament* 73 (1999): 7–31.

Liew, Tat-siong Benny, and Vincent L. Wimbush. "Contact Zones and Zoning Contexts: From the Los Angeles 'Riot' to a New York Symposium." *Union Seminary Quarterly Review* 56 (2003): 21–40.

Loomba, Ania. *Colonialism/Postcolonialism*. The New Critical Idiom. New York: Routledge, 1998.

Lopez, Davina C. *Apostle to the Conquered: Reimagining Paul's Mission*. Paul in Critical Contexts. Minneapolis: Fortress Press, 2008.

———. "Before Your Very Eyes: Roman Imperial Ideology, Gender Constructs and Paul's Inter-Nationalism." In *Mapping Gender in Ancient Religious Discourses*, edited by Todd Penner and Caroline Vander Stichele, 115–62. Biblical Interpretation 84. Leiden: Brill, 2007.

Mani, Lata. "Contentious Traditions: The Debate on Sati in Colonial India." In *Recasting Women*, edited by KumKum Sangari and Sudesh Vaid, 88–126. Delhi: Kali for Women, 1989.

Marchal, Joseph A. *Hierarchy, Unity, and Imitation: A Feminist Rhetorical Analysis of Power Dynamics in Paul's Letter to the Philippians*. Academia Biblica 24. Atlanta: Society of Biblical Literature; Leiden: Brill, 2006.

———. "Imperial Intersections and Initial Inquiries: Toward a Feminist, Postcolonial Analysis of Philippians." *Journal of Feminist Studies in Religion* 22, no. 2 (Fall 2006): 5–32.

———. "Inconsistent Consistencies and Improper Uses: Recent Approaches to Gender, Romans 1, and the Need for a Feminist, Postcolonially Queer Analysis." Paper presented at the annual meeting of the Society of Biblical Literature. San Diego, November 2007.

———. "Military Images in Philippians 1–2: A Feminist Rhetorical Analysis of Scholarship, Philippians, and Current Contexts." In *Her Master's Tools? Feminist and Postcolonial Engagements of Historical-Critical Discourse*, edited by Caroline Vander Stichele and Todd Penner, 265–86. Global Perspectives on Biblical Scholarship Series. Atlanta: Society of Biblical Literature, 2005.

———. "Mutuality Rhetorics and Feminist Interpretation: Examining Philippians and Arguing for Our Lives." *Bible and Critical Theory* 1, no. 3 (August 2005).

———. "'With Friends like These . . .': A Feminist Rhetorical Reconsideration of Scholarship and the Letter to the Philippians." *Journal for the Study of the New Testament* 29, no. 1 (September 2006): 77–106.

Martin, Dale B. "*Arsenokoitēs* and *Malakos*: Meanings and Consequences." In *Biblical Ethics & Homosexuality: Listening to Scriptures*, edited by Robert L. Brawley, 117–36. Louisville: Westminster John Knox, 1996.

Martínez-Vázquez, Hjamil A. "Postcolonial Criticism in Biblical Interpretation: A Response to Efraín Agosto." *Perspectivas: Occasional Papers* 6 (Fall 2002): 57–63.

Matthews, Shelly, Cynthia Briggs Kittredge, and Melanie Johnson-Debaufre, eds. *Walk in the Ways of Wisdom: Essays in Honor of Elisabeth Schüssler Fiorenza.* Harrisburg: Trinity Press International, 2003.

Mattingly, David J., ed. *Dialogues in Roman Imperialism: Power, Discourse, and Discrepant Experience in the Roman Empire.* Journal of Roman Archaeology Supplementary Series; International Roman Archaeology Conference Series 23. Portsmouth: British Academy, 1997.

Mazrui, Ali A. *Cultural Forces in World Politics.* London: James Curry, 1990.

McClelland, Keith. "Introduction." In *E. P. Thompson: Critical Perspectives,* edited by Harvey J. Kaye and McClelland, 1–11. Philadelphia: Temple University Press, 1990.

McClintock, Anne. "The Angel of Progress: Pitfalls of the Term 'Post-Colonialism.'" *Social Texts* 31/32 (1992): 84–98.

———. *Imperial Leather: Race, Gender and Sexuality in the Colonial Conquest.* New York: Routledge, 1995.

McKinlay, Judith E. *Reframing Her: Biblical Women in Postcolonial Focus.* Bible in the Modern World 1. Sheffield: Sheffield Phoenix, 2004.

McLeod, John. *Beginning Postcolonialism.* Beginnings. Manchester: Manchester University Press, 2000.

Meyers, Carol, Toni Craven, and Ross S. Kraemer, eds. *Women in Scripture: A Dictionary of Named and Unnamed Women in the Hebrew Bible, the Apocryphal/Deuterocanonical Books, and the New Testament.* Grand Rapids: Eerdmans, 2000.

Midgley, Clare, ed. *Gender and Imperialism.* Studies in Imperialism. Manchester: Manchester University Press, 1998.

Mills, Sara. *Discourses of Difference: An Analysis of Women's Travel Writing and Colonialism.* New York: Routledge, 1992.

———. "Gender and Colonial Space." In *Feminist Postcolonial Theory: A Reader,* edited by Reina Lewis and Mills, 692–719. New York: Routledge, 2003.

———. *Gender and Colonial Space.* Manchester: Manchester University Press, 2005.

Mohanty, Chandra Talpade. *Feminism without Borders: Decolonizing Theory, Practicing Solidarity.* Durham: Duke University Press, 2003.

———. "Under Western Eyes: Feminist Scholarship and Colonial Discourses." In *Feminism Without Borders: Decolonizing Theory, Practicing Solidarity,* 17–42. Durham: Duke University Press, 2003.

Mohanty, Chandra Talpade, with Biddy Martin, "What's Home Got to Do with It?" In *Feminism without Borders: Decolonizing Theory, Practicing Solidarity*, 85–105. Durham: Duke University Press, 2003.

Moore, Stephen D. *Empire and Apocalypse: Postcolonialism and the New Testament.* The Bible in the Modern World 12. Sheffield: Sheffield Phoenix, 2006.

————. "Postcolonialism." In *Handbook of Postmodern Biblical Interpretation*, edited by A. K. M. Adam, 182–88. St. Louis: Chalice, 2000.

————. "Questions of Biblical Ambivalence and Authority under a Tree Outside Delhi; or, the Postcolonial and the Postmodern." In *Postcolonial Biblical Criticism: Interdisciplinary Intersections*, edited by Moore and Fernando F. Segovia, 79–96. Bible and Postcolonialism. London: T&T Clark International, 2005.

Moore, Stephen D., and Fernando F. Segovia, "Postcolonial Biblical Criticisms: Beginnings, Trajectories, Intersections." In *Postcolonial Biblical Criticism: Interdisciplinary Intersections*, edited by Moore and Segovia, 1–22. Bible and Postcolonialism. London: T&T Clark International, 2005.

————, eds. *Postcolonial Biblical Criticism: Interdisciplinary Intersections*. Bible and Postcolonialism. London: T&T Clark International, 2005.

Naipaul, V. S. *The Mimic Men.* London: Deutsch, 1967.

Narayan, Uma. *Dislocating Cultures: Identities, Traditions, and Third World Feminism.* Thinking Gender. New York: Routledge, 1997.

Nicholson, Linda, ed. *The Second Wave: A Reader in Feminist Theory.* New York: Routledge, 1997.

Oakes, Peter S. "God's Sovereignty over Roman Authorities: A Theme in Philippians." In *Rome in the Bible and the Early Church*, edited by Oakes, 126–41. Grand Rapids: Paternoster/Baker Academic, 2002.

————. *Philippians: From People to Letter.* Society for New Testament Studies Monograph Series 110. Cambridge: Cambridge University Press, 2001.

————, ed. *Rome in the Bible and the Early Church.* Grand Rapids: Paternoster/Baker Academic, 2002.

————. "A State of Tension: Rome in the New Testament." In *The Gospel of Matthew in Its Roman Imperial Context*, edited by John Riches and David C. Sim, 75–90. Journal for the Study of the New Testament Supplement Series 276. London: T&T Clark International, 2005.

O'Brien Wicker, Kathleen. "Teaching Feminist Biblical Studies in a Postcolonial Context." In *Searching the Scriptures: A Feminist Introduction*, edited by Elisabeth Schüssler Fiorenza, 1:367–80. New York: Crossroad, 1993.

O'Brien Wicker, Kathleen, Musa W. Dube, and Althea Spencer-Miller, eds. *Feminist New Testament Studies: Global and Future Perspectives*. New York: Palgrave MacMillan, 2005.

Økland, Jorunn. *Women in Their Place: Paul and the Corinthian Discourse of Gender and Sanctuary Space*. Journal for the Study of the New Testament Supplement Series 269. London: T&T Clark International, 2005.

Olbrechts-Tyteca, Lucie, and Chaïm L. Perelman. *The New Rhetoric: A Treatise on Argumentation*, translated by John Wilkinson and Purcell Weaver. Notre Dame: University of Notre Dame Press, 1969. Originally published as *La Nouvelle Rhétorique: Traité de l'Argumentation*. Paris: Universitaires de France, 1958.

Ortiz, Fernando. *Contrapunto Cubano*. Caracas: Biblioteca Ayacucho, 1978.

Osiek, Carolyn L. *Philippians, Philemon*. Abingdon New Testament Commentaries. Nashville: Abingdon, 2000.

———. "Philippians." In *Searching the Scriptures: A Feminist Commentary*, edited by Elisabeth Schüssler Fiorenza, 2:237–49. New York: Crossroad, 1994.

Palmer, Bryan D. *E. P. Thompson: Objections and Oppositions*. London: Verso, 1994.

———. "Family Tree as 'Liberty Tree'?" In *E. P. Thompson: Objections and Oppositions*, 11–51. London: Verso, 1994.

Parry, Benita. "Problems in Current Theories of Colonial Discourse." *Oxford Literary Review* 9, nos. 1–2 (1987): 27–58.

Penner, Todd C., and Caroline Vander Stichele, eds. *Mapping Gender in Ancient Religious Discourse*. Biblical Interpretation 84. Leiden: Brill, 2007.

———. "Unveiling Paul: Gendering *Ethos* in 1 Corinthians 11:2-16." In *Rhetoric, Ethic, and Moral Persuasion in Biblical Discourse*, edited by Thomas H. Olbricht and Anders Eriksson, 214–37. Emory Studies in Early Christianity. New York: T&T Clark International, 2005.

Peterlin, Davorin. *Paul's Letter to the Philippians in the Light of Disunity in the Church*. Supplements to Novum Testamentum 79. Leiden: Brill, 1995.

Peterson, Kirsten Holst, and Anna Rutherford, eds. *A Double Colonisation: Colonial and Post-Colonial Women's Writing*. Dangaroo, 1986.

Pilhofer, Peter. *Philippi I: Die erste christliche Gemeinde Europas*. Tübingen: J. C. B. Mohr, 1995.

Polaski, Sandra Hack. *A Feminist Introduction to Paul*. St. Louis: Chalice, 2005.

Portefaix, Lilian. *Sisters Rejoice: Paul's Letter to the Philippians and Luke-Acts as Received by First-Century Philippians Women*. Coniectanea biblica: New Testament Series 20. Stockholm: Almqvist & Wiksell, 1988.

Pratt, Mary Louise. *Imperial Eyes: Travel Writing and Transculturation.* New York: Routledge, 1992.

Punt, Jeremy. "Towards a Postcolonial Reading of Freedom in Paul." In *Reading the Bible in the Global Village: Cape Town,* 125–49, 188–95. Global Perspectives on Biblical Scholarship. Atlanta: Society of Biblical Literature, 2002.

Quint, David. *Epic and Empire: Politics and Generic Form from Virgil to Milton.* Literature in History. Princeton: Princeton University Press, 1993.

Rajan, Rajeswari Sunder. *Real and Imagined Women: Gender, Culture, and Post-colonialism.* London: Routledge, 1993.

Rehmann, Luzia Sutter, "To Turn the Groaning into Labor: Romans 8:22-23." In *A Feminist Companion to Paul,* edited by Amy-Jill Levine with Marianne Blickenstaff, 74–84. Cleveland: Pilgrim, 2004.

Riches, John, and David C. Sim, eds. *The Gospel of Matthew in its Roman Imperial Context.* Journal for the Study of the New Testament Supplement Series 276. London: T&T Clark International, 2005.

Ringe, Sharon H. "Places at the Table: Feminist and Postcolonial Biblical Interpretation." In *The Postcolonial Bible,* edited by R. S. Sugirtharajah, 136–51. Bible and Postcolonialism. Sheffield: Sheffield Academic, 1998.

Rodgers, Rene. "Female Representation in Roman Art: Feminizing the Provincial Other." In *Roman Imperialism and Provincial Art,* edited by Sarah Scott and Jane Webster, 69–93. New York: Cambridge University Press, 2004.

"Roundtable Discussion: Anti-Judaism and Postcolonial Biblical Interpretation." *Journal of Feminist Studies in Religion* 20, no. 1 (Spring 2004): 91–132.

Rowbotham, Sheila. *Hidden from History: Rediscovering Women from the 17th Century to the Present.* New York: Pantheon, 1974.

Runions, Erin. *Changing Subjects: Gender, Nation and Future in Micah.* Playing the Texts 7. Sheffield: Sheffield Academic, 2002.

Said, Edward W. *Culture and Imperialism.* New York: Vintage, 1993.

———. *The Edward Said Reader,* edited by Moustafa Bayoumi and Andrew Rubin. New York: Vintage Books, 2000.

———. *Orientalism.* Revised edition, with new preface and afterword. New York: Vintage, 1994 [1978].

Sampley, J. Paul, ed. *Paul in the Greco-Roman World: A Handbook.* Harrisburg: Trinity Press International, 2003.

Schaffer, Kay. *Women and the Bush: Forces of Desire in the Australian Cultural Tradition.* Cambridge: Cambridge University Press, 1988.

Schottroff, Luise. "'Law-Free Gentile Christianity'—What About the Women? Feminist Analyses and Alternatives." In *A Feminist Companion to Paul,* edited by Amy-Jill Levine with Marianne Blickenstaff, 183–94. Cleveland: Pilgrim, 2004.

———. *Lydia's Impatient Sisters: A Feminist Social History of Early Christianity*. Translated by Barbara and Martin Rumscheidt. Louisville: Westminster John Knox, 1995.

Schüssler Fiorenza, Elisabeth. *Bread not Stone: The Challenge of Feminist Biblical Interpretation*. Rev. ed. Boston: Beacon, 1995.

———. *But She Said: Feminist Practices of Biblical Interpretation*. Boston: Beacon, 1992.

———. *Discipleship of Equals: A Critical Feminist Ekklesia-logy of Liberation*. New York: Crossroad, 1993.

———. "Paul and the Politics of Interpretation." In *Paul and Politics: Ekklesia, Israel, Imperium, Interpretation: Essays in Honor of Krister Stendahl*, edited by Richard A. Horsley, 40–57. Harrisburg: Trinity Press International, 2000.

———. *The Power of the Word: Scripture and the Rhetoric of Empire*. Minneapolis: Fortress Press, 2007.

———. *Rhetoric and Ethic: The Politics of Biblical Studies*. Minneapolis: Fortress Press, 1999.

———, ed. *Searching the Scriptures: A Feminist Introduction*. Vol. 1. New York: Crossroad, 1993.

———, ed. *Searching the Scriptures: A Feminist Commentary*. Vol. 2. New York: Crossroad, 1994.

———. *Wisdom Ways: Introducing Feminist Biblical Interpretation*. Maryknoll: Orbis, 2001.

Scott, James C. *Domination and the Arts of Resistance*. New Haven: Yale University Press, 1990.

Scott, Joan Wallach. *Gender and the Politics of History*. New York: Columbia University Press, 1988.

———. "Women in The Making of the English Working Class." In *Gender and the Politics of History*, 68–90. New York: Columbia University Press, 1988.

Scott, Sarah, and Jane Webster, eds. *Roman Imperialism and Provincial Art*. Cambridge: Cambridge University Press, 2003.

Sedgwick, Eve Kosofsky. *Between Men: English Literature and Male Homosocial Desire*. Gender and Culture. New York: Columbia University Press, 1985.

Seesengood, Robert. "Hybridity and the Rhetoric of Endurance: Reading Paul's Athletic Metaphors in a Context of Postcolonial Self-Construction." *Bible and Critical Theory* 1, no. 3 (2005).

Segovia, Fernando F. *Decolonizing Biblical Studies: A View from the Margins.* Maryknoll: Orbis, 2000.

———, ed. *Interpreting beyond Borders.* Bible and Postcolonialism. Sheffield: Sheffield Academic, 2000.

———. "Introduction: Configurations, Approaches, Findings, Stances." In *A Postcolonial Commentary on the New Testament Writings,* edited by Segovia and R. S. Sugirtharajah, 1–68. Bible and Postcolonialism. London: T&T Clark, 2007.

———. "Mapping the Postcolonial Optic in Biblical Criticism: Meaning and Scope." In *Postcolonial Biblical Criticism: Interdisciplinary Intersections,* edited by Stephen D. Moore and Segovia, 23–78. Bible and Postcolonialism. London: T&T Clark, 2005.

———, ed. *Toward a New Heaven and a New Earth: Essays in Honor of Elisabeth Schüssler Fiorenza.* Maryknoll: Orbis, 2003.

Segovia, Fernando F., and R. S. Sugirtharajah, eds. *A Postcolonial Commentary on the New Testament Writings.* Bible and Postcolonialism. London: T&T Clark, 2007.

Segovia, Fernando F., and Mary Ann Tolbert, eds. *Reading from This Place.* 2 vols. Minneapolis: Fortress Press, 1995.

Sharpe, Jenny. *Allegories of Empire: The Figure of Woman in the Colonial Text.* Minneapolis: University of Minnesota Press, 1993.

Sharpe, Jim. "History from Below." In *New Perspectives on Historical Writing,* edited by Peter Burke, 25–42. 2nd ed. University Park: Pennsylvania State University Press, 2001.

Sherwin-White, Adrian N. *The Roman Citizenship.* 2nd ed. Oxford: Clarendon, 1973.

Shohat, Ella. "Notes on the 'Post-Colonial.'" *Social Texts* 31/32 (1992): 99–113.

Sibeko, Malika, and Beverley Haddad. "Reading the Bible 'with' Women in Poor and Marginalized Communities in South Africa." *Semeia* 78 (1997): 83–92.

Smith, Abraham. "'Unmasking the Powers': Toward a Postcolonial Analysis of 1 Thessalonians." In *Paul and the Roman Imperial Order,* edited by Richard A. Horsley, 47–66. Harrisburg: Trinity Press International, 2004.

Spivak, Gayatri Chakravorty. "Can the Subaltern Speak?" In *Marxism and the Interpretation of Culture,* edited by Cary Nelson and Lawrence Grossberg, 271–313. Urbana: University of Illinois Press, 1988.

———. *A Critique of Postcolonial Reason: Toward a History of the Vanishing Present.* Cambridge: Harvard University Press, 1999.

———. "French Feminism in an International Frame." In *In Other Worlds: Essays in Cultural Politics,* 134–53. New York: Routledge, 1988.

―――. *In Other Worlds: Essays in Cultural Politics*. New York: Routledge, 1988.

―――. "Limits and Openings of Marx in Derrida." In *Outside in the Teaching Machine*, 97–119. New York: Routledge, 1993.

―――. "Marginality in the Teaching Machine." In *Outside in the Teaching Machine*, 53–76. New York: Routledge, 1993.

―――. "More on Power/Knowledge." In *Outside in the Teaching Machine*, 25–51. New York: Routledge, 1993.

―――. *Outside in the Teaching Machine*. New York: Routledge, 1993.

―――. *The Post-Colonial Critic: Interviews, Strategies, Dialogues*, edited by Sarah Harasym. New York: Routledge, 1990.

―――. "Subaltern Studies: Deconstructing Historiography." In *In Other Worlds: Essays in Cultural Politics*, 197–221. New York: Routledge, 1988.

―――. "Subaltern Talk: Interview with the Editors." In *The Spivak Reader: Selected Works of Gayatri Chakravorty Spivak*, edited by Donna Landry and Gerald MacLean, 287–308. New York: Routledge, 1996.

Spivak, Gayatri Chakravorty, with Ellen Rooney. "'In a Word': *Interview*." In *Outside in the Teaching Machine*, 1–23. New York: Routledge, 1993.

Stoler, Ann Laura. *Carnal Knowledge and Imperial Power: Race and the Intimate in Colonial Rule*. Berkeley: University of California Press, 2002.

―――. *Race and the Education of Desire: Foucault's History of Sexuality and the Colonial Order of Things*. Durham: Duke University Press, 1995.

Strauss, Gerald. "The Dilemma of Popular History." *Past and Present* 132 (Aug. 1991): 130–49.

Strobel, Margaret. *European Women and the Second British Empire*. Bloomington: Indiana University Press, 1991.

Sugirtharajah, R. S. *Asian Biblical Hermeneutics and Postcolonialism: Contesting the Interpretations*. The Bible and Liberation. Maryknoll: Orbis, 1998.

―――. *The Bible and the Third World: Precolonial, Colonial, and Postcolonial Encounters*. Cambridge: Cambridge University Press, 2001.

―――, ed. *The Postcolonial Bible*. Bible and Postcolonialism. Sheffield: Sheffield Academic, 1998.

―――, ed. *The Postcolonial Biblical Reader*. Malden: Blackwell, 2006.

―――. *Postcolonial Criticism and Biblical Interpretation*. Oxford: Oxford University Press, 2002.

―――. "A Postcolonial Exploration of Collusion and Construction in Biblical Interpretation." In *The Postcolonial Bible*, edited by Sugirtharajah, 91–116. Bible and Postcolonialism. Sheffield: Sheffield Academic, 1998.

―――. *Postcolonial Reconfigurations: An Alternative Way of Reading the Bible and Doing Theology*. St. Louis: Chalice, 2003.

————, ed. *Vernacular Hermeneutics*. Bible and Postcolonialism. Sheffield: Sheffield Academic, 1999.

Taylor, Barbara. *Eve and the New Jerusalem: Socialism and Feminism in the Nineteenth Century*. New York: Pantheon, 1983.

Thimmes, Pamela. "What Makes a Feminist Reading Feminist? Another Perspective." In *Escaping Eden: New Feminist Perspectives on the Bible*, edited by Harold C. Washington, Susan Lochrie Graham, and Pamela Thimmes, 132–40. New York: New York University Press, 1999.

Thompson, Edward John. *The Other Side of the Medal*. London: Hogarth, 1925.

————. *Suttee: A Historical and Philosophical Inquiry into the Hindu Rite of Widow-Burning*. London: George Allen and Unwin, 1928.

Thompson, Edward Palmer. "History from Below." *Times Literary Supplement*, April 7, 1966, 278–80.

————. *The Making of the English Working Class*. New York: Vintage, 1966.

————. *The Poverty of Theory and Other Essays*. London: Merlin, 1979.

Tolbert, Mary Ann, ed. *The Bible and Feminist Hermeneutics*. Semeia 28. Atlanta: Society of Biblical Literature, 1983.

————. "Defining the Problem: The Bible and Feminist Hermeneutics." *Semeia* 28 (1983): 113–26.

————. "The Politics and Poetics of Location." In *Reading from This Place*. Vol. 1, *Social Location and Biblical Interpretation in the United States*, edited by Fernando F. Segovia and Tolbert, 305–17. Minneapolis: Fortress Press, 1995.

Trinh, Minh-ha T. *Woman, Native, Other: Writing Postcoloniality and Feminism*. Bloomington: Indiana University Press, 1989.

Tyrell, Ian. *Woman's World/Woman's Empire: The Women's Christian Temperance Union in International Perspective, 1880–1930*. Chapel Hill: University of North Carolina Press, 1991.

Vander Stichele, Caroline, and Todd C. Penner, eds. *Her Master's Tools? Feminist and Postcolonial Engagements of Historical-Critical Discourse*. Global Perspectives on Biblical Scholarship Series. Atlanta: Society of Biblical Literature, 2005.

————. "Paul and the Rhetoric of Gender." In *Her Master's Tools? Feminist and Postcolonial Engagements of Historical-Critical Discourse*, edited by Vander Stichele and Penner, 287–310. Global Perspectives on Biblical Scholarship Series. Atlanta: Society of Biblical Literature, 2005.

Walters, Jonathan. "Invading the Roman Body: Manliness and Impenetrability in Roman Thought." In *Roman Sexualities*, edited by Judith P. Hallett and Marilyn B. Skinner, 29–43. Princeton: Princeton University Press, 1997.

Wan, Sze-kar. "Collection for the Saints as Anticolonial Act: Implications of Paul's Ethnic Reconstruction." In *Paul and Politics: Ekklesia, Israel, Imperium, Interpretation: Essays in Honor of Krister Stendahl*, edited by Richard A. Horsley, 191–215. Harrisburg: Trinity Press International, 2000.

——. "Does Diaspora Identity Imply Some Sort of Universality? An Asian-American Reading of Galatians." In *Interpreting Beyond Borders*, edited by Fernando F. Segovia, 107–31. Bible and Postcolonialism. Sheffield: Sheffield Academic, 2000.

Wansink, Craig S. *Chained in Christ: The Experience and Rhetoric of Paul's Imprisonment*. Journal for the Study of the New Testament Supplement Series 130. Sheffield: Sheffield Academic, 1996.

Washington, Harold C., Susan Lochrie Graham, and Pamela Thimmes, eds. *Escaping Eden: New Feminist Perspectives on the Bible*. New York: New York University Press, 1999.

Webster, Jane, and Nicholas J. Cooper, eds. *Roman Imperialism: Post-Colonial Perspectives*. Leicester Archaeology Monographs 3. Leicester: School of Archaeological Studies, 1996.

Weidmann, Frederick W. "An (Un)Accomplished Model: Paul and the Rhetorical Strategy of Philippians 3:3-17." In *Putting Body and Soul Together: Essays in Honor of Robin Scroggs*, edited by Virginia Wiles, Alexandra Brown, and Graydon F. Snyder, 245–57. Valley Forge: Trinity Press International, 1997.

West, Gerald O. *Academy of the Poor: Towards a Dialogical Reading of the Bible*. Interventions. Sheffield: Sheffield Academic, 1999.

——, ed. *Reading Other-Wise: Socially Engaged Scholars Reading with Their Local Communities*. Semeia Studies. Atlanta: Society of Biblical Literature, 2007.

Whitmarsh, Tim. *Greek Literature and the Roman Empire: The Politics of Imitation*. Oxford: Oxford University Press, 2001.

Williams, Craig A. *Roman Homosexuality: Ideologies of Masculinity in Classical Antiquity*. New York: Oxford University Press, 1999.

Williams, Patrick, and Laura Chrisman, eds. *Colonial Discourse and Post-Colonial Theory: A Reader*. New York: Columbia University Press, 1994.

Wire, Antoinette Clark. *The Corinthian Women Prophets: A Reconstruction through Paul's Rhetoric*. Minneapolis: Fortress Press, 1990.

——. "Response: Paul and Those outside Power." In *Paul and Politics: Ekklesia, Israel, Imperium, Interpretation: Essays in Honor of Krister Stendahl*, edited by Richard A. Horsley, 224–26. Harrisburg: Trinity Press International, 2000.

————. "Response: The Politics of the Assembly in Corinth." In *Paul and Politics: Ekklesia, Israel, Imperium, Interpretation: Essays in Honor of Krister Stendahl*, edited by Richard A. Horsley, 124–29. Harrisburg: Trinity Press International, 2000.

Wright, N. T. "Paul's Gospel and Caesar's Empire." In *Paul and Politics: Ekklesia, Israel, Imperium, Interpretation: Essays in Honor of Krister Stendahl*, edited by Richard A. Horsley, 160–83. Harrisburg: Trinity Press International, 2000.

Yee, Gale A. *Poor Banished Children of Eve: Woman As Evil in the Hebrew Bible*. Minneapolis: Fortress Press, 2003.

Yeğenoğlu, Meyda. *Colonial Fantasies: Towards a Feminist Reading of Orientalism*. Cambridge Cultural Social Studies. Cambridge: Cambridge University Press, 1998.

————. "Sartorial Fabric-ations: Enlightenment and Western Feminism." In *Postcolonialism, Feminism, and Religious Discourse*, edited by Laura E. Donaldson and Pui-lan Kwok, 82–99. New York: Routledge, 2002.

————. "Veiled Fantasies: Cultural and Sexual Difference in the Discourse of Orientalism." In *Feminist Postcolonial Theory: A Reader*, edited by Reina Lewis and Sara Mills, 542–66. New York: Routledge, 2003.

Yeo, Khoik-Khng. "The Rhetorical Hermeneutic of 1 Corinthians 8 and Chinese Ancestor Worship." *Biblical Interpretation* 2 (1994): 294–311.

Yuval-Davis, Nira, and Floya Anthias, eds. *Woman-Nation-State*. Hampshire: MacMillan, 1989.

Žižek, Slavoj. *The Puppet and the Dwarf: The Perverse Core of Christianity*. Short Circuits. Cambridge: MIT Press, 2003.

Index

Agosto, Efraín, 19, 38–41, 43–44, 56,
134nn31–32, 146nn24–29,
147nn54–55, 147n61, 148n63,
151n89, 170n36
Alexander, M. Jacqui, 117, 136n53,
137n60, 177nn4–5
anti-Judaism/anti-Semitism, 20–21, 37,
78, 119, 135n40
apocalyptic, 10, 39, 42, 48, 120, 121,
149n73
Augustus/Octavian, 96, 152n98

Bhabha, Homi K., 9, 13, 55, 57,
59, 69–75, 79–84, 87, 113,
129n13, 130n24, 148n69,
149n70, 153n109, 156n33,
157n38, 158nn41–48, 158n50,
159nn56–58, 159n60, 160n65,
160n67, 161n85, 162n96,
163n99, 168n22, 177n3
Blunt, Alison, 168n23, 172n50
Bockmuehl, Markus, 64–65, 67,
73, 148n68, 155nn14–18,
155–56n23, 159n53, 165n132,
174n64
Boyarin, Daniel, 72, 158nn50–51
Briggs, Sheila, 18, 134nn24–25,
135n34, 151n90, 166n140,
174n62
Buell, Denise Kimber, 76, 160nn75–76,
161n77, 161nn80–81, 161n84
Burke, Peter, 34–35, 139n73,
140nn82–83, 140nn85–86,
143n127
Butler, Judith, 156n33, 158n44,
159n60, 160n71, 162n96, 177n3

Cassidy, Richard J., 38–42, 44,
56, 145nn17–23, 146n23,
146nn39–43, 148n63, 170n36
Castelli, Elizabeth A., 63–68, 70, 72,
75, 79, 87, 131n29, 143n128,
148n67, 149n70, 154nn6–7,
155nn8–13, 155n20, 155n23,
156n23, 156n25, 156n28,
156nn31–32, 158n52, 160n65
catachresis, 121–22, 178n11,
179nn13–14
Chakrabarty, Dipesh, 30, 142n101,
142n103, 142nn106–7,
142nn109–10, 178n8
Chow, Rey, 9, 13, 59, 74–79, 81–82,
113, 122, 148n69, 159nn57–60,
160nn61–69, 160nn72–74,
161n76, 161n79, 168n22
Christ hymn, 13, 37–39, 41–43, 46,
48, 50–52, 56, 61, 106, 112, 118,
122, 151nn90–92, 154nn2–3,
175n78
class/economic status, 6, 8, 13, 22–23,
28–31, 33–34, 36, 50, 52–53, 70,
82–84, 87–88, 96–100, 102–3,
107–8, 114, 116, 118, 128n6,
129–30n22, 140nn88–89,
141n90, 141nn92–93, 141n96,
142n108, 145n22, 152n95,
164n126, 173n59, 174n60,
174n63, 174n70, 179n14
coercive mimeticism, 75, 78–81, 88, 105
colonialism
defined, 4
neocolonialism, 1, 3, 6, 8, 14, 17,
31, 33, 35, 69, 74, 94, 117, 122,
127n6, 128n6, 173n59

205

colonialism (*cont.*)
  Philippi as a *colonia*, 5, 13, 39–41,
    46, 55–56, 59, 68, 77–78, 85,
    87–88, 91, 93, 96–98, 100–109,
    113–14, 118, 156n34, 168n25,
    169nn28–29, 169n31
  contact zone, 13, 22, 53, 55–57, 78,
    91–93, 95–109, 113–14, 138n63,
    159n56, 167n11, 168n26, 174n69
    applied to Philippi, 22, 55–56,
      96–109, 113–14
    defined, 13, 22, 92–93, 95
    qualified, 93, 95, 97, 167n11,
      168n26, 174n69

D'Angelo, Mary Rose, 101–2, 152n99,
    153n105, 164n127, 166n36,
    171n49, 172n53, 174n64
destruction, 48–49, 51, 53, 62, 71, 77, 105
De Vos, Craig S., 103, 152n95, 156n34,
    157n34, 168n25, 169nn29–31,
    170n33, 173n60, 174n60, 174n67
Dirlik, Arif, 30, 142n103
Donaldson, Laura E., 7, 21, 94, 105,
    129n12, 129n16, 130n26,
    132n3, 132n6, 133n11, 135n36,
    135n44, 136n50, 136n53, 137n55,
    143n125, 153n103, 162n89,
    163n112, 167n16, 175nn72–73
Dube, Musa W., 5, 7, 12–13, 16–18,
    21–23, 35, 38, 44–45, 47–50, 55,
    84, 88, 91, 105, 112, 114, 128n11,
    129n13, 129n15, 129nn17–18,
    130n26, 131n1, 132n4, 133n7,
    133n12, 133nn15–18, 133n20,
    135n36, 135n42, 135n44,
    136n49, 136n52, 137nn55–57,
    138n64, 138n66, 138nn69–70,
    147nn59–60, 149n71, 149n73,
    150nn78–80, 152n101, 153n108,
    156n24, 157n36, 161n82, 162n86,
    164n128, 165n128, 166n139,
    166n141, 166n2 (chap. 4),
    170nn34–35, 175n71, 178n9

Elliott, Neil, 134n32, 137n61, 144n11,
    149n73, 150n85, 151n89
Epaphroditus, 46, 52, 61–62, 73, 78, 86,
    100, 102
ethnicity, 6, 9, 12–13, 24, 28, 33, 35–36,
    55, 70, 74–88, 92, 96–100, 103–4,
    107–8, 111, 113–16, 118–19,
    122, 128n6, 132n2, 133n8,
    159nn59–60, 160nn75–76,
    161n81, 161n84, 164n119, 174n70,
    176n1, 178n7, 179n13
  in colonial mimicry, 70, 74–88
  cross-ethnic representation, 13,
    75–77, 79, 84–85, 88, 104, 113,
    122, 159nn59–60
  ethnic reasoning, 76–77, 118,
    160n75, 161n84
  Paul's ethnic status, 76–77, 85–86,
    99, 108, 132n2, 161n81, 178n7
Euodia, 13, 53, 55, 85, 88, 89, 100–109,
    114, 152n96, 164n127, 165n132,
    171n49, 172n53, 173n60, 174n64,
    175n78

Fanon, Frantz, 78, 80, 84, 87, 89, 160n70,
    162n88, 162n93, 164nn120–21,
    166n138, 166n142, 171n48
feminism(s)
  defined, 4
  See also transnational feminism(s)
feminist, postcolonial analysis, 4, 7–8,
    10–16, 20, 26, 33–39, 44–45, 50,
    54–55, 57, 59, 67, 91, 93, 95–96,
    101, 106, 109, 111–13, 115–17,
    119–21, 123, 131nn29–30,
    139n78, 140n81, 144n129,
    164n126, 179n13
  defined, 4–10
Foucault, Michel, 63, 65–67, 75, 131n29,
    136n53, 142n109, 145n19, 154n7,
    156n23, 156n27

Georgi, Dieter, 42–43, 146n37, 147n49,
    150n85

Grewal, Inderpal, 9, 93, 95, 137n60,
142n108, 167n3, 167nn9–10,
168nn21–22, 171n48, 174n69,
175n75, 177n5
Guha, Ranajit, 30–32, 142n100,
142nn105–6, 142n109, 143n117

heavens, 13–14, 40, 99, 112, 118, 122
Heen, Erik M., 38–39, 43–44, 56,
147n50
history from below
  See people's history (history from
  below)
Hobsbawm, Eric J., 28–32, 34, 140n88,
141n91, 142n104
Hodge, Caroline Johnson, 76,
160nn75–76, 161n77,
161nn80–81, 161n84
Horsley, Richard A., 19, 25–26, 35–36,
28–44, 56, 132n2, 133n22,
134n29, 134n31, 134n33,
135n36, 137n61, 139nn72–80,
140n86, 144n1, 144nn4–11,
146n33, 146nn35–38, 146n48,
147n49, 149n73, 155n21, 157n40,
166n140, 170n33, 174n62
hybridity, 69–70, 72, 74, 81–82, 95, 113,
147n61, 149n69, 152n95, 158n41,
158n49, 158n51, 159n58, 161n22

imitation/mimicry, 12–13, 20, 47,
53, 55–90, 100, 104, 106, 108,
113, 118, 121–22, 148nn67–69,
149nn69–70, 153n106,
155nn10–14, 155nn19–20, 156n30,
156nn32–33, 157nn37–38,
157n40, 158nn40–42, 158n44,
158nn46–47, 158n52, 160n61,
160n65, 160n67, 160n71, 161n77,
162n96, 162n99, 163n99, 163n102,
164n119, 165n132, 177n3
imperialism
  defined, 4
  See also colonialism; Roman
  imperialism

imprisonment, 40–42, 46, 56, 98, 102–3,
114, 142n102, 145n17, 145n20,
146n23, 148n63, 170n36, 173n55
Irigaray, Luce, 80–84, 87–88, 156n33,
162n96

Junia, 102, 114, 173n56, 174n64

Kelley, Shawn, 20, 135n40, 135nn42–43,
161n83
Kim, Jean K., 21, 136n54, 151–52n92,
152n97, 153n103, 161n78,
166n135, 175n72
Kittredge, Cynthia Briggs, 18–19,
50–51, 68, 102, 106, 132n2,
134n24, 134nn27–28, 134n34,
135nn34–35, 137n61, 138n70,
139n77, 147n60, 148n62,
149n74, 150n83, 151nn89–91,
152n96, 152n100, 153nn111–12,
154nn1–2, 156n30, 164n127,
165n132, 166n140, 172nn52–53,
174n65, 175nn77–78, 176n82
Knust, Jennifer Wright, 134n30, 149n75,
166n135
Kwok Pui-lan, 7, 10, 12, 16, 18, 20–23,
35, 44, 47, 54, 69, 84, 91, 101, 112,
117, 129n15, 129n18, 129n20,
130n26, 132n4, 132n6, 133n9,
133nn11–12, 133nn19–21,
135n36, 135n40, 135n42,
135n44, 136n47, 136n49, 136n52,
137nn55–56, 137nn58–59,
137n62, 138n64, 138n66, 138n68,
143n125, 149n71, 152n102,
153n110, 157nn35–36, 162n86,
162n89, 163n111, 164n125,
166n139, 166n1 (chap. 4), 170n35,
172n51, 175n73
kyriarchy, 6–8, 14, 21, 34, 51–52, 56,
86, 94, 98, 103, 107–8, 114–17,
120, 122, 129n17, 129nn19–20,
130n23, 136n49, 151n90,
164n126, 179n13
  defined, 6–8, 164n126

kyriarchy (*cont.*)
    postcolonial feminist responses to,
      6–7, 21, 129nn17–21, 136n49
    use of *kyrios* in text and analysis, 6,
      40–43, 51, 53, 56, 99, 122

Levine, Amy-Jill, 135n36, 135n38,
    135n41
Liew, Tat-siong Benny, 97, 148n69,
    158n41, 159n58, 161n77, 169n26,
    176n1
Lopez, Davina C., 153n104, 178n7

Marchal, Joseph A., 1–3, 8–9, 20, 94, 103,
    112, 117, 119–20, 127nn1–2, 127–
    28n6, 135n43, 138n65, 145n22,
    148n62, 148n65, 151nn86–88,
    152n93, 152n96, 154n1, 155n22,
    159n54, 165n129, 165n132,
    169n25, 169n27, 169n30, 170n38,
    170n40, 172n53, 173n59, 174n68,
    175n79, 179n14
Marxist methodologies, 5, 8, 12, 28–33,
    129–30n22, 132n6, 137n60,
    140nn88–89, 142nn112–13,
    143n113, 159n57, 167n13, 178n11
    debates with/in feminism(s), 8,
      129n22, 130n22, 137n60, 140n89
    historiography, 12, 28–33, 140n88,
      142n112
Mazrui, Ali, 17, 133n15
McClintock, Anne, 9, 13, 17, 21, 59,
    79–89, 105–6, 113, 122, 128n11,
    133nn9–11, 136n53, 148n69,
    153n104, 161n85, 163nn101–12,
    163nn114–15, 163nn117–18,
    164nn120–24, 165n135, 166n137,
    166n142, 171n48, 173n59, 175n73
military, 2–3, 6, 14, 17, 21, 28, 51, 82,
    84–87, 90, 99, 103–4, 113, 127n2,
    138n65, 145n22, 148n62, 148n65,
    151n86, 151n88, 152n96, 155n22,
    164n126, 165nn129–32, 169n25,
    169n27, 170n40, 171n42, 172n53,
    173n59, 175n79

Mills, Sara, 9, 94, 100, 130n25, 132n6,
    136n46, 136n53, 148n69, 159n57,
    163n99, 167n8, 167nn11–13,
    168n19, 168n23, 170n35, 170n39,
    171n43, 171nn45–46, 172n50,
    175n74, 176n81, 177n2
mimicry
    See imitation/mimicry
missions/missionaries, 20–21, 33, 47,
    89, 98–103, 105–9, 114, 138n64,
    149n71, 153n104, 170n35, 172n51,
    178n7
    Paul's "mission to the Gentiles,"
      47, 89, 98–103, 105–9, 153n104,
      170n35, 178n7
    women in, 20–21, 101–3, 107–9,
      114, 149n71, 170n35, 172n51
Mohanty, Chandra Talpade, 9, 16–17,
    21, 32, 132n3, 132n7, 136n53,
    137n60, 143n120, 150n78, 167n3,
    177n5
Moore, Stephen D., 121–22, 128n9,
    131n1, 134n24, 142n113,
    143n113, 158n41, 159n56, 167n16,
    176n1, 178n11, 179nn12–13

Narayan, Uma, 32, 137n60, 143n120,
    153n108, 164n119, 177n5
Nero, 40, 42, 145n20

Oakes, Peter S., 38–39, 41–44, 56,
    91, 103, 145n18, 146nn30–34,
    146nn44–48, 147n49, 152n95,
    157n34, 165n132, 168n25,
    169nn27–30, 169nn32–33,
    170n33, 174n61
obedience, 46–49, 52–56, 60–61, 70–71,
    76, 86–88, 99, 103, 107, 148n62,
    149n74, 151nn91–92, 154nn1–2,
    172n52
O'Brien Wicker, Kathleen, 21, 128n12,
    136n54, 137n55
Økland, Jorunn, 100–101, 105, 152n94,
    165n133, 171nn44–45, 175n73
"ordinary readers," 9, 23, 56, 118,
    138n66, 178n9

Orientalism, 10, 20, 27, 78, 80, 93,
 130nn24–25, 135n40, 136n46,
 136n53, 148–49n69, 162n87,
 166n135, 172n50, 177n2

parousia, 39, 41, 46, 148n64, 170n37
Paul
 decentering scholarly focus upon,
  11, 13, 25, 59, 67–68, 72–74, 85,
  87–89, 100–101, 105–8, 113–16,
  119–22
 See also ethnicity: Paul's ethnic status
Paul and Politics group, 12, 18–19, 37
peace, 2, 14, 29, 53, 73, 152n98
 Pax Romana, 152n98
Penner, Todd C., 127n2, 138n65,
  145n22, 147n61, 150n81, 153n105,
  154n5, 155n22, 169n25
people's history (history from below),
  12–13, 24–36, 52, 55, 94–109,
  112–18, 121, 139nn71–73,
  139n81, 140n81, 140nn86–88,
  140n94, 141n90, 142n101,
  142n103, 143n129, 149n72
 in relation to feminist history,
  28–30, 33–35, 94–95, 112–17,
  121, 139nn77–79, 141n90
 in relation to subaltern studies,
  30–33, 112, 142n101, 142n103
 qualified by postcolonial feminist
  approaches, 31–33, 35–36, 94–95,
  112–18
 qualified by queer approaches,
  35–36, 117, 143n129
Polaski, Sandra Hack, 19, 135nn36–37
politeuma, 14, 38–41, 50–51, 56, 99
postcolonial biblical interpretation
  (not explicitly feminist), 2–3,
  8–10, 15–18, 40–41, 43, 111–13,
  115–16, 121–22, 128nn9–10,
  130n27, 131n1, 132n2, 134n24,
  143n113, 147n61, 148n69, 150n84,
  158n41, 159n56, 159n58, 176n1,
  179nn12–13
postcolonial/colonial studies (extra-
  biblical and not explicitly

feminist), 2–6, 9–10, 17, 59,
  69–79, 112–13; 130n24, 157n37,
  158nn42–48, 159nn56–60,
  160nn61–64, 160nn66–74,
  162n93, 164n121, 166n138,
  166n142
 See also feminist, postcolonial
  analysis
postcolonialism
 defined, 4–9
Pratt, Mary Louise, 9, 13, 92–95, 98, 101,
  104–5, 136n46, 136n53, 138n63,
  167nn4–7, 167n11, 167n15,
  168nn20–21, 168n23, 170n39,
  171n41, 174n69, 176n81
Prisca, 74, 102, 114
progress, 28, 33, 35, 46–49, 54, 60,
  73, 82, 86–89, 97, 101, 128n11,
  133n10, 148n63, 163n105,
  169n27, 171n41

queer theory/approaches, 35–36, 55, 117,
  119, 133n11, 143n129, 156n33,
  176–77n1, 179n14

race/racialization, 2, 6, 8–10, 17, 20–21,
  23–24, 28, 34, 51, 55, 70, 75,
  77–79, 82–84, 94, 99–100,
  116–19, 128n6, 129n13, 131n30,
  133n9, 135n40, 135n42, 136n50,
  136n53, 148n69, 149n72, 160n75,
  161n83, 161n85, 164n126, 167n13,
  171n48, 172n50, 173n59, 176n1
Rehmann, Luzia Sutter, 20, 135n38
rhetoric, 2–3, 11–13, 15, 18, 20, 23,
  27–28, 34–35, 37–38, 44–47,
  50–52, 55–57, 59–90, 91,
  93–94, 96, 99–100, 106, 111–14,
  116, 130n29, 131n29, 138n65,
  138n70, 144n2, 145n20, 147n60,
  148nn62–63, 149nn73–74,
  151n86, 151n88, 151n92, 152n93,
  152n95, 152n101, 154n1, 154n5,
  156n30, 161n80, 165n129, 168n17,
  170n40, 171n48
Ringe, Sharon H., 21, 136n54

Roman imperialism, 2, 5, 10, 12, 15–16, 18–20, 25, 37, 39–41, 45–47, 51–55, 57, 59, 68, 71, 77, 88, 96–102, 104, 109–11, 118–21, 130n28, 146n35, 150n85, 157n40, 165n134, 173n57, 178n8

safety (*sōtēria*), 39, 49, 51, 53, 62, 71, 73, 77–78
Said, Edward W., 4, 9, 128n7, 130nn24–25, 135n40, 142n111, 149n75, 161n78, 166n135, 177n6
Schottroff, Luise, 20, 135n39, 151n90
Schüssler Fiorenza, Elisabeth, 6–8, 18, 35, 64, 68, 84, 94, 101, 106, 112, 127n4, 129n12, 129n14, 129n17, 129nn19–22, 130n23, 130n26, 132n2, 134nn24–26, 135n34, 136n49, 136n51, 137nn54–55, 137n61, 138nn63–64, 138n66, 138n68, 138n70, 139n78, 143n128, 144nn2–3, 147n60, 148n62, 150n77, 153n112, 154n1, 155n10, 155n21, 156n30, 163n99, 164n126, 164n128, 165n128, 166n140, 167n12, 168nn17–18, 175n7
Scott, James C., 19, 132n2, 134n29, 134nn33–34, 139n77, 157n40
Scott, Joan Wallach, 29, 32–33, 141nn92–99, 143n124, 167n12
Sedgwick, Eve Kosofsky, 153n103, 177n3
Seesengood, Robert, 72, 147n61, 149n69, 152n95, 158n41, 158n49, 158n51
Segovia, Fernando F., 2, 10, 128nn8–9, 130n27, 131n1, 133n14, 134n24, 137n55, 138nn67–68, 143n113, 146n24, 157n36, 158n41, 165n128, 166n2, 167n14, 167n16, 176n1
sexuality, 1–3, 6, 9–10, 12, 17–18, 23–24, 27–33, 35–36, 40, 44, 80, 82–88, 91, 96, 100, 105, 107, 111, 115–19, 128n6, 137n56, 145n19, 149n75, 159n60, 165n135, 171n42,

174n64, 174n70, 175n78, 176n1, 177n2, 177n4
"porno-tropics," 17, 83, 163n112
Sharpe, Jenny, 136n46, 136n53, 167n12, 171n42, 176n81
Sharpe, Jim, 27, 140nn86–88, 141n90
slavery, 18, 51, 52, 92, 96–98, 103–4, 107–8, 114, 134n26, 135n40, 151n90, 151n92, 169n33, 170n33, 174n62, 179n14
Smith, Abraham, 132n2, 134n32, 135n43, 147n61, 170n33
Spivak, Gayatri Chakravorty, 2, 9, 16–17, 20–21, 31–33, 83, 94–95, 121, 130n24, 132n3, 132n6, 134n32, 135n45, 136n53, 142nn112–13, 143nn114–16, 143nn118–19, 143nn121–23, 159n57, 163n116, 167n13, 167n16, 168n22, 173n58, 178n11
subaltern studies, 13, 24, 27, 28, 30–32, 74, 94, 132n6, 142nn100–101, 142n103, 142nn105–7, 142nn109–10, 142n112, 143nn116–19, 143nn121–23, 159n57, 167n13, 173n58, 178n11
Sugirtharajah, R. S., 2, 10, 128nn9–10, 130n27, 131n1, 146n24, 150n84, 175n72
Syntyche, 13, 53, 55, 60, 85, 88–89, 100–109, 114, 152n96, 164n127, 165n132, 171n49, 172n53, 173n60, 174n64, 175n78

Thompson, Edward John, 31, 142n111, 143n123
Thompson, Edward Palmer, 28–34, 140n88, 141nn91–93, 141nn96–97, 142n103, 142n111, 143n122, 143n126
Timothy, 46, 52, 61–62, 73, 76, 86, 100
Tolbert, Mary Ann, 23, 127n5, 137n55, 138n68, 167n14
transculturation, 95, 99, 101, 105, 136n46, 167n4, 168n20

transnational feminism(s), 22, 117–19,
    137n60, 150n78, 167n3, 177nn4–5
travel, 12–13, 23, 44–48, 54–55, 91–93,
    96–103, 109, 113–14, 122,
    130n25, 131n1, 136n46, 137n60,
    142n108, 148n63, 148n66, 166n2,
    167nn3–7, 168n21, 168nn23–24,
    171nn47–48, 172n50, 174n69,
    177n5
Trinh T. Minh-ha, 21, 75, 136n53,
    160n65
type-scene of land possession, 91, 105,
    108, 114

Vander Stichele, Caroline, 127n2,
    138n65, 145n22, 147n61, 150n81,
    153n105, 154n5, 155n22, 169n25

Wan, Sze-kar, 132n2, 147n61, 161n81
Wire, Antoinette Clark, 18, 68, 73,
    106, 134n24, 134n26, 135n34,
    136n54, 137n61, 138n70, 139n78,
    143n128, 147n60, 152n95,
    153n111, 156n30, 159n55,
    166n140, 170n38
women
    as complicit in empire, 20–21, 88,
    98, 102, 107–9, 114, 172n51

as multiply oppressed, 6, 18, 98,
    103–4, 107, 114
roles in community at Philippi,
    13–14, 36, 53, 60, 85–90, 98, 100–
    109, 114–15, 162n127, 165n132,
    172nn53–53
roles in malestream Pauline scholar-
    ship, 18–19, 33–35, 85–89, 101,
    105–6, 114–16, 139nn77–78,
    165n132, 171n48
as site of contest, 16–17, 28, 31, 55,
    83, 105, 131n30, 153n103, 175n72
women's history, 25–26, 28–36,
    85, 89, 93–95, 106, 112–16, 118,
    141n90, 141nn92–99, 167n12
See also sexuality: "porno-tropics";
    type-scene of land possession
Wright, N. T., 38–40, 43–44, 50, 56,
    108, 144nn12–14, 145nn15–16,
    147nn56–58, 150n76, 150n82,
    176n83

Yeğenoğlu, Meyda, 9, 13, 59, 79–85, 89,
    106, 113, 122, 130n25, 148n69,
    162nn87–94, 162nn97–99,
    163nn99–100, 165n135, 166n138,
    166n143, 168n22

Pauline References

Romans
1:27-27   179n14
8:22-23   135n38
13   145n18
13:1-7   40, 145n18, 146n41,
                 150n85
13:1   145n23
13:5   145n23
16:3-4   102
16:7   102, 173n56

1 Corinthians
1–4   99
2:1-5   87

4:6   87
4:9-13   87
5:1-5   87
6:9-20   87
7:1-40   87
8   147n61
11:1   87
11:2-16   87, 147n61, 154n5
14:26-40   87

Philippians
1:1   102
1:3-11   52, 60, 148n68
1:5   77

Philippians (*cont.*)
1:7   53, 60, 61, 85
1:8   50, 159n54
1:12-14   52, 99, 148n68
1:12   46, 60, 61, 73, 86, 98,
               102
1:13   46, 85, 99
1:14   60, 61, 86
1:15-17   48, 62, 71, 99
1:15   48
1:17   48
1:20-23   46
1:20   159n54
1:23-26   52, 99
1:23   99
1:24-26   52, 61, 148n68
1:24   46, 60
1:25-26   60, 99
1:25   46, 73, 86, 99
1:26   46, 50, 73, 78
1:27-28   77
1:27   46, 47, 50, 62, 78, 99
1:28   47, 48, 50, 51, 62, 71,
               77, 105, 159n54
1:29   51, 73
1:30   60, 78, 85, 148n68
2:1-5   53
2:1-3   71
2:2-5   61
2:2   62
2:3   48, 53, 62, 99
2:4   62, 78
2:5-13   159n54
2:6-11   38, 39, 41, 43, 44,
               48, 61, 99, 106, 112,
               147n50, 151n90
2:6   43
2:7   43, 52, 151n90
2:8   42, 52, 61
2:9-11   56, 88, 151n90
2:9   42, 51
2:10-11   42
2:10   42, 51
2:11   51, 86, 122
2:12-16   86

2:12-14   71
2:12   46, 48, 52, 60, 61, 62,
               71, 73, 77, 78, 99, 105
2:13   47, 50, 52
2:14-16   60
2:14   48
2:15   48, 49, 62, 71, 77, 78,
               86, 99
2:16-18   52, 148n68
2:16   60, 77, 86
2:17-18   50
2:17   60, 61
2:18   60, 73
2:19-30   46, 73
2:20   61
2:21   48, 62
2:22   76, 86
2:24   46, 47, 62, 78, 99
2:25-30   102
2:25   61, 62, 85, 86
2:26   61
2:27-28   62
2:27   61, 159n54
2:28   78
2:29   62
2:30   61, 62
3:1   62, 71, 73, 77, 86, 105
3:2-11   49
3:2-3   71, 86
3:2   49, 62, 99
3:3-17   155n19
3:3   52, 76, 77, 86
3:4-11   99
3:4-6   52, 99
3:4   76
3:5-6   76
3:5   76
3:7-11   43, 52, 76, 87, 148n68,
               154n3
3:7-8   76
3:9   50, 159n54
3:10   154n3
3:13-14   170n37
3:13   86
3:14-17   47, 52, 53, 85

3:15-21	63
3:15	50, 53, 60, 62, 71, 77, 86, 105, 149n73, 159n54
3:16	62, 77, 99
3:17-21	40, 50
3:17	53, 59, 60, 62, 64, 78, 85, 86
3:18-21	13, 38, 39, 44, 49, 112, 146n41
3:18-20	41
3:18-19	40, 53, 71, 99
3:18	49, 62
3:19-20	51, 71, 77, 105
3:19	41, 49, 62, 145n19
3:20-21	39, 41, 50, 56, 99
3:20	14, 39, 40, 51, 53, 73, 99
3:21	39, 40, 41, 51, 53
4:1	53, 86, 99
4:2-3	53, 85
4:2	52, 53, 60, 104, 148n68, 152n96
4:3	85, 101, 104, 108, 149n73, 164n127, 172n53
4:5	77, 152n98
4:7-9	50
4:7	50, 73, 152n98, 159n54
4:8-9	47, 52
4:8	86
4:9	50, 61, 73, 78, 152n98; 159n54
4:10-20	49
4:11-13	148n68
4:11	49
4:13	50; 159n54
4:14-16	77
4:15-16	148n66
4:19	159n54
4:21-22	148n66
4:21	86
Philemon	
10–11	179n14